A
History of
Bucks
County Cricket Club

by Douglas Miller

ACS PUBLICATIONS
2006

First published in Great Britain by
Association of Cricket Statisticians and Historians
Cardiff CF11 9XR
2006

British Library Cataloguing-in-Publication Data.

A catalogue record for this book is available from the British Library.

ISBN-10: 1 905138 27 X
ISBN-13: 978 1 905138 27 2

Typeset by Limlow Books

Printed by City Press, Leeds

Contents

Foreword

It gives me great pleasure to write the foreword to Douglas Miller's superb book which records the detail of the history of the Bucks County Cricket Club, with many fascinating anecdotes and no punches pulled.

I didn't quite appreciate the vast amount of research and sheer hard work that would be necessary, when I suggested casually that a history of Bucks cricket should be published, and would be of great interest to all those who have played for or supported the county over the years, and also to future generations of Bucks cricketers. Douglas, being Douglas, rose manfully to the challenge and I hope he will feel the effort has been worthwhile – I certainly do!

As with all good books, once I started reading it I could hardly put it down, and of course particularly enjoyed the period when I was reasonably actively involved with the County. I well remember my first Bucks Committee meeting at the old Great Western Hotel in Paddington, over 50 years ago, when Walter Franklin was 'god' and it took a brave man to oppose his views, particularly if you were only 22 years old.

Oliver Battcock, a great character, Ben Barnett, a tremendous captain and motivator, Peter Stoddart, John Slack, Chris Parry and many others through to the present skipper Paul Atkins are all evidence of how lucky Bucks has been with its captains. There have also been a series of administrators, Tyson Chambers, Tony Prince, Paul Slatter, Jackie Tomlin and, of course, our present secretary Kevin Beaumont – all of them have served the County with great distinction.

I hope I will be forgiven if I give special mention, as Douglas has, to my guide and mentor Tom Orford, who started the Bucks Young Amateurs in 1946 and gave huge encouragement to all young cricketers in the County. Tom was a legend and taught us all how to play the great game and, as importantly, how to behave on the field (no sledging in those days!) and also how to reply promptly with dates of availability!

Enjoy this book – I'm confident you will and should you find any errors, do let Douglas know as he is always keen for a discussion! I'm sure you will agree with me that it is a marvellous read and does Bucks County Cricket Club proud.

I should add that I'm sure Douglas would also like to hear your views on his best Bucks Eleven of all time – personally I thought John Turner was unlucky not to make the side but, unsurprisingly, I never knew Charles Gresson!

Robin Peppiatt

Introduction

It was Tony Webb, a founder member of the Association of Cricket Statisticians and Historians ('the ACS'), who first approached me in his characteristically courteous and friendly way. "I hear you are from Buckinghamshire," he said, introducing himself. I had no reason to suspect that he had a proposal that would radically change the shape of my leisure hours for several years to come, but he soon began to explain. He was forming a team of statisticians who he hoped would unearth the scores of all the matches played by the minor counties since the formation of their championship in 1895.

Tony's unique brand of charm worked. I said I would help and take on the task of seeking out what I could find for Buckinghamshire. So began some years of visiting the County Library in Aylesbury to scour old newspapers and to delight in finding full-length reports and scores of most of the early matches. The County Club, meanwhile, in the persons of Kevin Beaumont, Michael Knox and others, offered every encouragement and support, and I was soon provided with an old suitcase, once the property of Ken Drucquer, in which resided all the score books from 1935. Michael Knox provided an almost complete set of yearbooks going back to 1905. Though these did not provide full scores I was better equipped than many others setting out on a similar journey of exploration and discovery.

Despite the implication of its three letters the ACS now includes historians. Within its membership are those to whom the game's statistics will always be paramount, but others prefer to dabble in the mix of fact and judgment that goes to make up history. It was Robin Peppiatt, at the time president of Bucks County Cricket Club, who first sowed the seed that all these statistics – now the product of 914 matches involving 609 different Bucks cricketers – should be turned into a published history. I am grateful to him for suggesting that the project should be expanded in this way. It seemed only right that he should pen a foreword to his brainchild. I am grateful to him for agreeing to do so.

Any history will have faults, real and perceived. That there are not even more in what I have written is due in no small way to the many people who have been involved in the original recording of scores and the processing of the annual statistics that flow from them. I refer to those now anonymous servants of the game who kept the scores in the earliest matches and ensured that what the newspapers published was accurate and comprehensive. I include also those who followed: the many years of Horace Perrin through to the scorers of more modern times, principally Lesley Hawkins, with whom I have sat down to try and reconcile apparent discrepancies, but also Bob Lane, John Goodman, Gilbert Knight and others who have kept the book in recent years. I blush to think how often my computations did not tally with theirs and how often I have had silently to bow to their greater accuracy. Of course earlier compilers of seasonal statistics have made errors, but they have not always had my normal luxury of a second source against which to check.

Within the wider ACS project Tony Webb's checking procedures and reluctance to admit that some fact or figure is unobtainable, which many sadly are, have been a model of thoroughness and dedication, for which the Association has rightly chosen him as its Statistician of the Year for 2006. The cross-checking procedures have also involved those working on the statistics of all Bucks' opponents. Here I should particularly like to thank Roy New (Berkshire), Bob Simons (Hertfordshire), Julian Lawton Smith (Oxfordshire) and Colin Munford (Suffolk), all of whom have gone beyond the call of duty in checking scores and offering other bits of advice and information. In all four instances I have had access to the histories or statistical summaries for their counties, to which I have referred freely.

For the early years of this history I have relied exclusively on the printed word, but the story of more recent times has benefited from the personal testimony of many of those who took part in the matches or the affairs of the County Club off the field. I have sat, with tape-recorder running, in home or hostelry with (in alphabetical order): Paul Atkins, Kevin Beaumont, John Cockett, Ken Drucquer, Ian Feasey, David Mackintosh, Chris Parry, Robin Peppiatt, Tim Scriven, John Slack, David Smith, Jack Tomlin and Stuart York. I have spoken more cursorily or on the telephone, sometimes at length, to: Ray Bond, Neil Burns, Paul Dolphin, Jason Harrison, Fred Hawkins, Brian Janes, Paula Johns, Michael Knox, Colin Lever, Brian Lucas, John Rogers, Tim Russell, Simon Stanway, Peter Stoddart, John Swain, John Tovey, Francis Whiting and John R Williams. Officers and older members of a number of local clubs have also kindly furnished information when, often as a total stranger, I rang asking questions about players of the past. I should particularly mention Colin Kightley for information provided about the early history of cricket at Wolverton.

I have made use of the following books of reference: Arthur Haygarth's Cricket Scores and Biographies, The Dawn of Cricket by T Waghorn, Fresh Light on 18th Century Cricket by GB Buckley, Fresh Light on Pre-Victorian Cricket by GB Buckley, The History of Cricket by Peter Wynne-Thomas, Cricket: a History of its Growth and Development throughout the World by Rowland Bowen, Barclays' World of Cricket, Playfair Cricket Annuals, Who's Who of Cricketers (Bailey, Thorn and Wynne-Thomas), Oxford and Cambridge Cricket by George Chesterton and Hubert Doggart, Wisden Cricketers' Almanack, the Wisden Book of Obituaries, Who's Who, Who's Who in Buckinghamshire, Bucks, Berks and Beds Contemporary Biographies (1907) and Walford's County Families of the United Kingdom.

My principal on-line source has been CricketArchive, which has been an invaluable reference point for first-class career records.

The newspapers that I have particularly perused are: Bucks Advertiser, Bucks Free Press and Bucks Herald. Many other newspapers have been consulted to trace scores. I am grateful to the staff of the Local Studies section of the County Library in Aylesbury, where I have been assisted in many ways and, in particular, in finding details of certain county families.

In addition I have visited the MCC Library at Lord's and looked through sundry editions of Cricket, the Cricketer and some club histories. I should like to thank Adam Chadwick and his staff for their unfailingly helpful attitude and, in particular, for allowing me access to minutes of committee meetings where there might have been deliberations relevant to Bucks' possible elevation to first-class status.

Throughout the writing of this history I have constantly referred to the work of Paul Slatter, produced for the centenary of the County Club in 1991. Working against the clock to meet a deadline and knowing that his health was failing, he achieved a brilliant résumé of the county's deeds to that date. I never had the good fortune to meet Paul, nor have I had his advantage of being at the centre of affairs in the county. What he knew at first hand I have gleaned through the reports of others. However, I now have one major compensating advantage – a comprehensive statistical base which has enabled me to fill in many of the gaps that Paul had to leave void, most notably details of early century makers. Moreover, I have had the time to explore the history of cricket in the county before the formation of the present County Club.

Among other ACS members who have offered help, I would particularly mention Don Ambrose, a mine of information on public school registers, and Peter Wynne-Thomas, a paramount authority on the game's earliest years. For information freely given on the military careers of those cricketers involved in World Wars I am indebted to Mike Spurrier. My thanks are also due to Bob Harragan for information about the aftermath of Bucks' match against Carmarthenshire in 1911. I am grateful to Peter Griffiths for work undertaken to prepare the manuscript for printing.

For many of the older photographs I am indebted to the Roger Mann Collection, whose pictures are identified in the text. In choosing those that might be suitable for the purposes of the history it has been a particular pleasure to find that Roger welcomes a challenge and then rises with unfeigned enthusiasm to meet it. I acknowledge also the provenance of two pictures that appear by courtesy of Bucks County Archives. A number of pictures have been made available through the Trent Bridge library, for which I extend thanks to Nottinghamshire CCC. Another source of more modern photographs is the Bucks Free Press, whose pictures have been made freely available for publication.

The photograph of PN Durlacher has been supplied by Wellington College, that of FN Bird by the Old Wellingburian Club. The picture of Harry Pitchford has been provided by kind permission of Sir Evelyn de Rothschild. Other photographs are, in the main, the property of the County Club or myself, but for the loan of personal pictures I am grateful to: John Cockett, Judge Simon Fawcus, Paula Johns, Chris Parry, Judge John Slack and George Whiting. I am grateful, too, to Paula Johns and Robin Peppiatt, whose generosity has helped to defray the cost of commercially obtained photographs.

It has been a privilege to write this short history, flawed as it may be. It has been written primarily for those with an interest in cricket in Buckinghamshire rather than for those whose preoccupation is with the game's statistics. However, I am delighted that the ACS, with its rigorous disciplines, has agreed to publish it. It is too early to talk of a series of such histories, but I hope that my attempt to show something of what lies behind the figures may help to persuade others involved with the ACS scores project to take the plunge and follow suit.

Douglas Miller
April 2006

The Early Years

First evidence of cricket in Bucks

When was cricket first played in Buckinghamshire? There can be no simple answer to this question; and what, in any case, do we mean by 'cricket'? This is still the word we might use today to describe the game that we see played on the beach: a soft ball game without teams, probably with one batsman rather than two, some under-arm bowling, perhaps a picnic box or a couple of children's spades acting as the wicket, with the incoming tide as an ever-shifting boundary and a dog as a supernumerary fielder. Of course such games conform to few of MCC's Laws, yet in many ways they may be closer to the cricket most likely to have been played in the 16th century, a form of competitive amusement, perhaps borrowing elements from other games that never flourished as cricket has done - games where participants hurled missiles and others struck them, in defence or attack, with some crude stick or bat.

We are talking principally of a game played by youngsters or by manual labourers at the end of their working day. There were no scores to report and no matches to advertise to the wider world in the hope of mustering a crowd of paying spectators, so it is hardly surprising that most early references to cricket should be found when the players started to make a nuisance of themselves. Cricket is most widely mentioned in the 17th century in records of court cases relating to injuries and damage to property caused in the course of playing the game, whilst high among the other misdemeanours for which the earliest cricketers risked prosecution was that most heinous of crimes, Sabbath breaking.

From such hazily charted origins our national game took root in the 17th century in The Weald, the area between the North and South Downs, primarily in Sussex but spilling over into Surrey and Kent. By the turn of the century it was gaining popularity in London, and it received an important boost as wealthy noblemen raised teams to compete for substantial purses with side bets adding to the importance attached to the outcome of the matches. The leading players of the day were found jobs on the great estates of their patrons, and cricket was dubbed a 'manly exercise' as those of social standing gave it their support.

As the game gained ground in aristocratic circles it began to find its way to the great public schools in the south of the country. Pupils at Eton, Harrow, Winchester and Westminster will have been caught up in its growing popularity. Horace Walpole, who was at Eton from 1727 to 1734, made reference to cricket being quite widely played at the school during his time there, though it had little appeal for him. It was not until the 19th century that success on the cricket field started to become a barometer of a school's prestige but, with Eton in those days lying within the boundaries of Bucks, the informal games of Walpole's time and previous decades will have been among the earliest cricket to be played in the county.

The first newspaper record of a match in Bucks came in October 1730 when 'a match of cricket was played by persons of distinction, on Datchett (sic) Heath, for £50'. We have to wait ten years for the next published mention of the game. On 8 September 1740 it was reported that 'a match was played between the gentlemen of London and eleven gentlemen of Buckinghamshire, Berkshire and Hertfordshire, which was won by the former with great difficulty.' A return match was to be played on the Artillery Ground, the principal venue for the great matches in the 1740s. It was on this ground, in 1744, that Kent played All England in what was long believed to be the first match for which the full scores have been preserved – it is, in fact, the second.

Cricket at the Artillery Ground in 1743

On 17 August 1741 the *Northampton Mercury* advised its readers that the gentlemen of Northants were to play those of Buckinghamshire for 20 guineas a side in the Cow Meadow near Northampton 'with wickets pitched at 10 and the game to be played out.' Demonstrating how the game was spreading its tentacles away from London, this is the first year in which newspaper references have been found of cricket matches in Northamptonshire and Bedfordshire. The earliest notices to be uncovered of matches in Hertfordshire are from newspapers of 1732 and 1737. The first match to be mentioned in Oxfordshire, relating to the University, is from 1727, exactly a hundred years before the first Varsity Match.

To place these dates in context, we are still some decades from the first authenticated mention of matches at Hambledon, so often misleadingly referred to as the cradle of cricket. Though cricket was probably played on Broadhalfpenny Down from 1756, the Hambledon Club itself may not have been formed until 1767 and its period of greatest prosperity was in the 1770s and 1780s. In fact, the game's progress in Hampshire was surprisingly slow given its proximity to Sussex, and the first reference to a match in the county does not come until 1749. So even if Bucks could not claim to compete with Hambledon in the quality of the matches played, the game may have been establishing itself in the county at an earlier date.

It was more common in publications of these early years to find notices of matches about to take place rather than reports on their outcome. An exception to this was in July 1761 when Wesburn Green near Beaconsfield became the first recorded venue in the county for a match on what was to become a popular pretext for a competitive game - married versus single. On this occasion the married men triumphed and took home a purse of £100.

A more modest prize was at stake in 1774 when Risborough, unusually prominent in early references, met Bucks at Wycombe Rye for a silver cup valued at five guineas and given by the innkeepers of High Wycombe, who no doubt hoped to profit from the crowd drawn to the match. The same year saw Risborough in action against Maidenhead at Lord Le Despencer's Park at West Wycombe, again for a cup, this time worth five pounds rather than guineas.

On 29 May 1775 there was 'a match of cricket for £50 a side' at Bray in which there was a victory by 151 notches for Maidenhead, assisted by Lumpy Stevens, the finest bowler of his generation, when they beat Risborough, who had a lesser luminary named Briggs to help them. Later that year there is report of Wendover beating Tring by an innings and a large number of notches 'although Tring were allowed two famous players from another place'.

An article in *The Cricketer* of 30 August 1924 celebrating Bucks' outstanding success in minor counties cricket around that time - they had thrashed Surrey Second Eleven by the little matter of 242 runs in the previous year's Challenge Match - pleads that the history of the county be set in print. It goes on to say, without further substantiation, that 'matches with Berkshire date back at least as far as 1784, when the counties met at Marlow and Datchet.' The following year the *Reading Mercury* announced that on 27 August Berkshire were scheduled to play Bucks for £25 a side on Langley Broom, Berkshire. That same summer the Gentlemen of Hertfordshire were entertained at Nettis Green near Beaconsfield. These appear to be the first references so far uncovered of a Bucks team purporting to compete against another county, but there is no evidence to point to a properly constituted club or selection procedures, and all the indications are that any further matches were few and far between.

Haygarth takes notice of Bucks

Cricket historians owe an incalculable debt to Arthur Haygarth (1825 - 1903), whose life was devoted to retrieving and publishing details of all matches of note played between 1746 and 1878. His *Scores and Biographies*, published in 14 volumes, provide a crude gauge of the game's health. After recording the single match at the Artillery Ground in 1744 Haygarth's next score is from 1771, but thereafter he shows cricket's popularity growing steadily through the last decades of the 18th century. However, decline was around the corner and as the 19th century dawned Haygarth found fewer matches that merited his attention.

Public morale around this time had been lowered by the enclosure of common land, and the rural population had suffered from depressed agricultural wages at a time when the price of grain was high. Those who had left the land and made their way to urban factories in the wake of the Industrial Revolution worked inhumanly long hours. Moreover, in the years before Waterloo, invasion was an ever-present threat. The mood of the people and their other preoccupations make it hardly surprising that the public should have had less taste for the sport of cricket, less time to play it and less approval of those participating in it.

By 1820 all this had begun to change. As cricket emerged from its dark age one of the first Bucks clubs to see the light of day was Stoke Green, claiming its foundation as a modest village club in 1815, when it is reputed to have played a game against an eleven from Eton College. A few years later came the formation of some of the county's foremost clubs - High Wycombe in 1823, Beaconsfield in 1825 and Marlow in 1829 - all pointing to a growing interest in the game in the south of the county.

Meanwhile Haygarth, whose publications overflow with the scores of Eton's matches, alighted upon another cricketing location in Bucks: Newport Pagnell, where we find the first of several references in 1838. On 24 and 25 August the home team beat the Royal Artillery Club by an innings and eight runs. In 1841 there was a heavy loss to Moor Park, a year later a comfortable win against the Gentlemen of Leicestershire. None of those who played in the matches would be counted among the great cricketers of the day, nor were any of the Newport Pagnell players later found playing for the county, but one man who was in the home team on all three occasions was Lord C Russell, possibly a kinsman of the Duke of Bedford.

Up to this point, games of cricket in Buckinghamshire were not to be counted among the great matches and, where neighbouring Hertfordshire could claim the rascally Lord Frederick Beauclerk, Bucks had thrown up no notable cricketing personalities. Notwithstanding the matches of the 1780s, none of the county's encounters had merited Haygarth's attention, and his first mention of a game involving a Bucks team comes in 1844. For his tardiness in including any of the county's earlier matches Haygarth was taken to task in the earlier quoted article from *The Cricketer*, where he was reproved for his failure to mention 'the game in which Buckinghamshire beat Surrey in Chelsea in 1814 for 200 guineas a side and 50 the odds.' Haygarth, in fact, collected full scores rather than mere references to matches, so the omissions are hardly surprising. Moreover, it was the presence of famous players that made a match noteworthy. However, in fairness to Haygarth, it is known that he strove to unearth the details of many matches that ultimately eluded him.

The 1844 match against Berkshire met Haygarth's criteria. Full scores survive and the match took place, very appropriately, on the Brocas at Eton. Moreover, at a time when it was common practice to hire professionals to undertake the more irksome task of bowling, the Bucks side was strengthened by the inclusion of three of the foremost cricketers of the day - Fuller Pilch, William Hillyer and James Dean. Pilch was the leading batsman of the period and Hillyer one of its most feared bowlers, while Dean, another fine bowler, thought nothing of keeping wicket and bowling alternate overs. These household names will certainly have commended the match to Haygarth, and though Pilch did little with the bat the two bowlers played a crucial part in steering Bucks to a three-wicket win against opponents who were themselves strengthened by three hired men, among them William Lillywhite. Emphasising that the cricket of the 1840s was seldom a batsman's game, the scores in this two-day match were: Berks 31 and 45; Bucks 47 and 30 for 7.

There is still nothing to suggest the formality of a county club at this stage. Indeed, when Bucks' activities next took Haygarth's attention in 1846, the selection of the side was left to a young aristocrat. The son of a high court judge, Charles Coleridge had taken the eye as an Eton schoolboy just two years earlier and he was destined to play with distinction for Oxford in 1849 and 1850. This time only one hired man, Hillyer, was enlisted and among the amateurs Coleridge invited to represent Bucks was JW Chitty, who had played with him in the Eton eleven. A familiar name in legal circles, his father was the author of *Chitty's Practice* and other law books. Young Joe Chitty went on to play alongside Coleridge for Oxford. Chosen as a wicket-keeper, he earned a place in the university's folklore for the amusement caused when his wig fell off in a collision on the field and revealed his bald pate.

After Berkshire had emerged victorious from another low-scoring match by 25 runs, the next three encounters between the two sides to be recorded by Haygarth, two in 1849 and one in 1859, all ended in draws or 'unfinished' in the parlance of the day. The next Bucks match to interest Haygarth was at Fenny Stratford in 1859 when Twenty Two of Buckinghamshire, strengthened by the inclusion of the Yorkshire professional William Slinn, pitted their skills against George Parr's All England Eleven. This was a wandering circus of players who used to earn a comfortable living by touring around and playing a succession of such matches across the country. Bucks lost by nine wickets, and Haygarth reports that 'in the second innings the first nine wickets fell for seven runs'.

A first County Club is formed

1864 is a pivotal year in cricket's evolution. It marks the legalising of over-arm bowling. It is the year in which *Wisden* was first published. It saw the young WG Grace, on the eve of his 16th birthday, first give evidence of his exceptional talent with an innings of 170 for South Wales against the Gentlemen of Sussex at Hove. It also heralded the formation of official county clubs in Lancashire and Middlesex, making them the sixth and seventh of the present first-class counties to be established after Sussex, Nottinghamshire, Surrey, Hampshire and Yorkshire. So when Bucks formed a county club in this same year it was in good company.

The avowed object of the committee was reported as being 'to encourage cricket among all classes in the County'. The qualifications for admission to membership of the club were 'birth, ownership or occupation of land, or one year's residence in the County.' Subscriptions were £1 for playing members and 10s (50p) for others.

HE Bull, an Oxford blue in 1863 and soon to be a pillar of the landed gentry in the Buckingham area, was installed as secretary. JC Maul, a driving force behind cricket around Newport Pagnell, became treasurer for one year before Bull took on both jobs. Under the presidency of The Hon Percy Barrington, the committee lacked nothing in social lustre. Its other members comprised: the Reverend ET Drake and TT Drake, both with the middle name Tyrwhitt as members of the family who owned Shardeloes, where the Amersham Club still plays; Thomas Fremantle, who would become the 2nd Lord Cottesloe and who lived at Swanbourne, where the family still resides, the present Lord Cottesloe having served as Lord Lieutenant of the county; the Hon. Charles Carington, the single 'r' denoting the family name of the present Lord Carrington; RA Fitzgerald, at the time Honorary Secretary of MCC;

HE Bull

the president's son-in-law AJ Robarts, an old Etonian banker and another prominent landowner from Lillingstone to the north of Buckingham; the Rev H Roundell and Charles Markham, who played a prominent part as a player.

If there was a strong aristocratic presence in the first committee there was nothing plebeian about those who first represented the county on the field. The team which gathered at Newport Pagnell to play another newcomer, Middlesex, on 2, 3 June 1864 included not one member of the Twenty Two from the 1859 match at Fenny Stratford. In batting order it read: Rev CDB Marsham, T Hearne, HE Bull, RDB Marsham, Rev CG Lane, G Hearne, Charles Marsham, C Powell, CW Scriven, EG Sutton, J Fremantle. Apart from the two ordained gentlemen, both players of distinction, the only men not to be styled 'Esq' are the two Hearne brothers, both of whom were professionals and who were also the only players to have previously appeared for a Bucks team, both having been in the side against Berkshire in 1857.

Of the two brothers Tom Hearne, born in 1826, was the more distinguished player. Fitting his Bucks matches into a career for Middlesex that stretched from 1859 to 1875, he made his mark comparatively late in life when he shared a first wicket stand of 149 with Robert Carpenter for the United against the All England XI at Lord's in 1859. Two years later he toured Australia, though with little success, but he took centre stage at Lord's in 1866 when he made 122 not out for the Players against the

Tom Hearne

Gentlemen. Tom Hearne's last match for Bucks was in 1868. He suffered a stroke in 1876, but made a remarkable recovery going on to earn great respect as manager of the ground bowlers at Lord's for more than 20 years. George Hearne, three years younger than his brother, did not play again for Bucks after this first match, making one of his rare appearances for Middlesex in the return fixture in1864.

If the Bucks team included a second paid player alongside Tom Hearne it was most likely to be Tom Plumb from Aylesbury, rated one of the finest wicket-keepers in the land. But the county's real strength lay in its amateurs, few of whom were more distinguished than the Reverend Edward Tyrwhitt Drake, who was most renowned for his under-arm lobs that twisted in from leg to off, and of whose batting it was said that he was 'one of the most slashing that has yet appeared'. In 1863 Edward Drake was installed as rector of St Mary's Amersham, where his family still hold the patronage, serving until 1904 when he was succeeded by another cricketing parson, the Reverend CE Briggs. Charles Edward Briggs had played six times for Hampshire before taking up his appointment. He was for many years captain of the Amersham club and made one appearance for Bucks. When he left St Mary's in1947 he and ET Drake had given the parish 84 unbroken years with a first-class cricketer as rector.

Henry Bull, a splendid long stop who seldom missed a match, and Robert Fitzgerald were both useful performers in the teams of the 1860s, but most notable of all were the three Marsham brothers, kinsmen of the Earl of Romney and all of them Oxford blues: the Reverend CDB, one of the best amateur bowlers of his day, Charles, who also served on the committee, and Robert, whose role in Bucks' first match is tinged with uncertainty.

In this match Haygarth credits Robert Marsham with batting at number four, but the *Bucks Herald* records that the player concerned was R Ridley, whose name is never seen again. Playing under an assumed name was not unknown in these times and one may speculate as to the reason. Might Robert have been mindful that for many years the Marshams' first loyalty had been to Oxfordshire? Or did he not wish to advertise his whereabouts as he absconded from some professional or social commitment? The match ended as a draw, the scores being Bucks 189 and 165, Middlesex 238. '592 runs for thirty wickets lowered!' gasps Haygarth, clearly unaccustomed to such dominance of the bat.

ET Drake

For Bucks the top scorer in the first innings was Robert Marsham (or Ridley) with 59, an innings that earned fulsome praise in the *Herald's* report. Another of the three Marsham brothers, the committee member Charles, scored 45. In the second innings a former Surrey player and double Oxford blue, for rowing and cricket, the Rev CG Lane made 55. Lane appeared only twice for Bucks; in the first innings he had had the misfortune to be dismissed cheaply - bowled by a shooter.

It is, perhaps, a sign of the public perception that Bucks was to be regarded as one of the premier counties that the expectation had been for a three-day match, the *Bucks Herald* reporting: 'The interest in the match subsided when it became known that only two days would be devoted to it, such a limit being entirely without precedent in a county match.' Two months later Bucks supporters had a different cause for disappointment when the teams met for the return game at Islington. This time the match stretched across three days enabling Middlesex to record an amazing win by 138 runs after following on no fewer than 218 runs behind on first innings.

A Bucks team at Shardeloes in 1869

Photograph courtesy County Archives

The Bucks team lacked the services of its clergy stars and Robert Marsham was also unable to play, but an innings of 109 from E Austen Leigh, a great-nephew of Jane Austen, and 74 from Charles Marsham helped the county to post a first-innings total of 294, after which Tom Hearne, with five for 26, was principally responsible for dismissing Middlesex for only 76. When the home team followed on no-one exceeded 78, but so consistent was the scoring down the order that Middlesex were able to reach 463, setting Bucks the formidable target of 246 to win. With a swollen knee preventing EG Sutton from batting and with two of their best batsmen run out, Bucks subsided for 107.

A match that eluded Haygarth brought MCC to Newport Pagnell on 9, 10 May 1865. Though county matches were also played at Marlow in 1869 and 1870, the ground at Bury Field in Newport Pagnell was Bucks' most favoured home venue, sometimes referred to as the county's headquarters. Situated about four miles from Wolverton station on the London and North-Western Railway, it was well placed for travellers from the capital, and the ground had been drained and the turf re-laid at great expense ahead of the first match in 1864. The news that Bucks were playing MCC attracted many carriages to the ground, but in later years it was the presence of the railway works in the town that guaranteed a good crowd of paying spectators for matches played at Wolverton.

The start of the 1865 match was delayed until one o'clock, but there was still time for MCC to be dismissed ahead of the 2.30 lunch bell for just 55, with Rev ET Drake claiming six of the wickets. Bucks now had to face the formidable attack of Alfred Shaw and James Grundy, two of the leading professional bowlers in the land, but with 22 from Drake they reached 96. Although a sprained knee kept Tom Hearne out of the attack, MCC were soon in trouble in their second innings. However, when they resumed next day at 52 for 4, RD Walker, one of the famous Southgate brothers, with 51, and HN Tennant of the theatrical family, with 26, combined to set Bucks 86 for victory. The county got home for the loss of six wickets, but not without alarms after ED Sutton had had to run for both Drake and Hearne before leaving it to Tom Plumb and RA Fitzgerald to finish the business.

Scores from 24 more matches involving Bucks were recorded by Haygarth, the last of them a single-wicket triumph at Bedford in 1871. This was an astonishing match in which Bucks recovered from being dismissed for 23 in their first innings to reach a target of 143 in their second attempt. Victory allowed one of the winning team to feel he could vent his wrath in the columns of the *Bucks Herald* without being regarded as 'one who cannot lose without grumbling'. The target of his attack was Walter Anstead, a Weybridge schoolmaster who had previously appeared with success for Surrey, and whose style of bowling had led to the first innings debacle. His disquieted opponent wrote: 'There is every reason to believe that with a little practice the new bowling will be overcome as easily as genuine bowling often is, but still in the interests of true cricket and personal safety I would ask is deliberate throwing to be admitted as a substitute for fair bowling?'

During the seven years from 1864 the team often styled itself 'The Gentlemen of Buckinghamshire', but with no notable change in personnel, especially when the side was strengthened by the inclusion of a professional. This usually enabled Plumb to play, though on one occasion the county hired James Southerton, one of the leading bowlers of the period, who was to appear in England's first Test match at the age of 49 in 1877. A few of the matches were against odds. A Buckinghamshire team took on Sixteen of Brackley and Seventeen of Great Marlow, and in the Brackley match Bucks deemed it necessary for some reason to include in their eleven no fewer than four well-known professionals – Humphrey, Jupp, Mortlock and James Lillywhite. However, proper eleven a side matches against Hampshire, Kent, Bedfordshire, Huntingdonshire and the Undergraduates of Oxford all featured on the fixture list.

RAH Mitchell

In 1868 MCC were trounced by an innings at Lord's, and later that year, on Mr AJ Robarts' ground at Lillingstone, Bucks beat a team styled by Haygarth as 'The World (so-called)' by 91 runs, with 88 coming from RAH Mitchell, an assistant master at Eton, who was regarded as one of the finest batsmen of his day. Others to make centuries were Robert Fitzgerald with 111 not out against Hampshire at Southampton in 1866 and FH Hill, an Oxford blue, who hit 105 against Bedfordshire at

Newport Pagnell in 1868. Mention should also be made of HC Maul. As a 17 year-old he made his debut for Bucks in 1867, going on to play a few useful innings before launching himself on a career with Warwickshire, then a second class county, for whom he hit a number of double hundreds including 267 against Staffordshire in 1888. Ten years earlier Henry Maul had toured Australia with the team led by Lord Harris, though he did not take part in the only Test Match played.

1871 is notable as the year in which WG Grace first played in Buckinghamshire. He appeared for a Gentlemen of England team against Twenty-Two of Wycombe in a rain-interrupted three-day match played in Wycombe Abbey Park. The venue is further described as 'Lord Carington's', though Haygarth errs in giving his Lordship a single 'r'. Grace, whose brother Fred also played, made 89 in his side's total of 219. Wycombe Abbey had earlier hosted a match against a relatively weak United All England Eleven in 1866 when they had beaten Twenty-Two of the Wycombe Amateur Club with Whale by 36 runs.

WG Grace and his brother were back in the county in 1872 playing for a strong United South of England Eleven, who beat Twenty-Two of Aylesbury by an innings and 27 runs. There was a further fixture in 1874 when the visitors were again successful, on this occasion winning by eight wickets. Once again the two Graces were playing and other leading players to appear in both matches were H Jupp, R Humphrey, E Pooley, H Charlwood, James Lillywhite and J Southerton. For the Aylesbury team, Tom Plumb played in both matches and Tom Hearne in the second, but none of the other local players had played for the county side.

The demise of the first County Club

With an influential committee and a string of successes on the field - 15 victories were recorded offset by only five losses - Bucks appeared to have all it needed to prosper, but after 1871 the County Club seems to have sunk into terminal decline. The reasons for this are not readily apparent, though many of the better players did not owe allegiance to only one county. The Marshams all played for both Oxfordshire and Northants, while Fitzgerald was the leading light in the formation of the Hertfordshire County Club in 1876 and Edward Drake also played for that county. Even as true a Bucks man as Henry Bull, the secretary, turned out at some time for Oxfordshire, Hertfordshire, Bedfordshire and Northants!

The apparent demise of the whole county organisation in Bucks certainly contrasted with a club game that was going from strength to strength. All the major towns were fielding teams and there were regular reports of new grounds opening, while cricket was thriving in many of the villages where it is still played today - and many where it is not. Some of the bigger clubs enjoyed an annual fixture with MCC, an occasion that was always eagerly awaited and contested with a determination well illustrated by the Vale of Aylesbury match in 1879 when fears that the weather might interfere with the game were well justified by a subsequent newspaper report that 'running was in some instances very difficult and the ball had to be waded for in pools of water'.

Scores and reports for club matches around the county lay beside those of more prestigious encounters: Eton v Harrow and the University match always merited full reports in the local press, and even details of England's first Test Match against Australia on home soil in 1880 reached the local sports page, as did the epic encounter at The Oval two years later. Yet space would still be found for matches of quintessentially parochial interest: Aylesbury butchers v Tring butchers; Brushmakers v Shoemakers at Chesham; Hazell Watson & Viney v Social Sons of Harmony; Choir boys of St Mary's North side v South side; Parishioners v The Establishment at Great Hampden.

During the barren years for Bucks there is evidence of adjoining counties playing a few matches. Occasional scores can be found in the *Bucks Herald* for Berkshire, Bedfordshire and Hertfordshire, but the last mention of a Bucks team comes in 1874, when the Gentlemen of Bucks let themselves down badly at Marlow. There was great disappointment that a weakened team should have been sent to play The Rovers in what the home club saw as a prestigious match. And it came as little surprise that the Bucks batsmen should buckle in both their innings and lose by nine wickets. One man who emerged with some credit was AC Bartholomew, who three years earlier had played for Cambridge in Cobden's match. Now he made 34 'by boldness and dash'.

By 1889 moves were afoot to set Bucks cricket back on the map. 'We are glad to find that the movement for the encouragement of County Cricket in Bucks has been well taken up,' reported the *Bucks Herald* of 25 May in noting that there had been a meeting of club secretaries from the south of the county at the Bear Hotel in Maidenhead. In mid-June their counterparts from the north gathered at the Bletchley Park Hotel where it was agreed to write to clubs inviting names of players who might wish to play for the North in the two trial matches that were planned for later that summer.

On 31 July, in lovely weather and before a good crowd, the two sides met for the first match at Buckingham. The South, seen as clear favourites, made a poor start, collapsing to the bowling of 20-year-old WJ Gough, a Buckingham hotel-keeper, for 61; but the North's batsmen could do little better, gaining a lead of just three runs. The South now showed their true ability as Percy de Paravicini, a former Middlesex player who was to become captain of Bucks in 1893, followed his first innings of 23 with 107. A target of 285 proved far beyond the capabilities of the North, whose batsmen surrendered meekly for 71.

The return match on the Dolphin Ground at Slough provided the stage for a stylish 108 from CW Parry of Stoke Green CC as he dominated the South's first innings of 154. AM Sutthery, who had won a blue at Cambridge two years earlier, made 36 for the North, but 19 from his brother was the only other double figure contribution as the ball dominated. Walter Hearne, another of that prodigious clan from Chalfont and the brother of JT Hearne, and who would soon gain a regular place in the Kent team, took eight for 43 as the North mustered only 107. Arthur Sutthery, with seven for 38, strove to keep his side in the match, but the South again ran out easy winners by 62 runs.

Mr. Leopold de Rothschild,
J.P., D.L., C.V.O.

There was now an appetite for county cricket and the next year Mr Leopold de Rothschild assembled a team at Ascott to take on Eleven of the County. The team included several members who would make their debut for Bucks the following year and they proved too strong for their host's eleven, winning by an innings and 43 runs. Cecil Parry again underlined his credentials in top-scoring with 68. A few months later he would be one of the 14 gentlemen who assembled in London to ensure that 1891 would see a Buckinghamshire team back on the field and when the next summer came round he would be its captain at the age of 24.

The Birth of
Minor Counties Cricket

The Bucks County Club starts up again

The county's first minute book, which still survives, records that the inaugural meeting to form a county club was held on Thursday 16 January 1891 at The Charing Cross Hotel. In the chair was EH Parry, the older brother of Cecil. The Parrys hailed from Stoke Poges, where their father, the Reverend E St John Parry, ran a small preparatory school, Stoke House, which was only a short distance from Stoke Green Cricket Club, where the family were all heavily involved. The two brothers were educated at Charterhouse and later followed their father into the teaching profession. Edward was an assistant master at Felsted until taking over Stoke House in 1892, while Cecil spent eight years on the staff at Wellington. Though he never played cricket for the county, Edward Parry was a fine sportsman, reserving his greatest achievements for the football field, where he captained Oxford University in 1877 before going on to win three England caps. Though Cecil Parry died at the early age of 34, Edward was still serving on the Bucks committee in 1920.

At the inaugural meeting Lord Rothschild was elected the club's first president, an office that changed annually in the early years. Edward Parry was confirmed as chairman, and the captain of the Marlow Cricket Club, GR Ward, a man of independent means who had been the prime instigator of the meeting, took on the office of secretary. CM Woodbridge, a bank manager from Iver, who played in a few of the early matches, was elected treasurer. The county's titled aristocrats and landed gentry were invited to become vice-presidents and the first committee included the names of several gentlemen who were to give sterling service to the cause of Bucks cricket beyond the turn of the century: PJ de Paravicini (Datchet), HE Bull (Buckingham), FD Clare (Chesham), CE Cobb (Aylesbury), AJ Thurlow (High Wycombe), E Warne (Winslow), W Curtis (Chalfont St Giles), JH Roberts (Datchet) and AA Somerville (Eton College).

HE Bull, jnr at Eton

Photograph courtesy County Archive

Another who would soon join their number was FT Higgins. In 1897 he was to take the name of his maternal grandfather, Sir Thomas Tyringham Bernard, who was the sixth and last Baronet of Nether Winchendon, and in that year he became known as FT Higgins-Bernard or simply FTH Bernard. He had been called to the bar in 1889 and his London residence was one of the venues for early committee meetings.

The minutes and contemporary newspaper reports contain no reference to the previously constituted club - despite the inclusion on the new committee of HE Bull. Whether this was Henry Bull, the earlier secretary now aged 47, or his 21 year-old son Herbert, who inherited his father's initials and who was destined to become secretary in 1904, we can only speculate. The younger Bull was certainly a close friend of other stalwarts on the newly formed committee, most notably Charles Cobb, and a later tribute to him refers to his involvement in the formation of the club. However, regardless of the date when his son first came onto the committee, HE Bull senior will not have been far from the action and would have been able to speak at first hand of the earlier attempt to form a county club.

It was felt that at least £100 would be needed to launch the club, and doubts were expressed about the shortage of professionals and the weakness of the game in the north of the county. The shape of Buckinghamshire has always presented difficulties, but if those involved with the governance of the club in its early days were truly concerned about the plight of the north it may well be wondered why the initial meeting in1891, and the Annual General Meetings in 1894 and 1895, should have been held not in Aylesbury, as they were in 1892 and 1893, but in Central London.

The first season's programme of matches began on 23 July at Oxford, where Bucks, without the services of their captain, lost by eight wickets. There was a return match against Oxfordshire at High Wycombe and home and away matches were played against Bedfordshire, with the home game taking place at Ascott, where the traditional hospitality of Mr Leopold de Rothschild ensured that they were all offered lunch. It was a disappointing first season for Bucks, whose record was two draws and two losses, but there was more cause for cheer the following year with wins away to Wiltshire and Bedfordshire offset by defeat to the former at Chalfont Park and a loss to MCC at Lord's.

By 1893 there was a more co-ordinated approach to arranging fixtures with counties sending delegates to Lord's and the secretary, George Ward, and Francis Higgins were deputed to attend for Bucks. The time for a formalised competition for the second-class counties, as they were then called, was drawing near.1895 is often quoted as the year that heralded the beginning of cricket's 'Golden Age'. It was a year in which the shape of the first-class game was undergoing radical change with the admission of Derbyshire, Essex, Hampshire, Leicestershire and Warwickshire to the County Championship. The minor counties, too, were on the move. At the start of the season the magazine *Cricket* had reported in its issue of 18 April on the inception of a championship for those without first-class status. This was the result of an initiative by the honorary secretary of Worcestershire, PH Foley, whose venture was supported by Bedfordshire, Durham, Norfolk, Oxfordshire and Staffordshire.

At first the Bucks committee adopted a cautious approach to the new championship. An invitation to play matches against the Isle of Wight had already been turned down on grounds of cost and, despite improving performances on the field of play, there was reluctance to commit to the eight matches that were mandatory for counties wishing to take part. An anomalous situation arose whereby, although the results obtained by Bedfordshire and Oxfordshire against Bucks in 1895 counted towards those counties' performance in the Championship, Bucks itself was excluded from the table. However, for modern record-keeping purposes, those who played for Bucks have been deemed to have begun county careers when selected for these matches and their runs and wickets are included in career statistics.

The County Ground

Around this time the committee had been much engaged with the laying out of a county ground at Aylesbury. Grounds elsewhere were felt to fall short of the standard required for playing county matches and it was decided that the County Club should have a single ground that could become the venue for all home fixtures. Aylesbury was favoured owing to its relatively central position in the awkwardly long and thin county, and it was an asset that there were three railway lines running into the town.

Few worked harder than Charles Cobb to see the new ground to fruition. He lived close by at Weedon and in 1895 assumed the office of treasurer of the County Club, a post he was to hold for ten years. After scouring the area for a suitable site he was grateful to be able to inform the committee of an offer from Lord Rothschild for the lease of 14 acres of land off the Wendover Road at the nominal rent of £2 an acre.

Tenders were invited for laying the square and levelling the rest of the ground. From the three individuals who responded the committee chose George Nash, a cricket coach at Eton College who was already well known to the members as he had been playing for the county since 1892. Nash was felt to bring the right experience to the task and his tender of £300 to cover an area of 150 yards square compared favourably with the estimate of George Hearne, the Kent professional and son of the cricketer of the same name who had played for Bucks in 1864.

Together with the cost of fencing and the building of a pavilion, as well as laying a football pitch, the total cost of constructing the ground was estimated at £1500. On top of this were anticipated annual running costs of £200, which included the groundsman's wage of £1 a week and the assistance of a boy, who would receive five shillings a week for 20 weeks' work during the summer. Such sums were quite daunting for the treasurer of the day, and appeals, bazaars and other fund-raising events were successfully undertaken to launch the project.

The post of groundsman was filled by George Nash. It was agreed that he should still be released to Eton for his more lucrative coaching assignment in the summer term, and he could further augment his income from match fees when playing for the county and from coaching engagements with other clubs.

Start of the Minor Counties Championship

It was a disappointment that the new ground could not be ready for the 1895 season, falling victim of a harsh winter followed by a drought in spring, so when Bucks met opponents who were participating in the new championship they had to entertain Oxfordshire at Wolverton, playing on The Big Field belonging to Mr Richard, and the Bedfordshire match took place on the London Road Ground at High Wycombe.

Bucks' first match of the season was against Oxfordshire on the County School Ground at Thame, where there was a contentious opening when the start was delayed as the pitch had been over-watered in a very dry spell, enabling the *South Bucks Free Press* to describe it as 'having the appearance of a bright green oasis in a desert of arid turf'. Bucks won this match by 65 runs and the return game by 51 runs. There was then a narrow loss, by three wickets, to Bedfordshire at Leighton Buzzard followed by a 72-run victory at High Wycombe. Friendly matches brought a win against MCC and two draws with Northamptonshire.

These successes meant that when it came to making plans for the 1896 season Bucks' position was unambiguous and Percy de Paravicini and George Ward were sent to the meeting at Lord's with a clear mandate to arrange the necessary fixtures to ensure that the county would be competing in the fullest sense of the word. Moreover, the new County Ground was now ready for the start of the campaign, and for the next three years this was where all home matches would be played. Thereafter, until 1902, Aylesbury hosted three matches a year while one went to Bletchley Park.

These early seasons were successful ones for Bucks. There were four wins to only one loss in 1896. Two of the matches were very close. The only loss was by one wicket against Hertfordshire at Watford, while one of the wins, against Oxfordshire at Banbury, was by eight runs with the penultimate wicket falling to a boundary catch that home supporters claimed had been taken as the fielder crossed the boundary line and Barber, the Bucks umpire, facing abuse for the decision he had made in favour of his own county. In 1897 the victories rose to five with two defeats. There was a poorer year in1898 with just one victory to offset two losses, but in 1899, under the curious rules of the day, Bucks were declared champions, jointly with Northants, despite winning only once with the seven remaining matches ending in draws. Glamorgan meanwhile had won six of their eight matches, but this was to no avail: avoiding any losses was the formula for taking the crown!

The leading amateurs

The Bucks team of this period conformed to a pattern that could be seen with many other counties. Typically there would be a handful of professionals, usually three with Bucks, who bore the brunt of the bowling, whilst the rest of the team was made up of amateurs of sharply differing ability but with the common thread of a public school background. A hard core played for many seasons, but others came and went after a few brief appearances.

PJ de Paravicini

For Bucks the leading amateur was Percy de Paravicini, who captained the team from 1893 until 1907. Though his appearances became infrequent in his final seasons he was seldom absent in the early years. A talented sportsman, he had first played in the Eton eleven of 1878 at the age of 15, becoming captain in the last two of his four years in the team. A four-year blue at Cambridge, he went on to play 62 matches for Middlesex between 1881 and 1892.

Until he was forced to retire from the game with a damaged knee de Paravicini was also an accomplished soccer player, who played at full back for England against Scotland, Ireland and Wales. He also played in two FA Cup finals for Old Etonians, ending on the winning side against Blackburn Rovers in 1882. In later life he was a keen golfer.

By the time he came to play for Bucks de Paravicini must have been past his best. He endured a wretchedly unsuccessful season in 1895, but came back strongly in subsequent years to register three centuries. Often promoting himself up the order when quick runs were needed, he ended his career with what was then a very respectable batting average of 25.86. In his younger days he was a fine outfielder and he allowed himself the very occasional over of slow bowling. But above all Percy de

Paravicini was a leader, and the newspaper reports of the day are fulsome in their praise of his cavalier approach to the game.

By all accounts he was a fun-loving man. The 1891 Census suggests that he was of independent means living with a bachelor brother and no shortage of servants, but later that year he married Lady Marcia Cholmondeley and by the end of the decade he had three young sons. The family lived by the Thames at Datchet, where a perennial hazard was the risk of flooding, and there are even reports of the river rising high enough for roach to find their way into the piano.

Another mainstay of the early campaigns was Charles Cobb, who had been a prominent Free Forester in the days before the County Club was formed. Cobb was a wicket-keeper of exceptional ability who exceeded a stumping a game over a 45-match career. It is a measure of his class that after his retirement it becomes more difficult to identify his successors from newspaper match scores and 20 matches elapsed before another stumping was recorded for Bucks. Cobb was also a useful batsman, usually in the middle of the order but quite often as an opener. He retired with a batting average of 24.47 and a top score of 111, his only century, which came against Berkshire at Aylesbury in 1898.

Another who began a distinguished career for Bucks in 1896 was Charles Gresson. Educated at Lancing, he was an opening bat. Less of a dasher than some of those who surrounded him, he was the key man to dislodge in the 1890s, never missing a match until 1900 when he was away for two years fighting in the Boer War. He returned for the 1902 season and continued to play until 1907, taking over the captaincy for almost the whole of the 1904 season, for most of which de Paravicini was unable to play. Gresson's outstanding season was 1899 when he scored 658 runs at an average of 65.80. He never quite matched this weight of run-scoring again, but ended his career with 2,978 runs at 27.57, and his record included three centuries.

The first professionals

The trio of professionals who played regularly in the first seasons were Jack Saunders, George Nash and Mat Wright. Saunders was a batsman who went in first wicket down. He had played a couple of matches for Middlesex in 1891 and went on to play for Bucks in every championship match until his retirement at the end of the 1900 season. A career average of 22.19 suggests that his overall contribution was a little disappointing, and he certainly had some poor years culminating in a return of only 134 runs from 12 completed innings in the final season before the committee decided not to retain his services. However, there were brighter moments, and Saunders has the distinction of being the first man to score a championship hundred for the county. This came when he made 114 against Northamptonshire in 1896 in the first match played on the County Ground at Aylesbury. It was the first time any Bucks batsman had passed fifty in a championship match, and Bucks' score of 339 speaks volumes for the quality of the Aylesbury pitch at this time. Jack Saunders was not a regular bowler, but he was a reliable slip fielder and very occasionally kept wicket.

The bowling was almost exclusively the preserve of the other two professionals, George Nash and Mat Wright. In 1895 they sent down just over 90% of all the deliveries bowled by Bucks. In the eight matches of 1896 the figure was just over 80%, the following year 81%. Thereafter injury and illness to Nash gave others more of a chance, but it had been quite common for the two professionals to bowl unchanged throughout an innings and sometimes an entire match. Naturally they ended up with the lion's share of the wickets, and it was the deadly combination of Nash and Wright that was the most crucial ingredient in Bucks' early successes. Their figures, even by the standards of the age in which they played, are remarkable:

	O	M	R	W	Average
1895					
Nash	186.4	67	374	47	7.96
Wright	174.3	83	273	25	10.92
1896					
Nash	405.1	148	716	65	11.02
Wright	402.4	214	492	42	11.71
1897					
Nash	408.1	120	913	62	14.73
Wright	452.2	238	618	55	11.24

If Nash was the bigger wicket taker Wright's economy rate is especially notable, and across the three seasons more than half his five-ball overs were maidens.

George Nash had made his mark with Lancashire before coming to Bucks. His career had not been an entirely happy one. Short in stature, he was a slow left-arm bowler who spun the ball sharply, but he had a distinctive action that aroused comment as to its legality. In 1879, after earlier engagements with Worcester CC, Barrow-in-Furness and Accrington, he signed for Lancashire, for whom he made 54 appearances, returning career figures of 232 wickets at an average of 12.35. It was Nash's misfortune that his time with the county coincided with that of John Crossland, whose action caused much greater furore, not least because he was one of the fastest bowlers in England. Controversy raged and Nash was swept up

George Nash

in it. Matters reached a head in 1885 when Lord Harris, as captain of Kent and with the support of his committee, refused to allow his county to play Lancashire at Tonbridge. Crossland was soon hounded out of the game on the technicality that living in Nottingham in the winter infringed his residential qualification for Lancashire, and Nash's career likewise came to an end in 1885 under a cloud of suspicion that he was a chucker, Lancashire by this time having less need of his services as another left-arm bowler, Johnny Briggs, was just embarking on his illustrious career.

After a time working as a publican in Darwen, Nash, who had been born at Oving near Aylesbury, found his way back south. His appointment as a coach at Eton College enabled him to secure a playing contract for Bucks as all the county's matches were then played in the school holidays. So, already well into his forties, he began a minor counties career that became more intermittent after 1900 as he struggled with ill health. George Nash's last season for Bucks was 1903, when he played in three of the eight matches. He died in November of that year at the age of only 53.

George Nash was the first bowler from all the minor counties to capture 100 championship wickets, a feat he achieved in only his ninth match. It came with the disputed boundary catch against Oxfordshire. Nash's career record for Bucks - 259 wickets at 13.25 - bears comparison with any bowler who has succeeded him. Frank Edwards alone could claim superiority, and even he must yield to Nash the record for the best ever match analysis for the county. This came in 1897 when he bowled unchanged in both innings against Oxfordshire on the County School Ground at Thame, recording figures of:

26.3	10	46	8
24.3	9	28	8

With Mat Wright conceding only 46 runs in the two innings Oxfordshire were hustled out for 84 and 54 leaving Bucks as victors by 110 runs.

Mat Wright

If George Nash's record was truly outstanding, his contribution pales beside that of Mat Wright, his fellow coach at Eton. Wright, who had played just once for Nottinghamshire in 1889, had taken part in a few Bucks matches in the early1890s. His championship debut in Bucks' first match of 1895 came shortly before his 37th birthday and he continued to play for the county until the end of the 1913 season. During this time Bucks played 150 championship matches and Wright took part in 143 of them. Measured just as a bowler his record is that of a titan: 811 wickets at 14.28. It was not until the sixth match of the 1899 season that he knew what it was to bowl through an innings without taking a wicket. On no fewer than seven occasions he took eight wickets in an innings and an equal number of times he took seven, most of these successes coming when he had lost the support of George Nash to spearhead the attack from the other end, and by which time he was taking well over 40% of the wickets that fell.

But this is only half the story for Mat Wright was an all-rounder, regularly batting at number four in his early days. Though his performances with the bat tailed off towards the end of his career, he could still point to a tally of 4,762 runs at an average of 22.25 with four centuries, the best of them 148 against Hertfordshire at Aylesbury in 1900, which was to remain the highest score by a Bucks batsman until surpassed by Dr E Weaver-Adams nine years later. The differential between Wright's batting and bowling average is 1.57, a measure of an outstanding all-round contribution in any company, bettered in the first-class game by a few of the immortals, but matched by no post-war English cricketer apart from specialist batsmen who occasionally bowled.

The image one has of Mat Wright bowling is of the easy rhythmic approach and unerring accuracy of a Derek Shackleton. With an action honed by long hours in the nets at Eton, his bowling was generally described as medium-paced and he was invariably able to keep a tight rein even though runs may have been flowing from the other end. It is confirmation of his accuracy and modest pace that throughout his career Wright gained victims through stumpings, and here he was fortunate to be supported in his early years by the skill of Charles Cobb and in his last three seasons by the genius of Walter Franklin, both of them keepers who were happy to stand up for him.

In an age of more formalised relationships Mat Wright fitted easily into a team where he would have been denied the appellation 'Mister' that all his amateur colleagues would have expected, but reports make clear the high regard in which he was held. It was an occasion for gracious speeches when, in his final match for the county, Mat Wright's benefit was marked by a presentation of a silver salver and a framed illuminated address. The Bishop of Buckingham, the Rt Rev ED Shaw, who had played for the county when he was vicar of High Wycombe, was able to eulogise about Mat Wright the man as much as the cricketer, and Mat himself was able to echo the most appropriate sentiments about a game he had served so long and well.

In 1932, towards the end of a long professional engagement at Eton that stretched from 1885 till 1936, Wright became a councillor for the Royal Borough of Windsor. He died at Windsor on 13 May 1949 at the age of 90.

The supporting cast

These pillars of the early teams received spasmodic assistance from others. Charles Allcock, a master at Eton who had won a blue at Cambridge in 1878, was the first amateur bowler to make a mark, his round-arm slows gaining him 57 wickets at 14.30 in the seasons up to 1898. JW Stratton, who had been educated at Cheltenham, was a younger man who was permitted a few overs when he joined the team after coming down from Oxford, for whom he made a solitary appearance in 1896, but his fast bowling earned him only 45 wickets from 27 matches.

CH Allcock

There were always places to be filled by those who seemed to make lightweight contributions with the bat. Many of these gentlemen were engaged with the running of the game in the county, none more so than Francis Higgins-Bernard. He had good playing credentials, having had the highest public school batting average of 1882 when he had captained Westminster. He later became the squire of Winchendon and, as Lt Col Higgins-Bernard, he stood for parliament as the Unionist candidate for St Austell. A blue for soccer at Oxford provided evidence of his all-round sporting talent. At a later date he won the Officers Sabre Competition and, for good measure, shortly after the turn of the century, he twice won the Bar point to point. He was still in action when he died on the tennis court in 1935. But despite the breadth of his athletic prowess his 23 matches for Bucks yielded a batting average of only 10.86.

CC Edmunds, a Haileyburian whose career stretched from 1899 to 1905, was another who was given his chance 24 times but could average no more than 10.21 with the bat. ENN Bartlett, another with an impeccable family background, served his stint on the committee and, like Higgins-Bernard, took a turn as treasurer, but his opportunities for Bucks appear to have owed more to his connections than to any conspicuous talent. He hit one breezy fifty in a career of 14 intermittent matches that brought him an average of 10.87.

Some occasional players performed rather better. One of undoubted ability was Captain SD Maul - his rank in newspaper reports sometimes rose erratically to colonel only to drop back to captain. The son of JC Maul, who had been secretary when the first attempts had been made at forming a county club in 1864, SD Maul had played for Uppingham in 1876 and shortly after joining the Army had made 217 for Sandhurst against Woolwich. A powerful batsman, he averaged 25.94 in a Bucks career that ended in 1902.

There were tantalising glimpses of talent from young players who made fleeting appearances. FH Mitchell burst on the scene in 1897, the year in which he had captained Eton. The son of RAH Mitchell, young Frank Mitchell made 98 not out against Hertfordshire at Aylesbury in his first match, but could play only six more times, scoring 96 against Wiltshire in 1899, when he shared in a fourth wicket stand of 205 with Wright, still a Bucks record. Mitchell played only three matches for Oxford, where he made more impact on the golf course, winning his blue and going on to become an England international. In later life he became Assistant Private Secretary to King George VI and earned a knighthood.

Lord Dalmeny

The Hon CW Cavendish, son of Lord Chesham, one of the County Club's first vice-presidents, made a promising start in 1898. He scored 32 and 87 in his first match, against Hertfordshire at Watford, but after just two more appearances, which were much less successful, he played no more and at the AGM in 1902 members heard of his death in the Boer War. Lord Dalmeny, who had made his debut for Bucks in 1899, played in five matches in 1900, his last year at Eton. Despite a good school record he made few runs for the county, averaging no more than 11.89 from seven matches, but reports suggest that he was the star fielder. He was later to play briefly for Middlesex before moving in 1903 to Surrey, for whom he made two centuries. He took over the captaincy of Surrey in 1905 and was always proud to recall that during his three years in charge he was responsible for awarding Jack Hobbs his county cap. In 1929 he succeeded his father, a former prime minister, to the title of Lord Rosebery. Many years later he was president of Surrey and of MCC, and he lived to the age of 92, still able to recall his days of playing for Bucks. He died at his home at Mentmore House in 1974, leaving a fortune of nearly £10 million.

Like other minor counties in the early days, the Bucks selectors were quick to find a place in the team for local clergy. By 1914 eight ordained ministers had played for the county. The Rev ED Shaw had the best credentials; an Oxford blue, he played once for Middlesex. The Rev LGBJ Ford brought most initials to the team and a few runs. Another who could point to an isolated half-century was the Rev Francis Symes-Thompson, an occasional wicket-keeper, who had made just one appearance for the university at Oxford. A lesser light, but one whose name crops up in countless friendly matches was the Rev SWR Holbrooke. For the county he achieved precious little with bat or ball. It may be a flight of fancy, but the score card recording him as absent for the first innings of the Hertfordshire match at Aylesbury in 1904 suggests a man ever willing to answer a last minute summons to make up the numbers. Was there someone to be buried first before exchanging clerical collar for flannels? These occasional absentees speak volumes for the communication and transportation systems of the day.

Another man of the cloth was CD Robinson. Cyril Robinson's is an intriguing story. As a 22 year-old he kept wicket for Bucks in two matches of the 1895 season when

CD Robinson

Charles Cobb was not playing. His season was then cut short as he joined a team touring America under the leadership of the Yorkshire amateur Frank Mitchell, a man not to be confused with Bucks' own Frank Mitchell mentioned above. Robinson, who played a few matches for Cambridge without winning a blue, made one further appearance for Bucks in the first match of the 1896 season after which no more was heard of him in local circles until 1907. By this time he had returned to South Africa, the country of his birth, and played for Natal with sufficient success to be selected for the South African team that toured England in 1907. By now ordained, he was the reserve wicket-keeper and vice-captain. He was never chosen for the Test team and played in only six games on the tour, but he was able to make himself available for Bucks' last two matches in which, as the Rev CD Robinson, he was the wicket-keeper.

Financial crises

The enthusiasm that had greeted the advent of competition for the minor counties in the 1890s soon gave way to worries that sprang from the misplaced optimism of those who plotted the future of the County Club. The completion of the County Ground had been voted a great success and its facilities had expanded as planned to allow for a lawn tennis section, where lady members could also play - though not on match days! A bowls section thrived and athletics events were also staged. But the cost of county cricket strained the budget. Matches were invariably attended by the great and the good with mayoral chains and clerical collars in evidence among the local gentry, but reports seldom spoke of much popular support. It was expensive to stage a match and even in good weather crowds could be disappointingly thin, with no more than £25 coming from gate money for four two-day matches in 1898 to offset expenses that topped £150. Moreover, there were ongoing costs in maintaining the ground, so it was just as well that there remained a healthy band of members paying their subscriptions.

The committee began to re-think its policy of making the County Ground the stage for all home matches. It was now argued that it was too far for supporters to travel from the south of the county to watch the cricket. From 1899 county matches at Aylesbury were reduced to three with the fourth home fixture moving further north to Bletchley Park. By 1903 Aylesbury was down to two matches and there was something to watch for those in the south of the county as High Wycombe was back on the list. In 1904 Slough hosted its first Bucks fixture and county cricket returned to Wolverton, where the ground now used was no longer The Big Field but the recently opened Wolverton CC Ground at Osborne Street, where the Wolverton Club still plays. By 1905 the County Ground had been reduced to a single match. With just one exception this was to remain its ration until the Great War, after which no county matches were played in Aylesbury until 1993. In what was a total reversal of the committee's original plan, the wisdom of retaining ownership of the ground itself would soon be called into question.

The move to Bletchley Park was an interesting one. This was a private ground on the estate of Mr Herbert Leon, a stockbroker who was to be created a baronet in 1911, the year in which he also held the presidency of the County Cricket Club. He had been a vice-president since 1896 and he and his wife could guarantee a hospitable welcome to the teams whilst there would be a reduction in the expenses associated with a match at a members' club. Sir Herbert died in 1926, but county cricket continued to be played at Bletchley Park each year until 1933. At the outbreak of World War II the Victorian style mansion and its grounds were acquired as a home for the code-breakers whose

Bletchley Park - the house today

special brand of genius unravelled the enemy's cipher device Enigma, thereby thwarting the efforts of the German U-boats. Sir Leon's old home and the huts that were erected around it still house much of the old deciphering equipment that is now on display to the paying public, providing a fascinating insight into some of the most closely guarded secrets of the last war.

Bletchley Park - the old pavilion - there is a preservation order on it

The mysterious world of the code-breakers would have been far from the minds of those who gathered in the more peaceful times of the early 20th century. There was always a party atmosphere at Bletchley Park with Sir Herbert greeting his friends at the matches. On one occasion, after Wiltshire had won with time to spare, the carnival spirit spilled over and the afternoon was taken up with boisterous challenges as the players competed in races with sprinters handicapped against others riding piggy back. A Wiltshire player weighed in at 18 stone but he was still carried to victory on the back of his captain.

The earliest surviving handbook is for 1905. This lists the vice-presidents and officers, reports on the previous season with potted summaries of the matches and full averages, provides a note on the playing record of each of the principal clubs, lists the forthcoming season's fixtures and shows the financial statement for the year. It is a more substantial booklet than the County Club felt able to produce in succeeding years, and it provides a timely reminder of how many matches were staged in addition to the championship. As well as a fixture with MCC, regarded as a full county match, there were 18 'Club and Ground' matches. These involved playing many of the principal local clubs, meeting a team of clergymen, taking on Eton College A team, assembling at Ascott Park to play a team raised by Leopold de Rothschild and entertaining wandering sides such as Free Foresters and Butterflies.

Later handbooks from this period seldom carried a written report, but they continued to list all the members' names. Another consistent feature was the inclusion of the accounts, and from these it is easy to see how the County Club found itself struggling. A press report showed that as far back as 1895 the sum of £22 11s 3d had been taken at the gate for a single match at Wolverton, where the thriving railway works would have ensured a good attendance. However, by 1904 admissions from five matches could bring in no more than £25 6s 0d, with Wolverton still attracting the most revenue. Two matches that both ran their full course on the County Ground at Aylesbury yielded a beggarly £5 2s 6d, and the next year takings were down again. Even with play on a Saturday gate receipts for a two-day match at Aylesbury were just 16s 6d (82p).

At successive annual meetings the treasurer had been obliged to report that the County Club was sliding ever deeper into debt, and it was carrying a deficit of £210 when the matter was addressed at a specially convened meeting in the Red Room at Wycombe Town Hall on Tuesday, 17 December 1907. The president of the County Club, Lord Desborough, shortly to become president of MCC, was in the chair and he told a well-attended gathering that he had been asked to propose 'that this meeting considers that it would be a great discredit to the County of Bucks if the County Cricket Club were to be discontinued'.

The problem of the shape of the county was acknowledged, and attention was drawn to the lack of members from the town of High Wycombe, where the local team was strong but did little to support the County Club. Speakers then fell over themselves to agree that it would be tragic if the county team were to be withdrawn from the Championship. The motion was carried unanimously as was a second, 'with acclamation', when Sir Coningsby Disraeli, a nephew of the former prime minister, proposed 'that this meeting pledges itself to support the Bucks County Cricket Club, by endeavouring to raise sufficient funds to enable it to pay off its debts and by securing enough new members to place the Club on a sound financial footing.'

The treasurer was soon able to announce donations exceeding £144, including £25 from Lord Rothschild, and securing more annual subscriptions brought in a further £43. But the good intentions of the meeting never really translated into effective long-term action. Only the short-term crisis had been addressed, and the accounts for 1908 still recorded an excess of expenditure over income of £69 3s 3d, a figure that rose to £99 2s 2d the next year, by which time liabilities were standing at close to £250.

Could the County Club continue? Was it in a position to arrange fixtures for the forthcoming season?

Another special meeting was held, this time at the George Hotel, Aylesbury. The possibility of disposing of the County Ground was discussed. Ground expenses were an annual drain on resources, and little was earned from lettings, but there were fears that the subscriptions of members living in the town, especially those who were using the club's facilities, would be lost to the county. Nevertheless the seeds were sown, and it would not be long before the County Club rid itself of its burden. The problem of insolvency was addressed by the chairman of the meeting, de Paravicini's successor as county captain Mr WF Lowndes, when he generously volunteered that, rather than see the county pull out of its fixtures, he would personally guarantee any loss incurred by the matches.

Despite this kind offer the 1910 season was even more disastrous adding a further £190 of losses to the balance sheet, which now showed total deficiencies of £227 15s 8d. Nor did it sound as though the ship was in the safest of hands. 'No letter or report received from Mr HG Hogarth' the minutes of the Annual General Meeting recorded when the secretary's report had been expected. The long-serving assistant secretary, Mr JCW Ellis, would no doubt have attended to the essentials, but the treasurer, the indefatigable Lt Col FT Higgins-Bernard, was also among those who were absent from this important meeting. He had at least apologised, which is more than can be said of Mr Hogarth, who had made little impact as a player - five matches, all as an opening bat, for an average of 5.88 - and who now melted from the administrative and playing scene, though he remained a member and became a vice-president in 1926.

Mr. H. E. Bull, J.P.

Herbert Bull, a tireless worker for the county cause who had been secretary for four years from 1904, was soon to take over as treasurer, and he had already been swift to voice his concerns about the financial situation at an extraordinary general meeting held in Aylesbury ten weeks earlier. That meeting had set in motion the relinquishing of the lease on the County Ground, and when the AGM came round a sub-committee had been able to report that the unexpired portion of the lease was to be taken over by the newly formed Aylesbury Sports Club for a price of £133 15s 0d, a figure that reflected a special valuation of the pavilion and fittings but gave the County Club nothing to reflect the costs it had incurred in creating a cricket ground and other sporting facilities from agricultural land.

There was still the matter of restoring the County Club to solvency deprived as it now was of its principal asset. This was the moment for Herbert Bull to speak out in committee and he received support for his proposal that 'steps be immediately taken to raise the sum of £400 in order to provide the expenses of next season's engagements and repay the amount of liabilities due, and unless £300 is raised by April 30th the Club must of necessity cancel its county fixtures'. A circular was prepared and the initial response was sufficiently encouraging for Bull's draconian proposal to be side-stepped.

The appeal raised £371 19s 3d, which went straight into the capital account. Yet once again the core problem remained. Some may have chosen to make donations instead of paying their annual subscription and members were lost in the Aylesbury area so at the year's end the treasurer had to report subscription income down to £173 - over £100 less than the sum that was coming in each year before the special meeting at

Wycombe only three years earlier with its fine words about 'securing enough new members to put the Club on a sound footing'.

Match expenses, which had been running at an average of £270 a year, had still to be tackled, and it did not help the cause that in 1911 the county team was required to play ten matches rather than eight including a tour to Wales, where new opponents were Glamorgan, Carmarthenshire and Monmouthshire. Nevertheless, with a strong amateur element in the team, the cost of the match programme that year was contained to £173 and the treasurer was able to go to the Annual Meeting in February 1912 and report a more modest deficit on the year of £70 2s 0d, adding that he had reason to believe that the position would improve. He was proved right: in 1912 and 1913, despite gate receipts that were now down to £10 for the season, the club could point to a modest excess of income over expenditure. Commenting on this 'absurdly low' figure for admissions to county matches the handbook report echoed the sentiment that 'it seems a great pity that the general public cannot be induced to take a little more interest in county cricket, even if it is second-class.' The committee could reflect that Bucks was not alone in finding that the public was now less easily wooed to spend its time watching cricket.

The years of struggle

The dwindling interest in minor county cricket in the early years of the new century was reflected in press reporting. No longer do we find local papers regularly devoting long columns to the deeds of the county team, and piecing together match scores becomes a more frustrating task. Moreover, for Bucks, the financial struggles were running parallel with those on the field, where it was becoming an ever harder task to find eleven men who could compete.

By 1904 Charles Cobb had retired, Percy de Paravicini, though still nominally the captain, was playing infrequently, Nash was dead and Gresson's best days were past, though he soldiered on until 1907. There was a great weight on the ageing shoulders of Mat Wright, who could still find himself bowling 40 overs in an innings - and they were now of six balls. The professional support for Wright could make no pretensions to the class of George Nash. There was all too little amateur talent coming through, and fickle commitment to the cause meant that there was seldom a settled side.

One who was now enjoying his best days with the county was FN Bird. A product of Trinity College Dublin, Frederick Bird had first played for Bucks in 1896 at the age of 20. He was always an outstanding fielder – he had taken the disputed boundary catch against Oxfordshire in his first season, but his intermittent appearances at first earned him few runs. However, his form improved and he became one of the mainstays of the batting so that by the time he moved away from the area in 1907 his 49 matches had brought 2,043 runs at an average of 27.42 with two centuries, the highest 133 against Berkshire at Slough in 1905.

FN Bird

A batsman with strokes all round the wicket, Bird tasted first-class cricket when he played half a dozen games for Gloucestershire in 1899 and 1900, and he appeared in a further ten matches for Northamptonshire, when he held the post of chaplain at Wellingborough School, having been ordained in 1908. He was briefly a housemaster at Cranleigh before becoming headmaster of Lowestoft College, when he turned out for his native Suffolk - he was born in Framlingham. Finally, when his teaching career ended with running a preparatory school in Exeter, he played some matches for Devon. Bird lived on until 1965, one of the last links with Bucks' very earliest days in the Minor Counties Championship.

To the end of the 1904 season Bucks had played 78 county matches and had won 29 of them with only 16 defeats, but the pendulum now swung as losses comfortably outnumbered victories. It was an inauspicious moment for a new captain to take over as WF Lowndes of Chesham did for the 1908 season. However, his predecessor had been able to play only very infrequently, the time was ripe for a change and all were agreed that the County Club was fortunate to have such a spirited enthusiast willing to take on the job.

Mr. W. F. L. Frith-Lowndes, J.P.

The Lowndes family had a distinguished history. A forebear of William Lowndes had been Secretary to the Treasury under William and Mary and had commissioned Sir Christopher Wren to build Winslow Hall in 1700. The family later accumulated substantial estates in the Chesham area, where they owned The Bury, the principal residence in the town, now offices occupied by solicitors. William Lowndes himself had been born William Frith, but on the death of his mother's bachelor brother in 1905 he had inherited The Bury and in 1906 he took the family's coat of arms and extended his name by Royal Licence to William Frederick Lowndes Frith-Lowndes. As his uncle had been before him, he was a man of great influence in the town and a considerable benefactor, rebuilding slum cottages and subsequently giving Lowndes Park to the town.

No sooner was he installed at The Bury than Lowndes found himself sucked into all manner of activities in and around the town. He sat as a Justice of the Peace, he virtually formed the local Conservative Association, very soon he would be a County Councillor and, when subscription lists were opened for local causes, his name was at the head of the donors. With professed interest in a wide range of sports – hunting, golf, lawn tennis and rackets as well as cricket – it was no surprise that he should be elected president and captain of the Chesham Cricket Club at the first opportunity. He immediately promised improvements to the ground, which suffered from the football club using it in the winter. Within a couple of years he had had a fence erected with a wire across the top to 'deter free galleryites'. Lowndes also promised the club a major attraction for his first season in charge: he would assemble a strong team to meet an Eleven brought down by WG Grace.

At the age of 37, William Lowndes came to the captaincy with limited credentials as a cricketer. He had not previously appeared for the county, but he had played in a couple matches for London County at the turn of the century and, the summer before taking over as Bucks captain, he had distinguished himself by making 49 in each innings in what was becoming an annual encounter against WG Grace's team. Moreover, he had captained Chesham with gusto and, invariably describing him as 'The Squire', the *Bucks Examiner* was able to report moments of success with the bat. As captain of the county, Lowndes now turned out regularly and, with the help of a fine 139 not out against Berkshire at Reading in the final match, he ended his first season as top run-maker, an achievement that was a tacit reflection on how few of his team played with any regularity.

In every way it was a difficult first year for Lowndes. A new secretary, Dr Bertram Abrahams from Amersham, had just taken over from Herbert Bull. The previous summer Abrahams had been given one game for the county, against MCC at Lord's where he had made a pair; but it was the enthusiasm he brought for the county's cause that commended him to his colleagues on the committee. Herbert Bull was looking forward to a season in which it would no longer fall to him alone to raise teams. Then, just before the season began, Dr Abrahams died at the age only 38. Amid the shock and sadness of his untimely demise the plans for the season were thrown into chaos. "I had no opportunity of finding out what he had done," said the new captain. The struggle to find teams to fulfil the county programme was back in the lap of Bull. It entailed the use of 25 different players. For one match, he said, he had written to no fewer than 40 players.

In the first four seasons of Lowndes' leadership the county managed to win only six matches and there were 22 losses. In 1910, for the first time, not a single victory was recorded. Six of the eight matches were lost, all by a substantial margin, and the county finished bottom of the table. Threadbare teams were fielded and most of the time they were barely competing. Typifying their misfortunes was the match at Bletchley Park against Wiltshire, where the visitors made 240 for 7 on a rain-interrupted first day and then made the most of a wet pitch to skittle Bucks for 48 and 84. The Bucks cause was not helped by the captain's car breaking down as he and his brother, PL Frith, made their way to the ground from Chesham on the second day. By the time they arrived it was too late for them to bat in the first innings.

The following year, when for some reason Lowndes did not play, Herbert Bull and the young Walter Franklin being among those who deputised, the ten-match programme saw Bucks' only successes coming at the expense of a weak Carmarthenshire team, for whom 1911 was to be their last year of competing in the Championship and whom Bucks now beat at home and away.

The three-match tour to Wales was a unique experience for a Bucks team, and it brought the players more excitement than they had bargained for after their victory at Llanelli. This was a time of industrial unrest on the railways and strikers in Wales were set upon imposing a blockade to prevent the free passage of trains. With militant protesters thronging the level crossings at both ends of Llanelli station, it was only with the help of an armed guard that the players managed to catch the last train out of the town that evening. Lucky to escape, they later heard that the Riot Act had been read out and troops had opened fire killing two bystanders. Amid the ensuing mayhem an ammunition train was blown up causing a further 18 deaths. The team managed to reach Cardiff, but the start of their match with Monmouthshire the next day was delayed when the players found that there were no trains running and they were obliged to find cars or taxis to complete their journey.

On occasions the margin of defeat in these dark years was embarrassingly emphatic with the batting especially liable to fail. The contrast in the averages for runs scored and conceded bears witness to teams that quite simply lacked talent:

	Scored	Conceded
1908	14.18	22.87
1909	14.83	22.63
1910	14.76	28.70

Only twice, in 1895 and 1903, had runs been so scarce, the 1903 season being memorable for Bucks' lowest ever total of 20, against Hertfordshire at Aylesbury. This sad landmark had been sandwiched in the middle of five completed Bucks innings none of which reached three figures. Never had wickets been nearly as expensive as in 1910; yet in 1911 their cost would rise again, to 29.26.

Among the more successful of the newcomers at this time was Dr E Weaver-Adams from Slough, who first played in 1903 and made 35 appearances spread over the next ten seasons to finish with a batting average of 26.27. He hit two centuries, his 162 against Berkshire at Reading in 1909 being the highest individual score for the county up to that time.

The doctor was not alone in finding time to play in only half the matches. Others who showed form that must have led to more invitations than they were able to accept were RH de Montmorency and E Southall, a Slough player. A distinguished all-round sportsman who also played for Hertfordshire, Reymond de Montmorency appeared just twice for Bucks in 1907 and once more in 1909 but still managed an average of 43.00 with a top score of 90 out of his side's total of 165 against Wiltshire at Bletchley Park in his final match. His daughter, many years later, was to marry EW Swanton. Southall's few matches are more puzzling as he remained involved in committee matters for some years and, like de Montmorency, the call came when Bucks were most in need of some ballast in the middle of the order. His seven appearances, interspersed between 1907 and 1909, brought him 431 runs at 43.10. He, too, had a highest score of 90, against Worcestershire Second Eleven at Kidderminster in his first match.

In the earlier years of this less propitious period the county will have been grateful for the commitment of EC Hobbs, an opening batsman from Slough, who began in 1902 and averaged 21.42 with seven fifties from 28 matches. Between 1905 and 1910 RW Orton from Amersham, managed 1,302 runs at 20.03 from 36 matches. A younger brother of Tom Orton, the Amersham Club's groundsman until 1944, Robert Orton's sudden loss of initials in 1909 suggests that the county committee felt it was worth paying him. Or perhaps he knew his value and held out for a match fee! EJ Leat, who was born in Somerset, played twice for his native county, though a Bucks career of 17 matches from 1908 that brought 588 runs at 21.78 suggests that he was hardly good enough for first-class cricket. Thomas Stacey, an Old Etonian from Buckingham, whose listed recreations - hunting, shooting and cricket - neatly encapsulated those of many of the other country gentlemen who assisted the county from time to time, usually played in matches at the convenient and congenial venue of Bletchley Park. Stacey stretched his 26 appearances over a long period in averaging 18.76 with three fifties. He occasionally turned his arm to good effect, once claiming four wickets for no runs against Bedfordshire with his leg breaks.

Mr. Thomas Stacey, J.P.

Modest as these players' figures are, they represent the efforts of a few of the more productive team members of the difficult years. As occasional players came and went, Bucks still attracted the occasional amateur of distinction. One such was the Hon JJ Astor, younger son of Viscount Astor, who was in the Eton XI of 1904 and 1905 and who opened the batting for Bucks in both those years, performing creditably. He never played for the county in later life, but went on to a distinguished journalistic career in the course of which he became proprietor of *The Times*. He served as president of MCC in 1937 and was created the first Baron Astor of Hever in 1956.

Even before George Nash died in 1903 it was clear that a void was opening up in the professional ranks. The Boddy family from Beaconsfield supplied at least two members, the absence of initials for professionals sometimes making it difficult to identify which appeared in certain matches. Ernest Boddy was the most regular member of the clan, performing erratically but scoring one century in 1900. After a gap of several years both he and GH Boddy were recalled to the colours in 1909 and 1910.

Another to be brought back after a long interval in these same desperate years was Herbert 'Laddie' Page, the professional at High Wycombe and a bowler who had made a promising debut in 1896 and played fairly regularly in the early 1900s. A total of 56 matches for Bucks brought him 143 wickets, a tally that might have been higher had others achieved the high standards he himself set in the field. Commenting on his misfortunes the handbook review of the 1904 season said: 'Page bowled fairly well but he was handicapped by not having an artist like CE Cobb at the wicket. The fielding of the team was at times fairly good, and at other times execrable. The catching was generally feeble.'

George Wilson

There was a single season, 1907, and three more matches in 1908, in which Bucks enjoyed the services of George Wilson, who had just retired from first-class cricket after a career of 160 matches for Worcestershire, in which he had taken 181 wickets and averaged nearly 27 with the bat. Though his batting for Bucks was disappointing he claimed 55 wickets, in a year when Mat Wright managed only 34, at a cost of 14.09. In 1904 there had been a single appearance for the county by Alec Watson, one the foremost bowlers ever to have played for Lancashire, who stands even today at number five in their list of all-time wicket takers. It was said that he never played for England in part because he was a Scot but also because his action, like those of Crossland and Nash, was questionable. Watson had begun his career as a fast bowler, later becoming an off-spinner. His figures in his one match for Bucks were an unremarkable 2 for 104 in 35 overs. More notable was his age - he had passed his 59th birthday!

For six seasons from 1905 Archie Vickerstaff played in every county match. He had been hired to replace George Nash at Aylesbury and, like Nash, he was available to clubs as a net bowler. He enjoyed days of success but 154 wickets at 23.01 was an expensive return for those days, especially when compared to the parsimony of Nash and Wright, and with the bat Vickerstaff was a fixture at number eleven. In the summer of 1910, with uncertainty surrounding the County Ground and the county's finances still haemorrhaging, there were concerns about Vickerstaff's future. It was hoped that a way of keeping him might be found, but he had received an offer from a club in the Lancashire League, and by the time the 1911 season came round he had gone.

One player who could be relied upon to stand by the captain in these difficult times was his younger brother, PL Frith, his vice-captain at Chesham. First appearing in 1909, Frith hardly missed a match thereafter and, though his early figures were modest, he improved to record one century and five fifties. His pace bowling but was rather expensive, coming into its own when there was no-one else to turn an arm, whilst on at least one occasion, when there was no proper wicket-keeper, he seems to have taken the gloves. There are only the sparsest of reports on the Welsh tour of 1911, but there was certainly an abundance of byes in the three matches, where no specialist keeper appears to have been taken and Frith was one of those sharing the wicket-keeping duties. Against Glamorgan he opened the bowling and later made a stumping.

EHD Sewell brings hope

In many ways 1911 was a pivotal season for Bucks in which some of the bricks that would build a stronger future first came to light. Foremost among these was the arrival of EHD Sewell. He came with a colourful past, but his overall contribution to the game still had years to run. Edward Humphrey Dalrymple Sewell was born in India and, returning there as a civil servant, he set new records as a batsman. He was the first man in India to score three consecutive centuries and likewise the first to pass 200 on two occasions. Returning to England he joined Essex as a professional, an unusual move for the son of an army officer and one educated at Bedford Grammar School. For his adopted county he batted with gusto, and when he played at anything but first-class level he was also a formidable bowler.

EHD Sewell

For a time Sewell was employed as a coach with Surrey and, after retiring from the game, he embarked on a career as a journalist, reporting on cricket for the *Daily Sketch*. A man of trenchant and sometimes unorthodox views, he had a regular seat in the Long Room at Lord's, where he was invariably engaged in discussion with his large circle of friends. He published several books on the game, in which he aired his opinions as well as indulging in selecting endless teams with an idiosyncratic flavour such as an eleven of those who batted left-handed but were right-arm bowlers or a team of cricketers with the names of a flower or vegetable.

This was the man, now living in Slough, who in 1911 threw in his lot with the Bucks County Cricket Club. He was by now almost 39 but, still seeking a new challenge, he began by taking over as secretary from the hapless HG Hogarth while he acquired his residential qualification to play for the county. At the Annual General Meeting before the 1912 season Sewell was elected captain. He later declined to take the post, preferring to serve as vice-captain to Lowndes, who was persuaded to carry on for one more year. The turnaround in Bucks' fortunes was in no small measure due to Sewell's arrival, and in his second season he assumed the captaincy.

In 1912, for the first time since 1904, Bucks' victories outnumbered defeats. Three wins were obtained, against Bedfordshire, Wiltshire and Berkshire, all by comfortable margins, and the only loss was to Wiltshire in the last match of the season after losing the toss and being asked to bat on a difficult pitch. In an especially wet summer two matches were abandoned without a ball bowled and two were drawn.

There was a more settled side this year, and Sewell's own contribution was outstanding. As an opening bat he averaged 40.63 and he bowled 350 overs to take 46 wickets at 14.09. Mat Wright, with 132 overs and 22 wickets, trailed some way behind, and from other quarters there was only modest support, PL Frith and DH Field doing best, the latter hitting 103 in his first match for the county, away to Bedfordshire. This was a match that Bucks won by an innings and 68 runs with victory set up by a first innings score of 505, still the highest ever recorded by the county.

Though their individual performances were still often modest, this was a time when a number of younger players of talent first made their mark. Two sons of the Rev ED Shaw, Edward and Bernard, both played for Bucks and in the run feast at Bedford they had contributed 76 and 65. EA Shaw's first match had been in 1908, two years before he was to leave Marlborough as its captain of cricket, and on one occasion that year he played alongside his father, who was shortly to become Archdeacon and then Bishop of Buckingham. BHG Shaw, also a Marlburian, followed into the team in 1911. Both brothers were wicket-keepers who also batted, Edward gaining a blue at Oxford, but their chances to perform behind the stumps were thwarted by the arrival in 1911 of Walter Franklin, soon to become one of the giants of Buckinghamshire cricket. It was a cricketing curiosity that the Bucks team, for three matches in 1912, should have contained both wicket-keepers from that year's Varsity match, Franklin having won his blue at Cambridge.

Another to play for Buckinghamshire for the first time in 1912 was WE Hazelton, a Wellingborough schoolboy, who came with a reputation as the outstanding bowler in public schools cricket that year. He achieved little in his solitary match in 1912, but 26 wickets from only four matches the next year provided evidence of a talent that would serve Bucks long and well. Another whose main contributions would come after the war was PW Le Gros, who had been in the eleven at Rugby School in 1910 and who first played for Bucks in the opening fixture of the following year, not missing a match until the end of the 1925 season.

Mention should also be made of NDC Ross, a product of Uppingham and Cambridge University, who first appeared in 1910 and went on to average over 40 in 1911 when the highlight of his season was an innings of 144 scored in just over two hours against Carmarthenshire at Slough. That day he shared a partnership of 147 with WL Jackson of Amersham Hill, who was making his Bucks debut and was soon to become a pillar of the county's batting.

EHD Sewell's first year as captain of Bucks in 1913 was much less successful with five defeats and only two victories. Sewell himself again had a fair season with the bat, but his 35 wickets were more expensive, and Mat Wright, no longer styled as a professional, managed only a dozen wickets in what was to be his last season. In a less settled side there were plenty of opportunities for those who were clearly unable to cope with the demands of minor counties cricket and the Annual Report made specific reference to the feebleness of the slip catching.

It was the one drawn match that was in many ways the most satisfactory for Bucks. This was at High Wycombe, where the county faced a daunting task after Hertfordshire had amassed 505, by a strange coincidence the same score as Bucks had made at Bedford the previous year and now the highest ever to be recorded against the county. Initially the reply was feeble as the Bucks score stood at 95 for 8, but Walter Franklin then joined forces with Wright, hitting 119 not out in a partnership of 141 that still stands as a county record for the ninth wicket. The follow-on was not saved, but in the second innings Sewell promoted himself to open with TR Kent from Slough. They added 217, with both batsmen scoring centuries, as they set a first-wicket record that has yet to be beaten. Tommy Kent's 123 was the first flowering of a talent that had lain dormant in earlier seasons and now took him to the top of the averages, while Sewell went on to hit his second century for the county the following day in the match against Bedfordshire at Aylesbury.

The 1914 season was cut short after only two of the scheduled matches had been played, and by the second week of August most of the minor counties were abandoning their playing commitments in preparation for a much bigger battle in Europe. Bucks' second game, which ended on 30 July, brought victory by an innings and eight runs against Dorset at Aylesbury. David Sewell, EHD's son, who had been in the Sandhurst eleven that summer, broke the visitors' batting with six for 44, while the batting hero was Edward Shaw with a commanding 117. Young Sewell would return to play again in 1920; Shaw would be less fortunate.

The two matches that Bucks had been able to play in July were notable in shaping the course of the county's history - they marked the first appearance of Frank Edwards. He was a left-arm bowler, converted from pace to spin, who was to become a legend of the minor counties game. Edwards had started with Surrey and had opposed Bucks in the second of their matches against that county's Second Eleven in 1908, though without bowling a ball! The next year he played a fuller part, though it was his colleagues that routed Bucks. His career at Surrey was stuttering and after the 1911 season it came to an end as the county sought to make economies and dispensed with his services and those of EHD Sewell, who had been their coach.

That autumn, through the offices of Sewell, Edwards was in discussion with Bucks and soon began a period of qualification. He took up residence in Slough and spent his winter working at Stoke Poges Golf Club. In the summer he tended the ground at Marlow Cricket Club, playing when required for the club, for Slough and in Bucks Club and Ground fixtures. The county minutes record that Edwards was to be offered '£3 and no expenses per county match, and half a guinea with expenses for Club and Ground matches.' There is a further reference to a three-cornered agreement between Marlow Cricket Club and the County Club to secure Edwards' services for Bucks, an agreement which Marlow was later felt to have repudiated and which led to solicitors being consulted. The Marlow Club was subsequently requested to make a contribution to the legal costs. Meanwhile Edwards had been obliged to write in for money that was owing to him. It was not a promising start, but Edwards was still able to take the field for the county for the first time on 16 July 1914. His first two matches, which brought him just three wickets at a cost of 50 each, gave little indication of what lay in store.

Between the Wars:
Bucks' Golden Age

The aftermath of War

The county handbook was produced as usual in 1915. It made brief reference to the two matches played the previous summer, but its report gave greater prominence to the names of all Bucks cricketers who had 'responded to the call of King and Country'. Already the war was taking its toll. Lieutenant BHG Shaw, the second son of ED Shaw, now Bishop of Buckingham, was the first Bucks player to fall, dying at Neuve Chapelle on 19 December 1914. Three days earlier Captain Stephen Ussher, the youngest son of the vicar of Westbury, had also been killed in the trenches at Givenchy. He had played in Club and Ground matches, while his two brothers, Beverly and Richard, had both appeared for the full county team.

Tragedy would strike both families again. Captain Beverly Ussher, a regular Army officer like his brother Stephen, met his death on Gallipoli Peninsula on 19 June 1915, while Bishop Shaw's eldest son Edward, who had bowed out in such splendid style in the final match of 1914, perished on the Somme in 1916. By the end of the war the list of those killed in action would extend. When publication of the handbook resumed in 1919 the names of DH Field, WG Garforth, ER Mobbs and P Broughton-Adderley were added to the Roll of Honour. All had played for the county team, but the last named has a special poignancy. In 1911 he played his only game for Bucks; he did not bowl and, entering at number eleven, he was out first ball.

Despite the loss of young life a gratifyingly large number of those who had represented Bucks before the War survived the carnage, many earning citations for their gallantry. The Distinguished Service Order was awarded to AM Grenfell, AHC Kearsey and JT Weatherby, while the Military Cross was won by GEW Bowyer, SG Fairbairn, H Jennison, HW Priestley and F Weatherby. None of these played many times for Bucks, Hubert Jennison, an opening batsman from Wolverton with eleven appearances being the closest to a regular player. Another to have shown promise was Sydney Fairbairn, an Old Etonian who had been in the Sandhurst Eleven in 1911 and toured West Indies with MCC in 1912-13. He had made his debut for the county in 1913, taking 23 wickets as an opening bowler. After the War Fairbairn spent some time in East Africa, and he accomplished the astonishing feat of crossing Equatorial Africa on foot. He was at one time commissioned to collect wild animals for British zoos, a venture that apparently met with little success.

SG Fairbairn

Franklin takes command

Fifteen of those who had represented Bucks returned to play at least once more in post-war matches. They were: ET Brocklehurst, F Edwards, WB Franklin, RN Hamilton, WE Hazelton, OP Horlick, WL Jackson, RA Janes, H Jennison, TR Kent, PW Le Gros, DLL Mackey, H Pitchford, DAD Sewell and SL Trevor. Some on the list were the makeweights of the difficult pre-war years, men who had contributed little on the field and were to add little more; but the 15 names included one man who would stamp his presence on Bucks cricket for more than 20 years. Walter Franklin had first joined the committee in 1912 while still an undergraduate and in 1919 he was elected captain, a post he held until 1946. During these years he became renowned as one of the fiercest competitors in minor counties cricket. "He hated to lose," says one who remembers opposing him, and there is little doubt that many of those who played under him lived in fear of his sharp tongue and withering stare if their standards slipped.

Widely regarded as one of the finest wicket-keepers in the land and a useful if inconsistent batsman, Franklin played regularly for the Gentlemen and, had he chosen to do so, could have enjoyed an impressive first-class career. In the opinion of HL Collins, captain of the Australian touring team in 1926, Franklin was the best wicket-keeper in England and he was invited to tour Australia with APF Chapman's team two years later, but he could not spare a winter away from his profession at the bar. However, life as a barrister with its long summer vacation was ideally suited to a minor county career. Injury cost Franklin four matches in 1921, but thereafter he missed only two more games until he retired at the end of the 1946 season having played 200 championship matches for Bucks.

Franklin in action in the Gents v Players match.
The batsman is Percy Holmes

Those from the pre-war teams who had survived the war with Franklin and were to become his key players of the early seasons were: Philip Le Gros, vice-captain and number four batsman; opening bowler Wyndham Hazelton; Will Jackson, an opening batsman from Wycombe; and the incomparable Frank Edwards as a left-arm spinner. Of the others survivors Captain Spencer Trevor, who had played in 1914, was elected the first post-war secretary, while EHD Sewell's son David became his assistant in 1921. Oliver Horlick, with just two matches before the war and two more in 1920, was a more modest performer on the field. His greatest contribution to the cause began when he took over from Herbert Bull as treasurer in 1920 and stretched on throughout the decade, first as Trevor's replacement when he left the area, then as assistant to his successor.

Bucks were fortunate to enjoy the services of Spencer Trevor. A man who would later play the part of Period Blimp in the film 'The Life and Death of Colonel Blimp', Trevor's dedication to the cause was captured in the columns of *The Cricketer*: 'Climbs into the ground before play starts on the second day, and copies rough score sheet into vellum-bound score-book, scrutinizes the *Sportsman* report to make sure no Bucks runs have been missed, wades into *Bradshaw* for intricate train services back to Bucks, assures himself that all boots are spotlessly white and bats properly oiled and fills in accidental moments with little thoughts on championships.' On the field Trevor was a useful lower order batsman and occasional strike bowler.

SL Trevor

The Minor Counties Championship was not resumed until 1920, but Bucks played a full programme of matches in 1919, suffering only one defeat - by eleven runs at the hands of a strong MCC side at Lord's. There were centuries for RN Hamilton and TR Kent against Herts at Slough, but neither of these survivors of pre-war Bucks teams was to be much of a force in future years, Hamilton moving overseas and not reappearing until 1931, when he played a couple of games, and Kent seldom making the runs to warrant selection, though still reappearing as late as 1933.

Championship successes

As Bucks awaited the resumption of championship cricket the handbook reflected the committee's confidence: 'The 1919 Bucks side has every prospect of ranking with the best sides produced by the County in the past.' These high hopes were not misplaced: the inter-war period remains the golden age of Bucks cricket. Between 1920 and 1939 the county could boast of 89 victories against 28 losses with 57 matches drawn and one tied. In the 20 seasons that spanned the two wars Bucks contested the Challenge Match six times, losing on only one occasion with one other match, against Berkshire in 1932, abandoned before the completion of a single innings.

In 1920 five of the eight matches were won with a solitary loss, to Berkshire by 31 runs, depriving the county of the chance to challenge Staffordshire for the title. The key to success, as it would continue to be, lay in the bowling. Of 136 wickets to fall to bowlers two men accounted for 97. Wyndham Hazelton, who had promised so much before the war, took 50 at 14.26, but the star performer was Jack Whiting with 47 at 10.21.

Jack Whiting

There were two Whiting brothers from Newport Pagnell. Earning their livelihood as farmers, they found it difficult to play together. Frank Whiting, whose son played three times for the county in the 1940s, had announced himself in 1919 with a whirlwind innings of 130 in 50 minutes for the Club and Ground against Wolverton. He made a few useful scores for the county, but it was the younger of the two brothers, fast bowler Jack, tall and well built, who was the unchallenged star of the 1920 season and of whom it was said that he was one of the three fastest bowlers in England. Among his outstanding analyses were: eight for 23 against Wiltshire at Bletchley Park, seven for 42 in the return fixture at Trowbridge and seven for 39 against Berkshire at Slough. The next year saw him make two first-class appearances, when he played for HDG Leveson Gower's XI against both Oxford and Cambridge. Among his six victims was DR Jardine.

There were some useful overs of left-arm spin from CL Powell, who would go on to play 65 times for Bucks though bowling less and less as the seasons passed and graduating to opening batsman in his later years. It was hardly surprising that Bucks should have had less need for Powell's bowling after 1921 because this was the first year in which the county could call on the slow bowling of Major Henry Aubrey-Fletcher and, more importantly, it was the season that marked the return of Frank Edwards. A man who would serve the county in many different capacities from secretary to president, Aubrey-Fletcher's best years as a bowler were 1921 and 1922 when he proved a valuable foil to Edwards, whose left-arm spin was soon to make him a legend of the minor counties game.

Edwards, it should be remembered, had achieved very little in his two pre-war matches, and he had been virtually forgotten when cricket resumed in 1919. There are no references to him in the minute book or handbooks, and rumours even circulated that he had died in action. In fact, he had been lucky to survive having endured a particularly unpleasant war, in which he had suffered shell shock and been severely gassed in France. But he had a stroke of good fortune in 1917. Not for the first time, he had been invalided from the front and had spent time recuperating in England. Re-graded A1 and fit to return to action, he was awaiting a troop ship at Felixstowe when he strolled down to the local cricket club one evening. There he chanced to meet JWHT Douglas, who had led the MCC team to South Africa in 1913/14 and who would captain England again after the War. Invited to turn his arm over, Edwards was quick to impress the England captain with his accurate spinners. Johnny Douglas soon set about pulling a few strings and, with the connivance of his brother, managed to have Edwards re-classified as C2, enabling him to spend the rest of the war at Felixstowe, where he played for the garrison with Frank Woolley.

Frank Edwards

After the War Frank Edwards, now almost 34, entertained hopes that Surrey might wish to re-engage him, but he was turned down and found a post caring for the ground at North Park, where the Surrey Wanderers played, and umpiring their matches. One day the team found themselves a man short for their match against St Thomas's Hospital. Edwards was asked to fill the gap and took eight wickets. As soon as stumps were drawn a doctor was on the telephone to Bucks, and when the news reached Oliver Horlick he soon made sure that Edwards was back in the fold for the 1921 season.

By the heady standards Bucks set themselves in these early post-war years, 1921 was an indifferent season and the county slipped down the table to eighth, the lowest position the team would occupy in the 1920s. It was a major blow that injury should keep Jack Whiting out of all the matches, especially as Hazelton also missed several games and was not at his best when he was able to play. Moreover, with 48 wickets at 16.10, Frank Edwards' first full season was one of his least fruitful. To add to the team's problems, Franklin broke a finger in the first match and, when he was able to return for the last three games, it was only as a batsman.

Now opened the most glorious passage in the county's history as Bucks reached the Challenge Match in three of the next four seasons, emerging triumphant on each occasion. In 1922, a year when scoring was otherwise very low, Hertfordshire's 453 for eight at Watford was the only occasion on which the Bucks bowlers were mastered. Escaping from this match with a draw, the county's only other upset was a loss at Bedford in which poor fielding left the batsmen requiring 79 for victory, a modest task that proved beyond them as Bedfordshire ran out winners by 14 runs. The match against Cambridge at Fenner's was abandoned without a ball bowled, but winning their other five matches meant that Bucks earned the right to challenge Norfolk for the title.

In the words of the *Bucks Free Press* the match at Lakenham had 'more incidents than was good for people with weak hearts'. Bucks won the toss and with 67 from Franklin, the highest score by any Bucks batsman in the entire season, a respectable score of 225 was posted, to which Norfolk replied with 218, Edwards and Hazelton sharing the wickets. The Bucks batting then collapsed as opener Will Jackson fought a lone battle to be ninth man out for 41 when the score had reached 75. A few lusty swings from Jack Whiting raised the total to 89, setting Norfolk 98 to win. Hardly enough, spectators felt, until Norfolk plunged to 39 for five to swing the match in Bucks' favour. A stubborn stand between their captain Michael Falcon and Richard Carter regained the initiative for Norfolk as they took the score to 81. Four wickets then fell without addition to the score, first Hazelton then Edwards capturing two in successive balls.

With all resting on the last pair, Edwards appealed vainly for lbw. Another appeal, this time for a catch behind the wicket, was turned down. A possible catch eluded mid off. Eight precious runs were garnered; eight more would level the scores. Then Edwards tossed up a shorter ball tempting the Norfolk tailender to hit against the spin. The batsman's eyes lit up at the prospect of a leg-side six, but he could only send up a skier. Four fielders converged on the ball as it descended in mid pitch. Edwards and Franklin collided but the captain clasped the ball and hung on to give Bucks victory by eight runs and Edwards his sixth wicket, at a cost of 35.

In 1923 seven matches were won, the closest a two-run victory against Oxfordshire at High Wycombe. This narrow win came hard on the heels of Hertfordshire taking first innings points in the previous and only unfinished match, though when rain brought that game to a premature conclusion it was probably the visitors who were the more relieved. This year Bucks' record placed them at the top of the table, giving them the privilege of playing at home when challenged by Surrey Second Eleven.

When the two teams had last met it had been a story of humiliation for Bucks. The four matches in 1908 and 1909 had all ended in innings defeats with Bucks' pitiful scores reading: 42, 42, 124, 69, 34, 100, 61 and 37. Now there was the chance for revenge. Bucks batted first in difficult conditions and, with some inexperienced players at the top of the order, were soon 23 for three. In strode Philip Le Gros and, with Jackson and then Franklin in support, he struck 71 in only 80 minutes. The value of his innings soon became apparent as Surrey could manage no more than 95 in reply to Bucks' 181. The next day Bucks built on their lead and, with Eton schoolmaster WN Roe making 56, totalled 232 to set Surrey the formidable target of 319 to win. Before the close of the second day they had collapsed a second time for only 76. There were match figures of nine for 62 for Hazelton and nine for 80 for Edwards as Bucks ran out winners by 242 runs.

This match marked the end of Edwards' most prolific season. With eight wickets against MCC he had taken 104 for Bucks. Unfortunately this figure has been misconstrued over the years to accord to Edwards the distinction of taking a hundred wickets in Minor Counties Championship matches alone, the canard first appearing in the report published in the 1924 handbook. His 96 victims against county opposition came at an average of 10.29.

Bucks' batting around this time was often uncertain and various young hopefuls were tried for a few matches only to melt away. Some, like the former Brighton College player WRN Philps, shone in the field, but for weight of runs Philip Le Gros was in a class of his own. Good enough to be chosen for the Gentlemen in 1920 and for the Minor Counties in 1924, for each of the first five seasons after the War he was the county's leading run-maker and, as he had in the Challenge Match against Surrey, Le Gros was a batsman who could turn a match with his commanding stroke-play. Tall and well-built, he had a pronounced stoop at the wicket, from which he uncoiled to strike the ball with rare power. He once made 164 in little over the hour in a Club and Ground match at Northampton, reaching his century in 40 minutes. As tribute to another innings a photograph hung for many years in the High Wycombe pavilion showing a row of cars with their windscreens smashed by the ferocity of Le Gros' hits.

Le Gros' highest score for Bucks came when he hit 155 against Hertfordshire at Watford in 1923, but it was the Leicestershire Second Eleven bowlers who had most reason to remember his capabilities. When the teams met for the first time in 1924 the match at Hinckley did not begin until two o'clock on the second day. Within two hours Leicestershire were all out for 35, Edwards taking six for 10. The Bucks innings was also moving at a slow pace until Le Gros exploded, taking 26 off the last over bowled. His 70 not out enabled Franklin to declare at 5.35 with a lead of 86. This gave Edwards enough time to take another five wickets as Leicestershire stuttered to 43 for 6, counting themselves fortunate to escape an innings defeat in half a day's play.

Three weeks later the two teams locked horns again at High Wycombe. Leicestershire again chose to bat first but could muster no more than 33. This wretched score nevertheless sufficed to give them a first innings lead of nine. Hazelton and Edwards had done the damage in the first innings and they were soon in action again, but the visiting batsmen fared better in their second attempt, reaching 118. Needing 128 for victory, Bucks then slumped to 27 for 3 overnight. The odds must have favoured Leicestershire, but the next day Le Gros took command. With Aubrey-Fletcher giving staunch support, he drove his way to 80 not out to secure a seven-wicket victory for Bucks.

These matches with Leicestershire came in the season that broke Bucks' sequence as champion of the Minor Counties. In a wet summer Franklin had the misfortune to lose the toss in every match. The season began with not a ball bowled at The Oval and in the next two games there was no play on the first day. The handicap was too great for Bucks, who nevertheless managed to chalk up three wins, their only loss coming when Surrey Second Eleven squeezed home by 24 runs at High Wycombe to avenge their heavy defeat of the previous year.

This season Frank Edwards found a new ally to bowl at the other end. AU Payne, the brother of the Reverend EJ Payne of The Lee, had played seven matches in 1923 but only as a batsman. In 1925 he was to win a controversial blue in a very strong

Cambridge team on account of his fielding, but it was with the ball as a fast medium bowler that he served Bucks most conspicuously. While Edwards took 69 wickets at 9.03 in 1924, Alan Payne was close on his heels in the averages with 32 at 10.75. There were 26 wickets for Hazelton in what was virtually a three man attack.

Problems off the field

Though these were years of outstanding success for Bucks, many of the problems that beset the county before the War remained. The constancy of Franklin, Edwards and Le Gros helped to compensate for a continuing stream of amateurs whose star shone briefly or whose services were only offered for a couple of seasons. For instance, the only century in 1924 came from WN Roe, yet his Bucks career comprised just four matches. Those in the services came and went, while others had long overseas postings at a time when it was fashionable to pursue careers that meant uprooting to far corners of the Empire.

PN Durlacher

One of the more talented young men who promised much but was soon lost to Bucks was PN Durlacher, who played in the last five matches of the 1920 season when he still had a year to go at Wellington College. A fine sportsman who was in the winning pair at the Public Schools Rackets Championship the following winter, Patrick Durlacher opened his Bucks career with innings of 80 and 46 not out against Berkshire at Reading, ending the season with an average of 33.14. Next year, when the school holidays arrived, Bucks eagerly awaited the return of young Durlacher, who had accepted an invitation to play in all the county's fixtures.

Two days before the first match at Bletchley Park Walter Franklin received a telephone call from Durlacher's father seeking to withdraw his son's acceptance as he had been asked to play for Middlesex. First-class play, Mr Durlacher would later contend, would be more beneficial to his son's development and improve his prospects of winning a blue. Such pleas cut little ice with Franklin, who nevertheless reluctantly agreed to the withdrawal. However, far from letting the matter rest, the Bucks captain persuaded the committee that it should be brought up at the next meeting of the Minor Counties Association and drawn to the attention of MCC.

'The Durlacher Case' became a cause celebre as other minor counties were persuaded to register their indignation at the practice of first-class counties poaching their players. Years later Durlacher senior was still a member of the County Club. His son played five matches for Middlesex without any notable success. In the autumn of that fateful year of 1921 he went up to Cambridge, where he won a half blue for cross country but he never took the field for the cricket team, and never again did he play for Bucks.

In contrast to this nationally publicised case the committee was soon embroiled in a more parochial storm in a teacup. There had long been a tradition that players who had made three appearances for the county should be awarded their cap, though the rules declared that such awards were at the discretion of the captain. In 1921 H Thorpe of Slough CC played in six matches averaging 18.71 with the bat and taking a couple of expensive wickets. He had not received a cap and his club saw fit to raise the matter. There was some support for their plea in committee, but Franklin was not a man to be stampeded. In his view Thorpe was not good enough and that was that. On the casting vote of HE Bull, who was in the chair, Franklin won his point.

If the committee thought that they had heard the last of the matter they were in for a rude shock. There was a further exchange of letters, the full contents of which are not recorded, which caused the committee to express regret at the tone of the Slough secretary's missive. The Slough captain, WJ Newberry, who was on the county committee, maintained that his club's secretary had not conveyed the true view of the committee members, but enough damage had been done for David Sewell to cancel the Club and Ground fixture with Slough for 1922, a decision that the committee ratified. Eighteen months after the original rumpus the matter was still rumbling on with the newly installed president, the Bishop of Buckingham, asked to make conciliatory approaches to the Slough club. Thorpe, meanwhile, never got his cap and he never played for Bucks again.

Success continues

Champions again in 1925, Bucks had to endure another season of wretched weather. The away match with Hertfordshire never started and there was no decision on first innings in the return fixture or in the match against Surrey Second Eleven at High Wycombe. But in a year where the ball invariably dominated affairs Frank Edwards captured 62 wickets at a cost of 7.39 each. The season began in dramatic style at Bletchley Park where, after a blank first day, Kent Second Eleven won the toss and batted, only to be dismissed for 34 with Edwards and Payne sharing the wickets. There

The 1925 Team
At back: **GH Quint** *(scorer)*
Standing (l to r): **F Edwards, WT Brindley, LG Baker, EA Fawcus, OG Battcock**
Seated: **JN Buchanan, PW Le Gros, WB Franklin, WE Haselton, AO Payne**
On the ground: **EF Robson**

were four new faces in the Bucks team and one of these men, WT Brindley, on leave from Ceylon, where he became chief of the harbour police, now played the first of several valuable innings as he made 45 in Bucks' modest reply of just 95. An hour later the match was over with Kent all out for 15 (Edwards eight for 7). This remains the lowest innings score ever made against Bucks.

Only one day's play was needed at Oxford where Edwards returned match figures of fourteen for 41 as the home team made 60 in each innings. Oxfordshire's batsmen were even less successful at High Wycombe totalling just 33 and 41 to give Edwards thirteen more wickets for 24.

The bat came into its own at The Oval where a century from Hazelton gave Bucks first innings lead in a drawn match. At Bickley Park, Kent looked like exacting revenge for their earlier humiliation as their bowlers skittled Bucks for 66, enforcing the follow on with a lead of 108. It was Brindley who rode to the rescue. A battling 50 and a partnership of 93 with Le Gros helped to overhaul the deficit and set Kent 81 for victory. With Edwards keeping one end quiet, Brindley now took over with the ball, returning career-best figures of seven for 20 to lead Bucks to an unlikely win by 26 runs.

These results earned Bucks a trip to Jesmond to challenge Northumberland, who had won all their matches. Brindley top-scored with 50 in Bucks' first innings total of 205, after which there were ten more wickets for Edwards at a cost of 64 as, for the fourth time this year, opponents failed to reach 100 in either innings. Easy winners by 157 runs, Bucks will seldom have sent a stronger attack into the field. With Payne and Brindley in support of Edwards, it barely mattered that Hazelton could play in only four matches. Moreover, among the newcomers to the team was 21-year-old OG Battcock, who would become the mainstay of Bucks bowling in later years and succeed to the captaincy in 1948. Oliver Battcock played in five matches in 1925, but the handbook saw him as 'a promising left-hand bat' and he bowled not one ball.

Another whose talent with the ball went virtually unused in 1925 was EA Fawcus, a capable all-rounder who played for the RAF and who enjoyed three seasons playing for Bucks while serving at Halton. This was also the only year in which the county had the services of JN Buchanan, who had captained Cambridge in 1909 and had later served on the committee of MCC. Buchanan had been in the Grenadier Guards with Aubrey-Fletcher during the War and he was another Bucks man to have won the Military Cross. Thirty eight years of age when he first played for Bucks, Buchanan proved a useful opening partner for Brindley. Though his bowling was not needed he maintained his formidable reputation in the field, being described as 'one of the most brilliant slip fielders in England'.

With Brindley back in Ceylon, Buchanan injured all summer and Le Gros restricted to one match through pressure of business, Bucks did well to end the 1926 season in joint second position. There was only one loss, and among the five victories was a cliff-hanger at High Wycombe in the final match when Edwards claimed an lbw decision off the last ball of the penultimate over to beat Surrey Second Eleven by 102 runs. There was jubilation at the outcome and the *Bucks Free Press* congratulated the team on 'a glorious victory' as it relished the prospect of another Challenge Match, this time against Durham. However, the celebrations were to prove premature. In the words of the handbook: 'It can be imagined with what disappointment Bucks subsequently received the news that Oxfordshire were placed above them in the Championship table.' With three teams level, all with identical playing records, Oxfordshire were ultimately accorded second place by virtue of having a higher 'nett batting average'.

There were 74 wickets for Edwards this year and Franklin recovered his best form with the bat; but the loss of so many leading players gave opportunities to several young players, of whom the most successful was Leslie Baker with 367 runs at 26.21. Baker had first played for Bucks in 1924, but this was the first year in which his stylish batting had brought him many runs. He was the son of Harold Baker, a pace bowler and Jessopian hitter of the pre-War era who had played nine times for the county. A true stalwart of the High Wycombe club, Harold Baker was soon to embark upon a long stint as treasurer of the County Club, while his son was to become one of the select band who have made more than a hundred appearances for the county team and he in turn was to give long service on the committee.

Bucks took third place in the Championship in 1927. Once again there was one dramatic match, against Hertfordshire at Ascott, on which the county's fate hung. Thanks to a sound batting performance with half centuries for Franklin and Powell, Bucks gained a first innings lead of 152. Herts then batted with more resolution in their second innings, scoring 238 to set Bucks 87 to win. Wickets soon began to tumble and, with two overs to go, five were still needed with four wickets in hand. With Aubrey-Fletcher unable to score off the penultimate over, the tension began to mount. Battcock was now facing the final over from fast bowler Redhouse. The first ball rattled into his stumps and he departed for a well played 32. This brought a nerve-wracked Jim Pitchford to the wicket. He failed to connect with his first two balls then managed a single to get Aubrey-Fletcher back on strike. A heave to leg brought three more runs and the scores were level, but Pitchford failed to score off the last ball. Bucks believed that they had taken first innings points but, under the Law as it then stood, MCC ruled that the match was a tie, and at the end of the season this was to cost Bucks second place and another Challenge Match.

Edwards was still a major force this year with 69 wickets at 8.57, but he had to yield top place in the averages to Harry Pitchford, another professional who had played only intermittently in earlier seasons with little use made of his bowling. One of a family of 15, Pitchford was the brother of the unfortunate Jim, whose game against Hertfordshire was one of only three appearances for Bucks. Their youngest brother, Leonard, played briefly for Glamorgan. Harry Pitchford worked for the Rothschild family at Ascott from 1912. For many years he was responsible for the care of the ground that the county has been privileged to use through the generosity of succeeding generations of the family. In the winter he used to help the gamekeeper.

A greatly loved man, Harry Pitchford coached several members of the Rothschild family including Sir Evelyn de Rothschild, the present owner of Ascott, whose father

Harry Pitchford in his role of groundsman

Anthony played ten times for Bucks and served as president in 1912 and 1913. Another who was introduced to the joys of cricket by Harry Pitchford was Peter Stoddart, who went to Ascott Park for coaching in the late 1940s and who captained the county for seven years from 1959. "He was such a nice man," he says, "he was the one who really got me going. And around that time he was producing just about the best batting wickets in England."

Whenever Harry Pitchford played for Bucks the Rothschilds saw to it that it was at no cost to the county, and in 1927 Bucks will have been especially grateful for his right-arm spinners that perfectly complemented Edwards and earned him 42 wickets at 8.12, form that led to an invitation to play for the Minor Counties against the West Indians the following summer. Pitchford had a few useful knocks for the county, but he never again repeated his golden year with the ball and he played his last match in 1929.

A newcomer to the Bucks ranks in 1927 was 20-year-old JWA Stephenson. In later years his fast medium seamers brought him success in services cricket and for Essex. After taking nine for 46 for the Gentlemen against the Players at Lord's in 1936, many considered him unlucky not to be picked for the tour to Australia that winter. However, when he and his brother, FMR Stephenson, played for Bucks both were regarded primarily as batsmen.

JWA Stephenson

This same summer saw the start of another career that would soon flower impressively when AG Skinner, a 16-year-old schoolboy from Oundle, made his debut against Kent. He took a little time to find his feet in minor counties cricket, but before long he had made the number three spot his own and his stylish batting in 66 matches brought him 2,515 runs at an average of 28.58. For several years Graham Skinner was lost to Bucks cricket when his business career took him to India, where he scored a century for Bengal against Nawanagar in the Ranji Trophy, but the county was always delighted to welcome him back. He played his last match for Bucks in 1952, thereafter remaining one of the county's staunchest supporters until his death in 1997. Bucks cricketers of today continue to reap the benefit of his generous legacy to the county, which has provided funding for coaching and enabled interest-free loans to be made to clubs wishing to improve their facilities.

In 1928 Bucks ended the season in fifth position. Needing only to draw their last two matches to earn the right to challenge Berkshire, the team contrived to lose both. There were two notable newcomers this year. The first played just once for Bucks: RJ Shaw was an officer in the Royal Navy, but he was the third of Bishop Shaw's three sons to take the field for Bucks, stirring memories of his two older brothers who had both given their lives in the War. The other debutant was RH Rutter, who would play 82 times for the county. Educated at Tonbridge, Ronnie Rutter had played for the Public Schools at Lord's earlier in the summer before making his Bucks debut against Hertfordshire at Broxbourne. A tall man with a beautiful rhythmic action, he took six for 93 against a strong Surrey Second Eleven at High Wycombe. Two years later he had taken over the mantle of Wyndham Hazelton as spearhead of the pace attack.

A pillar of the Beaconsfield club, Rutter was a much valued and popular figure in Bucks cricket on and off the field. In a career that stretched on to one final post-war season in 1947, he took 366 wickets for the county. On occasions he could hit out to good effect, often being promoted when quick runs were needed. His one century for Bucks came in 1932 when he hit 106 against Oxfordshire at High Wycombe in just 45 minutes, believed to be the fastest three-figure score in Bucks' history.

The third young man helping to maintain Bucks' supremacy around this time in the triumvirate with Skinner and Rutter was RHJ Brooke, one of the finest batsmen ever to wear a Bucks cap. A product of St Edward's Oxford, he was just 20 when he burst on the scene in 1929, scoring what was then a Bucks record of 822 runs in 19 innings. His figures were less startling in the next two seasons, but in 1932 Hubert Brooke averaged 49.33 and his 740 runs included 164 not out at Bedford School, an innings which surpassed by two runs the previous best for Bucks set in 1909.

This was also the year in which Brooke won a blue at Oxford, hitting four centuries for the university that had scorned his talent when he first went up. He went on to teach for 30 years at Shrewsbury, returning to play for Bucks in 1934 and 1935, though without the success of his best years. Apart from taking the cricket at Shrewsbury, he taught French and English to the lower forms. A former pupil remembers him fondly as a bit of an eccentric who used to enjoy getting his class to sing songs and one who imposed order in jocular fashion by shouting 'This is war' if his charges were getting out of hand. The late disc jockey and broadcaster John Peel was another who came under Brooke's wing at Shrewsbury, years later paying tribute to 'RHJ' for encouraging him to shut himself away and make his own music. In later life Brooke was ordained and spent his last years as rector of Great Canfield in Essex.

Brooke's fine batting and a normal quotient of 72 wickets from Edwards were the major factors in steering Bucks back to second in the table and earning the county another Challenge Match in 1929. The season had begun with defeat at The Oval, but not before Hazelton had batted splendidly for 124 not out, his second century for the county and the highest of his career. It looked as though Bucks might be on the way to another defeat at Ascott when they trailed Norfolk by 40 on first innings and later needed 238 to win, but the two young lions of the batting line-up, Brooke (86) and Skinner (104), combined to steer the county home by six wickets. After the match the three rising stars, Brooke, Skinner and Rutter, were all awarded their county caps.

Three more victories and first innings points in a further three of their ten-match programme allowed Bucks to challenge Oxfordshire. Along the way the team had twice denied Staffordshire, and the great Sydney Barnes, in taking first innings points, with Oliver Battcock winning eternal fame by twice hitting the former Test bowler into the river at High Wycombe. The Challenge Match was played on the Merton College ground. Franklin won the toss and may have regretted deciding to bat on a difficult pitch, from which Oxfordshire gained an early advantage that they never surrendered, winning the match by ten wickets after Bucks had been dismissed for only 61 on the second morning.

A highlight of the 1930 season was a return of nine for 29 for Frank Edwards against Oxfordshire, the best innings analysis ever recorded by a Bucks bowler. Later in the season he took eight for 13 and seven for 31 against Kent Second Eleven – yet he still ended up on the losing side. Needing just 51 to win in this low-scoring match, Bucks were bowled out for 24, sliding to one of the county's most ignominious defeats and one that surrendered the chance of another Challenge Match.

After taking fourth place in the table in 1930, Bucks moved up to third the following year, a season in which the team was often thwarted by the weather. The ever enterprising Franklin devised what was then a novel stratagem to conjure full points for a victory against Hertfordshire at High Wycombe, when he proposed that both sides should declare their innings closed after just one ball. There might have been another Challenge Match for Bucks had Franklin managed to persuade Oxfordshire to take the same approach after a blank first day in the match at Banbury, but the home captain would have none of it.

Ten victories in ten matches

The Bucks team had been regular contenders for the Championship title and in 1932 they made no mistake. The nucleus of an outstanding side was Brooke and Skinner in commanding form as top order batsmen, reinforced for a few matches by the return of JWA Stephenson and the arrival in mid-season of SS Peters, a fine if sometimes impetuous stroke-maker from Aylesbury, who was also a brilliant cover point. In an otherwise subdued season Leslie Baker chipped in with one century.

With the ball Frank Edwards captured 79 wickets at 7.67. This was his swansong as a true sorcerer - never again would his average be below 12. With 63 wickets at just over ten apiece for Ronnie Rutter there was little scope for others to shine, though Henry Aubrey-Fletcher's son John, who had made his debut the previous year at the age of 18, was starting out on a useful career as an all-rounder that would see him representing the Minor Counties in 1933. Behind the stumps Walter Franklin was directing affairs as shrewdly as ever and with few signs that his wicket-keeping skills were diminishing.

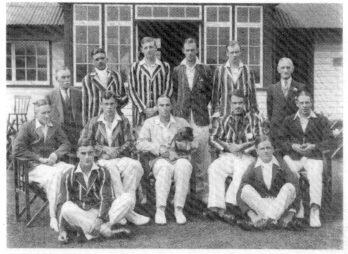

The 1932 team that won all its championship matches.
Standing: **GH Quint** *(scorer)*, **JWA Stephenson, JHL Aubrey-Fletcher, CV Raffety,**
BO Byass, H Baker *(Hon. Treasuer)*
Seated: **LG Baker, RH Rutter, WB Franklin** *(Captain)*, **RHJ Brooke, F Edwards**
On ground: **AG Skinner, AP Powell**

This was the team, with only Franklin and Edwards over the age of 30, that was to win all ten of its matches, five of them by an innings. Victories by four wickets with a weakened team away to Norfolk and by five wickets against Bedfordshire at Bletchley Park were the closest the county came to defeat. The players were deprived of the icing on the cake that they so richly deserved when the Challenge Match against Berkshire did not start until 12.15 on the second day and was abandoned shortly after lunch on the third. The match had not started propitiously for Bucks. At one time they had been 23 for 6, but a brave recovery was led by Graham Skinner whose 72 not out, with help from Aubrey-Fletcher and Edwards, took the score to 164 for nine. However, the abandonment meant that, as the challenged county, Bucks were still crowned champions.

Fortunes decline

Minor counties will often struggle to assemble their best teams, and for the next few years the vagaries of overseas postings and players' other commitments combined to reduce Bucks' competitive potency. The 1932 champions immediately fell to 15th in the table; the following year they slipped one place lower. A rise to ninth in 1935 was then followed by the indignity of dropping to 20th in 1936. Brooke missed the 1933 season and never captured his best form again, Stephenson had played his last match for Bucks in 1932, Skinner could play less regularly in 1933 and by the summer of 1934 his work had taken him to India for four years. Rutter bowled manfully in 1933, but thereafter he could no longer promise to play in all the matches and he was missing altogether in 1936 and 1937.

Franklin was seldom the force he had been with the bat, but the most critical decline was in the form of Edwards. In 1933 his 57 wickets were obtained at twice the cost of the previous year and, whereas between 1922 and 1932 he had taken an average of 70 wickets a season at 9.52 each, from 1934 his annual bag was only 30 and his wickets were costing 14.50. In 1935 Edwards passed his fiftieth birthday, and it was small wonder that his powers were on the wane.

During these disappointing years Leslie Baker and Sam Peters were the mainstays of the batting, while the supporting cast continued to turn over as promising young men were given their chance, struggled to make much impact and then disappeared from the scene. One who batted with some consistency in the difficult years was Algie Busby, a farmer from Buckingham. As far back as 1926 Charles Clover-Brown had played for Bucks while still at Harrow, and his return on leave in 1933 was awaited with keen anticipation. The previous winter, Clover-Brown and WT Brindley had shared an opening stand of 79 for Ceylon against DR Jardine's MCC team, when the tourists made their customary break on their voyage to Australia. For Bucks Clover-Brown made 83 not out against Norfolk in his final match, but otherwise achieved little. In 1935 it was Brindley's time for some home leave. He returned, as he had in 1930, to take up his place in the county side, but he could not repeat the success he had enjoyed when he had first played in 1925.

There were two seasons for PHC Badham, the son of the vicar of Great Missenden. Though he had played a few matches for Oxford University, Peter Badham seldom revealed his best form for Bucks. Among the more capable batsmen was AP Powell, who had played once for Middlesex in 1927. He enjoyed a fine season for Bucks in 1933, but his form soon suffered a decline. Robert Campbell, a teenage left-hander from Chesham, played for two seasons, making a century against Bedfordshire at Ascott Park in his second match in 1935, when he shared in a stand of 223 for the fifth wicket with Leslie Baker, still a county record. Campbell ended the summer as leading run-maker, but he could not sustain this good form and after 1936 he played no more. Campbell's principal sport was rugby, at which he played war-time internationals.

AH Birtwell

The bowling could no longer rely on two or three players to run through the opposition. Typifying the new regime in which Franklin would toss the ball to more of his players, AH Holliman, captain of Dulwich College in 1934, played in 30 matches in which his googlies brought him 41 wickets, but at the high cost of 26 each. Another spin bowler who devoted three seasons to Bucks was AJ Birtwell, who took 34 wickets with his leg breaks in 1934. Thereafter he proved rather expensive, but after leaving the area to practise as a solicitor in the north he went on to bowl with great success in the Lancashire League and make a few appearances in the county team.

Champions again

Things began to look up for Bucks in 1937 when the team claimed seventh place in the table and then, in 1938, they were back at the top. The batting was strengthened by the return of Graham Skinner for just this summer. John Aubrey-Fletcher had developed into an opening batsman who was hard to dislodge. Leslie Baker, who partnered him, enjoyed his best season, winning a place in the Minor Counties side to play the West Indians the next summer. Peters was in good form and there were a few good innings from Geoffrey Walker from Wing, a solid batsman who had made a favourable impression the previous year.

Meanwhile the bowling, which had become a perennial problem, benefited from the return of Rutter for some of the matches and, most conspicuously, from having Oliver Battcock also available for six games - for the first time since 1930. He now took 45 wickets at 9.56 each to top the averages for all the minor counties. Adding further power to the attack was Vic Lund, a swing bowler from Slough. After making his first appearance for the county in 1929, he played in only two more matches before gaining a regular place in 1936. He had enjoyed an outstanding season in 1937. This was the year in which he had lengthened his run-up but reduced the pace at which he bowled his prodigious inswingers. With greater control and well supported by his leg trap, where there was often a ring of four close fielders, Lund topped the averages with 43 wickets at 9.37. That same year he became yet another Bucks player to be selected for the Minor Counties.

Nor were these the only bowlers of class now at Bucks' command. One who played eight times between 1937 and 1939 as well as returning to play all matches in the 1947 season was DH Macindoe. A four-year Oxford blue, who later became master of cricket at Eton, in 1937 he took six wickets as a freshman in the Varsity Match and was chosen to open the bowling for the Gentlemen a week later. However, it seemed that his exertions had drained him and, as in other years, he was never able to show for Bucks the form that he revealed at Oxford. Another to disappoint for the county around this time was Alan Ratcliffe. In 1931, after coming into the Cambridge team only as a late replacement for an injured player, he had made the first double-century in the history of the Varsity Match; for Bucks he made 68 in his second match but few scores of significance thereafter.

The 1938 season opened with a seven-wicket win against Hertfordshire followed by three victories, all by an innings, in the same week. The value of winning these matches so easily, the handbook shrewdly pointed out, was that the team did not have to tire themselves out with travelling through the night. Two more comfortable wins assured the county of a place in the Challenge Match and two draws to complete the programme meant that Bucks would be hosts at High Wycombe and it was Lancashire Second Eleven to travel.

The visitors' team included two future Test players, Winston Place and Ken Cranston, and there was a familiar face in their line-up - Alex Birtwell, who had been playing for Bucks only two years earlier. In miserable weather Lancashire won the toss and batted, obliging Bucks to bowl in a drizzle with a wet ball. A run out was missed off the first ball, but Battcock still managed to take a wicket in his first over and the Lancashire batsmen were contained to 69 for 3 at lunch. Then Battcock really got to work as the last seven wickets fell for just 12 more runs.

A stubborn opening partnership was followed by a forceful 51 from Peters and an invaluable 30 not out from Franklin as Bucks built a lead of 104. Sterner resistance was expected from the visitors when they batted a second time, but instead there was a spineless display with wickets falling steadily as Bucks cruised to victory by an innings and 25 runs. With 12 for 65 Battcock had been the star performer, and with solid support from Lund and Rutter, there had been no need for Edwards to bowl.

The revival in Bucks' fortunes was maintained into 1939. A heavy defeat by Hertfordshire in the first match was the only loss and Bucks ended fourth before the curtain came down once more, suspending championship play until 1946. The final match before the war, against Norfolk at Ascott Park, brought a debut to 17-year-old John Tovey from High Wycombe. Described in the *Bucks Free Press* review of the season as 'a forceful batsman with plenty of skill and confidence', he is believed to be the sole survivor of those who played under Franklin. After the war he played for Berkshire, his family having moved to Reading, but he still recalls vividly his one appearance for Bucks and the traditional needle between the two captains, Norfolk's Michael Falcon having played for his county even longer than Franklin, starting in 1907 and captaining from 1912. Inserted by Franklin, Norfolk made only 50 in their first innings, Lund taking seven for 24, but their captain led a fight back in the second knock to set Bucks 46 for victory. At 10 for 3 young Tovey, who had made 17 in his first innings, was in again. His brief second innings included the unusual sensation of seeing his off stump rock back without a bail falling to the ground, but at 30 for 5 he was back in the pavilion nervously watching some bold blows from Macindoe as Bucks reached their target without further loss.

"I remember Franklin," John Tovey says, "very autocratic and very formidable for a 17- year-old schoolboy. I was fielding on the boundary - I had quite a good arm in those days – and, when I threw it in not quite straight, he put his hand on his hip and glared at me and the ball nearly hit him on the chin. He had one peculiarity I remember: at the end of the over he used to walk from wicket to wicket with his hands clasped behind his back." If Franklin was a daunting captain for the raw recruit there were others who made him more welcome: "I was privileged to play with Frank Edwards, a very kindly old pro, a very nice man. And there was Leslie Baker, who had been my mentor at High Wycombe. He had his dental surgery just opposite the ground."

Before leaving the inter-war years mention might be made of some of the lesser lights who played their part in keeping the flag flying. AJS James, a civil servant from Beaconsfield, had moments of success in the 42 matches he played as a middle order batsman between 1926 and 1937. Vezey Raffety, another prominent member of the Beaconsfield club, promised much when he first played in 1924. A Cranleigh schoolboy, he made his Bucks debut fresh from having played for the Public Schools at Lord's but, despite selection to play for the Minor Counties in 1931, 17 matches for Bucks brought only two fifties. There were also just two fifties in 35 appearances for BH Stevens-Davies, an enthusiastic cricketer and brilliant fielder whose friendship with Maurice Turnbull brought him one non-first-class game for Glamorgan. BO Byass from Gerrards Cross opened the batting in the all-conquering team of 1932, but the runs he was expected to score never materialised.

Bucks, some had said in the glory years, were too good for minor counties cricket. What is more, back in 1921 they had been asked to join the first-class counties, but they had declined through lack of facilities. So runs the story that has long been the received wisdom of Bucks cricket, but is it more than folklore? For such a momentous move there might at least have been debate in committee, but the minute book is silent on the matter. So, too, are the handbook and the local newspapers. Nothing has been uncovered in an extensive, though not perhaps exhaustive, scrutiny of MCC Committee minutes. Moreover, though Glamorgan joined up in 1921, before that season began the Bucks County Club was still climbing back to its feet; it had a poor pre-war playing record and assets of just £148 7s 0d. Fourth in the table in 1920, and eighth a year later, hardly suggest dominance on the field. Moreover, Franklin and many of those who played alongside him could only do so in late July and August.

If playing credentials were to count then a move to first-class status would have been more credible at a later date, but the character of the cricket remained a world apart from the first-class game. Perhaps the idea was floated informally or in jest – "You're too good for us, Franklin, you ought to be playing with the big boys!" Either way there is certainly nothing to suggest that Bucks ever seriously entertained the idea of playing cricket throughout the summer with the likes of Middlesex, Yorkshire and Lancashire, though it should be said that some of those who mooted promotion for minor counties envisaged that they could take part in the first-class game without playing a full programme of matches throughout the summer.

Back on the Field:
The Early Post-War Years

Franklin's last fling

'On behalf of the Committee, I have the pleasure to inform you that the activities of the Club will be renewed in 1946.' Thus began the notice dated 1 January and circulated to the club's 246 members by H Tyson Chambers, who had succeeded to the office of secretary after it had been in the worthy hands of George Brocklehurst, with just one year's break, since 1927. The notice invited members to pay their annual subscription of one guinea (£1.05), but the plea fell on many deaf ears, just £146.17s being recorded as members' donations by the end of the year.

The cessation of hostilities in Europe had been marked by a handful of friendly matches the previous summer, the most memorable against the Australian Services team captained by Lindsay Hassett. This match at High Wycombe was marked by an explosive innings of 114 from Cec Pepper, which contained nine sixes. A game had also been played against Alf Gover's Eleven and, when Northants were entertained, it was the first time that Bucks had taken a match to Agar's Plough, the principal Eton College ground. For the next five years the county always played one match at Eton.

As the first-class counties prepared for a full season, their minor brethren resumed with more circumspection. Just six matches sufficed for qualification in the Championship, though Bucks elected to play eight. Leading the county once more was Walter Franklin, now aged 55. He was not alone in taking up the challenge at such an advanced age. Michael Falcon, his old adversary from Norfolk, also served one more year after the war, even topping the batting averages at the age of 58.

Frank Edwards, now 61, had expressed his eagerness to join his old skipper and wheel away for another season, but in his case age counted against him and the committee decided to award him a testimonial instead. Edwards was, however, chosen for one match, against Dorset at Canford, though he never set foot on the field of play as Bucks made 204 for 8 between interruptions for rain, still batting on when play resumed at 4.15 on the second day.

In a wretchedly wet summer Bucks began well with a seven wicket victory over Berkshire, for whom the 17-year-old PBH May was playing his only match. The future England captain made an inauspicious debut: lbw b Lund 0. Hereafter five of Bucks' matches failed to reach a decisive result on first innings. Under the scoring system of the day, later changed at Bucks' instigation, these 'no result' games suited the county's cause better than taking the points available for a first innings lead. This led to a farcical conclusion to the final match against Hertfordshire at Watford. Once again most of the playing time was lost to the weather and, when Bucks finally dismissed the home team for 91, two hours remained for them to bat. With two victories and one first innings lead, Bucks' average points per match would fall if they were to overtake the Herts' score, whereas another 'no result' match would take them to the top of the table.

Franklin was in no mood to respect the spirit of the game, instructing his batsmen that they must not pass the Herts' total. Arthur Grimsdell, Herts' long-standing wicket-keeper and captain for the match, had other ideas. Telling his bowlers to aim wide of the stumps, he proceeded to let the ball pass through to the boundary. A saturated outfield did not help the Herts' plan but, to Franklin's consternation, Grimsdell claimed the extra half hour, only relenting and coming off when Bucks, with the aid of four wides and 18 byes, had reached 80 for 3.

Matches with Hertfordshire always had an extra edge of competitiveness in the years to come and Franklin's attitude at Canford, coming after he had left Dorset two hours to chase 363 at High Wycombe and then made little attempt to take wickets, meant that matches with that county were discontinued. But the Bucks captain succeeded in his objective: with two wins his side were top of the table, while Suffolk, with five wins and three first-innings leads from their eight matches, came second. In the end justice was served as Suffolk swept to victory by 70 runs in the Challenge Match at High Wycombe, skittling Bucks twice for scores of 70 and 94 in another contentious match where the captains were in constant dispute about the fitness of the ground for play.

For Walter Franklin it had been his 200th match for the county. In his final season he had been well served by two stalwarts of the pre-war era. At the age of 44, Vic Lund, with 24 wickets at 6.92, was the leading bowler in the Championship, and Oliver Battcock was close on his heels with 32 at 8.16. The batting was more uncertain with the best of the pre-war players, Leslie Baker and Sam Peters, both having lean seasons, though Baker hit one of the summer's five hundreds when he equalled his previous best for the county with 131 against Bedfordshire on his home ground at High Wycombe.

Jack O'Connor

Peter Isherwood from Slough, who had played five times in 1939 as an 18 year-old and who was destined to become the last link with the pre-war era, hit the first of his four centuries. Another hundred came from Bill Yates, a former professional footballer with Bolton Wanderers and Watford, who was soon to become better known locally as the sports manager at the Slough Community Centre. The newly engaged professional Jack O'Connor, the former Essex all-rounder who had played four times for England, made 112 against Berkshire. Appropriately this was at Eton College, where he was now head coach. Bucks' fifth hundred came in the same match from Tony Prince, another newcomer, later to become secretary of the County Club for 15 years.

Life after Franklin

Heading the averages in this first post-war season, with a top score of 99, was Claude Taylor. A master at Eton, he had won a blue at Oxford and played for Leicestershire in the 1920s. It was he who was to become Bucks' first new captain for a quarter of a century. In a summer that will always be remembered for the runs that flowed from the bats of Compton and Edrich, Bucks' batsmen enjoyed the hard August pitches of 1947, indulging themselves as never before and posting a record team average of 31.59 per wicket that was not surpassed until 1983. Taylor himself led the way with three centuries and an Eton colleague Donald Bousfield, who had played a few matches for Hertfordshire in the 1930s, joined to open the batting and also averaged over fifty.

There had long been a pronounced public school flavour to Bucks teams and Taylor now further strengthened the Etonian presence by bringing back David Macindoe, another teaching colleague and former pupil of the school, later to become its Vice-Provost, who had played for the county before the war. Taylor and Macindoe were both great theorists, and both in their time ran the cricket at Eton. They were soon to team up again to write an instructional book *Cricket Dialogue,* which took the form of a conversation in which the pair addressed themselves primarily to youngsters who might be taking up the game, offering advice that went far beyond keeping the left elbow up:

Claude Taylor
(without hat in the centre)
leaving for Canda on a pre-war
MCC tour

M. Just to ram home the points that we have made about appearance by drawing a picture of the Impossible Cricketer.
T. Good idea. Well, he arrives late.
M. Without a shirt to wear.
T. His pads are dirty.
M. His boots are muddy.
T. And several spikes are missing in them.
M. His batting gloves are riddled with holes.
T. So are his trousers, because he omitted to put them in moth-balls last winter.
M. He wears a wrist watch while playing.
T. His loose change is jangling in his pocket.
M. His uncut hair flops in his eyes because he doesn't wear a cap.
T. He wears dark blue socks.

Oliver Battcock

With Lund fading away, Battcock now carried the attack almost single-handed, taking 50 of the 117 wickets that fell to bowlers, while Macindoe struggled once more, his ten victims costing 62 apiece, and Ronnie Rutter, returning for five matches, also made little impression. The weakness of the attack was compounded by poor fielding, while there was no obvious successor to Franklin behind the stumps. Yates, who had bowled a few leg breaks in 1946, was the first to be tried as keeper but he lost confidence and the county appeared to be searching high and low for someone to take the gloves. The call went to David Cooper of the little-known Amersham Hill club, who let through 24 byes in a total of just 242 at Stoke-on-Trent, where 'there were an astonishing number of shooters'. Then Roy McKelvie, a tennis and squash reporter later to become a singularly unpopular press officer at Wimbledon, was given a chance. Finally, for the last match of the season, a man was found who would keep throughout the following summer: JFN Mayhew, another Etonian, had won a blue at Oxford in 1930.

Sliding down the table to thirteenth place, Bucks had had a poor season and for this the captain took much of the blame. His instinct to pile up large scores was in sharp contrast to Franklin, whose victories in the inter-war tears had typically been achieved by dangling a carrot and letting Edwards get to work, often on dodgy pitches. In fairness to Taylor, conditions in 1947 did not favour this tactic, nor had he an attack to press home an advantage; but he still fell foul of Tyson Chambers, a blunt Lancastrian who seldom favoured kid gloves. So Taylor's brief career for Bucks ended in his resignation when, even at 44, his fluent batting still had much to offer. Alone of those who have played as many as his 16 matches, he departed with an average of over fifty.

Battcock takes over

It was now the turn of Oliver Battcock to assume the captaincy, a position he would hold for four years. One of the great characters of Bucks cricket, Battcock had been educated at Harrow and his adult life was divided between the stage and the cricket field. After making his name in the West End – it was Oliver Gordon on the stage – he ran the Theatre Royal, Windsor for the duration of the war, taking the opportunity to indulge his passion for pantomime. After the war he continued to return to the theatre as a guest actor, invariably being roped in to play the dame at Christmas. His freelance status ensured that the summer could be devoted to cricket. Apart from his matches for Datchet, for whom he took over 2,000 wickets, he turned out for MCC, Incogniti, the Butterflies and the Forty Club, frequently captaining sides and taking teams abroad.

The new captain had an unhappy baptism. After travelling to Stone, he lost the toss and by the close of play Bucks had bowled 96 overs, seen a strong Staffordshire side rattle up 505 for 6 to equal the highest score ever recorded against the county, and still had time to reach 91 for 3 by close of play. Defeat by an innings and 45 runs came the next day.

There were three debutants in the Bucks team that day. Francis Whiting was the son of a pre-war player and the nephew of the fearsome Jack Whiting of the early 1920s; the young Whiting achieved little. Albert Hayhurst, now 41, was a medium pacer and useful batsman. He had played a few games as a professional for Warwickshire in the 1930s and would chip in usefully over the next five years. The third newcomer was Alf Hughes of High Wycombe. Since the war Bucks had felt a desperate need for a spin bowler of quality. An initial return of one for 105 gave scant indication that Hughes was to be the answer; but by 1958 his 391 wickets, captured at 15.26 each, would take him to third place in the all-time list of Bucks' wicket-takers behind Frank Edwards and Mat Wright.

There were three defeats in a row to set Battcock on his way, but the third, by ten wickets at Bedford School, came after a daring declaration in which he had invited the home county to score 133 in 85 minutes. Twenty third place out of 28 reflected very weak batting. Taylor had departed, Bousfield was able to play only three matches and Prince and Isherwood both lost form. In the search for an opening batsman the county turned to the 40-year-old Aidan Crawley, who had played with distinction for

Aidan Crawley

Oxford University and Kent. He was now Labour MP for Buckingham, and he would soon carve out a distinguished career as a television journalist before returning to the Commons as a Conservative. In 1948 his batting was rusty. Seven innings brought only 100 runs with a single fifty reminding spectators of what might have been.

One man who bucked the trend and now batted with authority was Tom Busby from Buckingham, the younger brother of Algie, who had been a regular pre-war player. Squat and chunky in appearance, and with a voice that branded him of good farming stock, he had made two earlier appearances in 1936, scoring just one pre-war run before announcing himself purposefully with a century against Bedfordshire in 1947 when he shared an unbeaten partnership of 298 with O'Connor, still the second highest stand in the county's history. Now playing more regularly, Busby was the mainstay of the batting in Oliver Battcock's team.

Two other pre-war players also returned in 1948. John Aubrey-Fletcher, whose father had succeeded to the presidency on the death of Dr PH Eliot, Bishop of Buckingham, two years earlier, played nine matches but could not re-capture his pre-war form and did not reappear again. Jim Hastie, who had played once as a 19 year-old in 1939, embarked on a more substantial post-war career that stretched to 1954 and saw his aggressive left-handed batting and brilliant fielding in the covers win him a place in the Minor Counties team to play Kent in 1951.

There was an elderly feel to the side with the new captain almost 45 when he took over, but plans were afoot to ensure a steady flow of young talent in the years to come. For this Bucks will always be indebted to Tom Orford. Elected to the committee in 1945, he was to devote his life to the service of youth cricket. His Colts team, soon to be re-christened Bucks Young Amateurs, first took the field in 1946. In November 1995, just two months before his death, Tom Orford, now president of the county, was able to speak without notes at the dinner to celebrate the golden jubilee of his brainchild.

In 1948 the first of a long line of Orford's protégés took his place in the full county side when Robin Peppiatt was chosen to play against Staffordshire at High Wycombe. The young Peppiatt had taken 45 wickets as an opening bowler for Winchester, but he had not found favour with *Wisden's* acerbic reporter of public schools cricket, EM Wellings, who described him as 'a youngster in whose person are combined all the modern bowling faults.' He was one who 'presented a full view of the trundler's chest to the batsman' in search of the increasingly fashionable inswinger. It was an action that did not sustain Peppiatt into adult cricket. There were a few early wickets for the county, but the sharp swing of his youth soon deserted him and, playing intermittently through to 1965, his later contributions were as a middle-order batsman, dependable slip fielder and occasional captain. His greater contribution to the Bucks cause was off the field, where he joined the committee in 1952, in fear of uttering a word with Franklin in the chair, but serving without a break until he became president on the death of Tom Orford.

Robin Peppiatt looks back fondly on his induction to adult life as he set off for his second match, against Norfolk at Kings Lynn. "This should look after you, boy," his father had said proffering a fiver to cover his son's expenses. "Then we stopped at a pub on the way and I found myself in a poker school with Oliver Battcock. I'd only got this fiver, so he'd got me taped!"

Things looked up for Battcock in 1949, though there was a dire start to the season at Christ Church, where Bucks chose to insert the opposition and had to wait until the Oxfordshire score had reached 264 before claiming their first wicket. Jack Mendl, one of the finest of all minor counties cricketers, made 195 that day. A loss by ten wickets in this match was followed by two drawn games, after which there was a splendid run of six consecutive victories. Another win in the final match, against Bedfordshire at

High Wycombe, would have brought the chance to challenge Lancashire Second Eleven for the title, but Battcock's men were comprehensively beaten by nine wickets.

Behind the upturn in Bucks' fortunes lay the arrival of new players who would make a major contribution to the side over the next ten years and beyond. John Cockett, who played his local cricket at Amersham and was to win a blue in his last year at Cambridge in 1951, brought useful quick runs to the middle order and the athleticism that befitted a future Olympic hockey player to the fielding. After becoming a schoolmaster at Felsted, he was able to play with great regularity each August, amassing 81 appearances for Bucks. Another important newcomer was the ever

Alf Hughes

competitive Chris Pickett, whose left-arm swing brought variety to the opening attack, where the captain was still bowling the bulk of the overs. Alf Hughes now came into his own, his off-breaks bringing him 41 wickets. With a ring of leg-side catchers in support, twice that summer he exploited wearing pitches to take seven wickets in an innings. A Welshman, sometimes described as a cussed soul and not the easiest man to captain, Hughes was another whose competitive spirit knew no bounds. "He'd appeal for anything – and expect to get it!" says Jack Tomlin, who played several years of club cricket with him at High Wycombe.

In 1949 hundreds were hit by Isherwood and Busby, for whom there was a new opening partner for many of the matches, RFB O'Callaghan, who had last played for Bucks in 1939. "Bush O'Callaghan," says Robin Peppiatt, "he had an enormous moustache and he played more wandering cricket than anyone could ever imagine. Extraordinary character, he had either a Rolls Royce or a Bentley and he travelled round to all the matches in it." John Cockett remembers "an enormous bag with every cap known to man in it." With endless games for all these teams, O'Callaghan was the antithesis of the player whose loyalty lay to a local club. Such players were not always welcome in Bucks sides and after this one season he was not seen again.

Bucks slipped back a bit in 1950, finishing twelfth with only two wins from their ten matches. Despite his advancing age Battcock still had his customary clutch of inexpensive wickets, 47 at 12.04; Hughes was close behind and Pickett confirmed his early promise. Tony Prince's career came to a sadly early end through illness. "He was a very good player," says Robin Peppiatt, "and he held the finest catch I can remember seeing – at long on against Norfolk at Kings Lynn." But this popular figure was not lost to the county, taking over as secretary in 1954 and serving until 1968. Prince apart, the old guard played its part on the batting front, while the Colts programme was beginning to pay dividends as more players graduated to the full county team. The Butler brothers, Norman and Ken, both made their debuts and played in most of the matches, there was a first appearance for fast bowler Rex Avery and Charles Robins, son of RWV, played a couple of times. "Do you bowl the same sort of stuff as your father?" a team mate remembers him being asked, to which the self-assured reply was, "Yes, but you can spot father's googly!" Young Robins played only five times for Bucks before moving into the first-class game where, whether his googly was spotted or not, he was conspicuously less successful than his Test-playing father had been.

A longer impact on Bucks cricket would be felt from the batting of Norman Butler from Burnham. There was a modest start in 1950, but by 1968 he had amassed 4,735 runs with six centuries, while brother Ken played 53 times, capturing 121 wickets with his medium-pacers and enjoying one moment of glory with the bat when he reached 96 against Oxfordshire on the Morris Motors ground in 1955.

Archie Campbell from Chesham was another newcomer in 1950. His younger brother Robert had scored a century and shared in a record stand in his second match in 1935. Now Archie made it a family tradition with 130 at Lakenham on his maiden appearance, his first-wicket partnership of 217 with Busby equalling the Bucks record set by Sewell and Kent in 1913. As with his brother, this was to be Archie Campbell's only century for Bucks. He was already 35 and further chances were denied by the demands of a distinguished civil service career that soon took him to a series of overseas postings. Archie Campbell's son Andrew, a left-hand batsman, won a blue at Oxford in 1970 and played 14 matches for Bucks in the early 1970s.

Dwarfing these other newcomers in 1950 was David Johns. One of the finest of all Bucks cricketers, he began with three fifties in his first four innings before making exactly 100 in his fifth, against Oxfordshire on his home ground at High Wycombe. When he finally retired in 1966 he was only the third man to have exceeded 4,000 runs for the county and no-one could match his eight centuries.

Ben Barnett and another Championship

The 1951 season was notable for the arrival of Ben Barnett. Australia's wicket-keeper for the 1938 Test matches, he had qualified for the county after coming to work for Aspro in Slough. At last Bucks had a worthy successor to Franklin behind the stumps, and a man who matched him in ferocity of intent. John Cockett remembers how it manifested itself: "He would appeal for anything that was within a foot of the stumps, and if it was given not out he would look down at the chap's pads, look up at the umpire then look down again as if to say, 'Are you sure, umpire?'" His aggressive

The 1951 Team
Back row (l to r): **L Wickson** *(scorer)*, **KWA Butler, DFV Johns, DR Peppiatt, D Rickard, NV Butler, H Tyson Chambers** *(Hon. Secretary)*
Seated: **AJ Hughes, JH Hastie, A Hayhurst, OG Battcock, P Isherwood, JA Cockett, BA Barnett**

left-handed batting was a bonus, bringing him 531 runs at the exceptional average of 75.86. With Johns and Hughes both in good form, there was disappointment that Bucks could finish no higher than ninth, due in part to the unsettled August weather that brought seven drawn matches.

Tyson Chambers was stepping down as secretary at this time, handing over for just two years to Hugh Bayley, but he chose to remain a member of the selection committee and one suspects his influence in engineering the appointment of Barnett to take over the captaincy. In what was to be his last season, Battcock's sharp outswing had still been good enough to bring him 32 wickets, but he had passed his forty-eighth birthday and those who sought change believed that Barnett could bring an extra dimension to Bucks' cricket - the Australian brand of competitiveness. With 379 victims Battcock stands fourth in the all-time list of Bucks bowlers. He had brought boundless enthusiasm and commitment to the county's cricket, and he was deeply hurt by the decision to replace him. Though still playing cricket until shortly before his death 20 years later, his time with Bucks was over.

Barnett's supporters were soon proved right. Going for a win wherever possible, the new captain opened his 1952 campaign with a crushing defeat of Norfolk at Lakenham, the first of seven victories before the summer was out. Coming to Ascott Park for their final match, the team knew they must beat Bedfordshire to gain home advantage in the Challenge Match. Victory hardly looked probable when the visitors' first innings closed on 375 for 5, but after two more declarations Bucks were set to score 206 in 115 minutes. Norman Butler, who had made 130 in the first innings, came within seven runs of a second century, something no Bucks batsman had yet achieved, as he and the captain opened with 97 in 49 minutes. This was the skipper leading from the front and, when he was out, Cockett maintained the pace and Bucks got home by five wickets with 15 minutes to spare.

Ben Barnett

Peter Isherwood, with 107, led the way when the challengers, Kent Second Eleven, came to High Wycombe and Bucks posted a useful 294. Early wickets for Don Rickard, a former Colt, maintained the advantage and when Bucks batted again with a lead of 82, Cockett, with 87, ensured that Kent were set an improbable 311 to win.

Tigrish fielding made certain of victory, by 109 runs, and enabled the club to celebrate with a dinner at the Red Lion, High Wycombe, where the celebrity guests included Denis Compton and Bill Edrich and the toast of the County Club was proposed by Walter Robins. Not since 1946 had one of the minor counties been crowned champions in a competition dominated by county second elevens.

For David Johns this had been his annus mirabilis. He set a new county record with 846 runs, and the highest of his three centuries, 191 at Bedford, surpassed O'Connor's record. Moreover, for the first time, he became a force with the ball, his left-arm spin complementing Alf Hughes as the pair shared 83

David Johns

wickets. Cockett, Barnett and Norman Butler all made runs, and there was a century in his second match for an Aspro team-mate of Barnett, Ron Clements, whose season then ended with a broken finger. Though he returned to play seven more matches the next year, Clements met with little further success. Pickett, back after injury, was able to lead the attack once more, and Rickard offered useful support.

Barnett was always one to set and take up a challenge, but for all his aggression on the field he was one of the most popular of all Bucks captains. "The most fun of all the captains I played under," says Brian Lucas, who first played as a teenager in 1951. "He was very level-headed, he never seemed to get upset and he got the best out of everybody." Under Barnett's leadership the county finished second in the Championship for the next two years, though in neither season were the team involved in a challenge match. In 1953 they had already lost to Berkshire, the ultimate champions, and their chance of taking the title disappeared when the final match, against Norfolk at Ascott Park, ended in an eight wicket defeat. In 1954 Bucks only moved into second place after a bizarre ruling that Devon, having gained first innings lead in a drawn Challenge Match, should have their result entered in the table, thereby lowering their average and dropping them to fourth.

There were centuries this year for five different players. Mike Tilbury of Gerrards Cross, on his first appearance for the county, made 113 at Lakenham, and his lead was followed by Jack Parton of Aylesbury, who made exactly the same score in the next match against Oxfordshire, again on debut. Neither batsman enjoyed much success thereafter, Tilbury playing 25 matches but never again approaching fifty and Parton scoring just seven more runs in three knocks. Another Aylesbury newcomer, Harry Taylor, enjoyed a golden year as an opener with two hundreds and an average close to fifty. Invariably a slow starter, he had a wide range of shots when under way and is remembered as one of his club's very finest post-war players. Against Bedfordshire John Cockett hit his only hundred for Bucks, and in the same match Brian Lucas, then from Slough but later of Beaconsfield, also reached three figures for the only time. Lucas played off and on until 1964, his presence in the covers always giving an added edge to the fielding, though a tendency to play across the line restricted his run-making.

A hard act to follow

Though he had accepted the captaincy for a fourth year, Barnett found that his business commitments enabled him to play in only two of the matches in 1955 – he had missed none in the previous three years – and his vice-captain, Geoff Reynolds from Chesham, stepped in for one season. An increasingly useful batsman and occasional off spinner, he was an immensely popular cricketer, but he was a quiet and gentle man with no pretensions to the dynamism of Barnett. Moreover, he led a weaker team in which Hughes played only five matches and Norman Butler just one and from which, even more crucially, Johns was absent all year. To add to the captain's woes, Taylor, who had made such a big impact in his first season, struggled all year and soon after left the district to return to his native Durham. With all these difficulties, a drop to twelfth place in the table was no surprise.

This glorious warm summer had its compensations, however, as two newcomers established themselves. Peter Stoddart, who had captained Eton in 1952, played in all the matches, making over 500 runs as a very correct opening batsman. Making an equally favourable impression this year was Colin Smith, then playing for Ernest Turner's but later of Aylesbury, who had played a few games the previous summer. Mixing outswingers and off cutters, he made a formidable opening partner for Pickett and ended as the leading wicket-taker with 44.

Next year, with Johns and Stoddart batting well, Bucks rose to seventh. This was the first of three seasons in which David Johns was captain, but his reign was not marked by great success. Working in the diamond trade, the new captain had employers who were not sympathetic to him taking time off to play cricket, so he could manage to play in only seven of the ten games. Superb player as he was – "he always seemed to have so much time and the middle of his bat seemed a yard wide," said a contemporary – Johns, for all his personal popularity, was not a natural captain. An intensely serious competitor, he was also a great theorist, but some of his players found his outlook a bit defensive after the more cavalier approach of Barnett. Curiously, too, for one of such exceptional talent, Johns was always nervous before batting, and this could sometimes impair the confidence of other members of his team.

In 1957, when Pickett was away, having taken up an appointment as professional with Haslingden in the Lancashire League, Bucks slipped to nineteenth. Three of the matches were only narrowly lost, making the overall performance seem worse than it had really been, though one of Bucks' only two victories came in the tightest of finishes when two leg byes were scampered off the last ball to beat Oxfordshire with the last pair at the wicket.

Bill Atkins

A newcomer of interest this year was Donald Steel, later to become a respected golf correspondent and course designer. He played in just six matches, always opening the batting, but 62 on debut was his only fifty in a disappointing season. More significant were the first appearances of two of the county's finest post-war players, Bill Atkins and Fred Harris. Amersham's Atkins, christened Gerald but always known as Bill, had captained the Young Amateurs and, when he played the last of his 107 championship matches in 1972, his nuggety left-handed batting had brought him 4,689 runs. But it was as a world-class cover point that he will always be best remembered, the blue he won at Cambridge in 1960 owing much to his ability to swoop on hard-hit balls and return them with unerring accuracy to the top of the stumps. His reputation alone saved Bucks countless runs and gained many crucial run outs.

Fred Harris from Chesham, played in the final match of the 1957 season. The most widely respected of opening bowlers in local club cricket, Harris is remembered by those who played against him as one off whom it was exceptionally difficult to score – "especially on a green top at Chesham," adds one High Wycombe opponent. Deadly accurate, he bowled inswingers and off cutters at a lively pace. Though Harris may not have been regarded as an out and out pace merchant, his speed in a match at Folkestone nevertheless earned from Ben Barnett the accolade of being, on that day, the quickest bowler to whom he had ever kept. Like so many of the strictly amateur players who comprised the Bucks teams of the period, he seldom played in all the matches, but his Bucks career stretched into the mid-1970s, bringing him 323 wickets for the county.

In the depressingly wet summer of 1958, Bucks finished twelfth. Johns, who averaged 53.33, suffered a foot injury and missed half the matches. His deputy, Geoff Reynolds, led the team to one sensational victory at his home club Chesham. With eight wickets down, Kent Second Eleven had settled for a draw when the final over began. Reynolds, who had not previously bowled in the match, decided to try his luck. Off his first ball Barnett achieved a stumping and from the last Stoddart snaffled a catch to bring Bucks a 40-run victory.

This was the first summer in which Bucks had had to compete without Alf Hughes. One who might have filled the gap was Reg Dare, who had played 109 matches as a left-arm spinner for Hampshire and who was now employed as groundsman at Ernest Turner's in the Totteridge area of Wycombe, where he earned a reputation for producing some of the best pitches in the county. From 1965 the ground would be used to stage county matches and for a few years Turner's made an immense contribution to Bucks cricket. Cricket-mad Norman Turner, who ran the company, was a vice-president of Bucks and his firm soon became a much favoured employer for those who sought days off to play for the county. Between 1958 and 1963 the popular Dare played 20 matches for Bucks, though without any startling achievements.

Reg Dare

The Stoddart years

Peter Stoddart

In 1959 Peter Stoddart was elected captain, a position he retained for seven years. He was in splendid personal form with over 600 runs, and after six matches his team were still undefeated, but availability problems made for a difficult end to his first season when the last four fixtures produced three losses and a single victory. The one win came on the Morris Motors ground in bizarre circumstances as Bucks sought the last Oxfordshire wicket. The final over was in the hands of Brian Taylor from Amersham. Bowling what should have been the last ball, he overstepped the crease. His indiscretion earned him another delivery, with which he claimed an lbw decision.

In one of the hottest summers of the century batsmen flourished across the country while bowlers struggled. There were six centuries for Bucks, four of them from the established players Stoddart, Atkins, Butler and Reynolds, while two others to take their opportunity were hard-hitting Michael Hardy, remembered as the captain of the Territorial Army Eleven, and Lionel Hitchings, a left-hand bat and fine stroke player from Tring Park, both of whom played a full season.

The retirement of Alf Hughes from minor counties cricket created more openings for Reg Plested. His left-arm spinners had been a feature of Chesham cricket since 1946, and he would continue landing it on the spot for the club and bemusing batsmen with his flight until 1977. In 1959, his 220 overs, in seven matches, were the most sent down by any Bucks bowler. Another to be given his chance was Ernie Clifford from Burnham, who distinguished himself by bowling 14 consecutive maidens against Suffolk at Chesham. Clifford sometimes made useful runs and he combined with Plested against Norfolk at Slough to post a record eighth-wicket stand of 111, which has still to be surpassed.

For the 1960 season Bucks engaged the former Hampshire opening bowler Vic Cannings, who had become cricket coach at Eton. An immensely popular figure, always happy to offer advice, he played in all ten matches, his accurate

Vic Cannings

medium pacers claiming 33 wickets. With Fred Harris able to play in only three games, John Mills, also from Chesham, partnered Cannings for most of the season. Dubbed 'Taurus' by his opening partner, Mills was a swarthy character with prominent sideburns, who hurled the ball down at ferocious pace. "Just like the village blacksmith" in one player's memory. Eight wickets for 22 against Hertfordshire was the harbinger of what lay in store for Mills, who enjoyed conspicuous success the following year, when Cannings did not return.

With the team chopping and changing throughout 1960, the batting was often weak and no centuries were hit; yet five victories were secured, several by narrow margins, to take the team to third place in the table. The win against Norfolk at Lakenham in the first match, by 34 runs, was set up by Atkins' brilliant fielding. Within a period of twelve minutes the home team's second innings was in disarray as first Bill Edrich and then Ted Witherden fatally misjudged Atkins' capability in the covers. The next match, against Suffolk at Ipswich School, saw Bucks complete a memorable East Anglian double when a ninth wicket partnership of 46 between Harris and Smith ended with a six over long on from the Aylesbury bowler's bat with just two minutes remaining. There was the satisfaction of twice defeating Hertfordshire, Stoddart's least favoured opponents. "Robin Marques could be a bit too competitive," he has said. The defeat of Oxfordshire at Slough completed the best summer of Stoddart's tenure, and it was followed by another good year in 1961 when the side finished fourth, again with five wins. Atkins had a particularly good time with the bat, David Janes, a 17-year-old left-hander from Beaconsfield, who had played for the Public Schools earlier in the year, first established himself, and 'Taurus' had by far his best season with 46 wickets.

The weather was against Bucks in 1962, but it was an indication of Stoddart's positive intent – and the way matches were played in those days - that in eight of the ten matches he declared the Bucks innings, though his enterprise brought him only two victories. Vic Cannings returned for just two matches, taking 19 wickets at 6.21, while the main strike bowler was the somewhat ungainly Rex Avery from High Wycombe, whose career of 27 matches stretched over 14 seasons and who took 34 of his 70 wickets during this one year. Bucks' regular wicket-keeper was now Derek Taylor, soon to progress, via Surrey, to a long and distinguished career with Somerset. He and his twin brother Michael had both started their cricket at Amersham Hill before moving to Chesham and they had made their Bucks debut together the previous year. At this stage, Mike Taylor was regarded purely as a batsman – he never bowled an over for Bucks – but once he had been engaged by Nottinghamshire his usefulness as a net bowler was translated to the middle and for 16 years, first at Trent Bridge and then with Hampshire, he was a highly successful medium pacer.

Around this time plans were being laid for the first one-day knockout competition. 'There is a possibility that some minor counties will be invited to take part,' the Bucks yearbook for 1962 informed members. The possibility came to fruition in1964, but finishing sixteenth in the Championship the previous summer meant that Bucks could not seize their chance. There would not be long to wait. In 1964 Colin Lever struck a rich vein of form to become the only Bucks batsman to exceed a thousand runs in a season. He started with a bang, adding an unbeaten 263 with David Janes against Hertfordshire at Tring, still a county record for the second wicket. Lever's 1,011 runs included three centuries, winning him the Wilfred Rhodes Trophy as the leading minor counties batsman of the year and helping Bucks to seventh place in the table - good enough to qualify for what had now become the Gillette Cup.

A schoolteacher, Colin Lever was a member of the strong Chesham club. One of Bucks' most talented players, he was the older brother of England fast bowler Peter Lever. A regular player for Bucks in the mid-1960s, his appearances became fewer after he had taken up a teaching post in Liverpool in 1968. After his move north, he found that the sound method and steely application that had brought him such consistent success for Bucks led to the offer of a weekend job as a professional in the Lancashire League. For nine seasons he played for Heywood, usually opening the batting and the bowling in the manner expected of league professionals in those days. He recalls an early problem: his bowling was not up to the club's requirements. "I was a declaration bowler for Bucks," he modestly asserts, "bowling little off spinners. So they sent me on a two-week crash course before the season started and I learnt to bowl properly." Thereafter, until 1978, Lever continued to do his best to play a few games for Bucks. As the years passed he moved down the batting order and the consistency of his run-getting declined, but his medium paced bowling became a more potent force, while he remained an outstanding fielder in the covers.

Colin Lever with Norman Butler

Qualification for the 1965 Gillette Cup brought Bucks a plum tie – they were drawn to play Middlesex at Lord's on 23 April. For this memorable match the committee entertained old players, members and friends in a box in the now demolished Clock Tower, and the team were issued with new blazers for the traditional photograph in the Harris Garden. There had been thoughts of inviting Denis Compton to play for Bucks. Living in the county, he was certainly well qualified, though it was eight years since his last season of county cricket. However, after much discussion, the committee decided that it was unfair to drop one of the players who had helped the county to win a place in the competition. Later committees might have reached a different conclusion!

Peter Stoddart leading the team out at Lord's

Batting first in chilly conditions, Middlesex were checked by two Atkins run outs and their last wicket fell with six of their 65 overs unused. However, there was no fairy tale outcome; the home side's total of 269, with 86 from Bob Gale, proved more than enough as an attack spearheaded by the England bowler John Price, and with Fred Titmus in support, soon put the shackles on Bucks, for whom David Janes hit out well to make the top score of 32 in a total of 111.

David Janes hits out

The rest of the season was to prove anti-climatic. Though no matches were lost in the Championship, only two of the ten fixtures were won. Eleventh place was not good enough to qualify for the Gillette Cup, and the ultimate irony was that failure sprang from the desire to play positive cricket when acting captain Robin Peppiatt sacrificed first innings points, when they were there for the taking, in pressing for victory in the final match against Hertfordshire at Slough. Peppiatt now looks back ruefully on a decision for which the team manager berated him, but he was not to know that so many other counties, still with a couple of rounds of matches to play, would struggle against the weather, and that most of the late season games would end as draws.

The coup

There was a settled pattern to the fixtures around this time. The counties were able to choose their opponents, to be played home and away, and not since 1958 had there been any change in those Bucks elected to play. Each summer began with a tour of Hertfordshire, Norfolk and Suffolk and there were games with neighbouring Berkshire and Oxfordshire. There was also a regular cycle of grounds used for the home fixtures. Until the inclusion of Ernest Turner's in 1965 there had been no new venue in Bucks since 1951, when a match had been taken to the Aspro Sports Ground, Ben Barnett's home club, for the first of four years. Thereafter, the appointed grounds were Ascott Park, Chesham, Slough and High Wycombe, where two matches were always played.

This apparently happy arrangement suited the county better than the clubs, who were irked to be out of pocket on Bucks matches, especially as they often felt they had players whom the county should have been choosing. Instead, they saw others with little involvement with the local club scene come sweeping in. This discontent would fester on for more than 20 years and come to a head at a vitriolic AGM in the 1980s, but it first found expression in the spring of 1966. The malcontents at this time also harboured objections to what they saw as preferential treatment often given to those with a public school background.

The Bucks teams of the period were in fact drawn from all walks of life, and plenty of those who played regularly had certainly not attended independent schools. Nevertheless there was some substance to the objectors' case, especially with the Young Amateurs, whose ranks were often tapped to make up teams. Though no-one in Bucks cricket was regarded with more universal affection than Tom Orford, his unabashed concern about the educational establishment his Young Amateurs had attended, and his invariable practice of pressing the claims for county selection of those who had been to 'good' schools caused murmurs of complaint. One former grammar school pupil spoke of the Young Amateurs' captaincy going to a boy from one of the major schools "although he had no character whatsoever." Another very capable teenage cricketer could recall how, as a labourer, he found no-one making him welcome in the dressing room - middle-class gaucheness and teenage shyness probably cost the county a cricketer of talent.

After seven years in charge, Peter Stoddart was happy to hand over the reins; but with the committee finding no willing successor, he was persuaded to carry on and, as their choice, he was expected to be elected for an eighth year. But, without the knowledge of the Bucks hierarchy, others had been planning a coup. Leading the rebellion were members of the High Wycombe club, one where the public school ethos counted for little. 'The factory side,' as they had been unkindly dubbed, found support at Chesham and Slough. The rebels packed the AGM and, as the constitution of the day allowed, without any prior warning they presented the meeting with an alternative skipper for the forthcoming season.

Their chosen man was Brian Janes, unrelated to the Marlburian David Janes. Though he was not at the centre of the mutiny, many felt it was disloyal of Janes to allow his name to go forward as he was a member of the committee whose choice had been Stoddart. However, as a successful captain of High Wycombe and a powerful figure in the club, Brian Janes was in many ways a logical alternative around whom the rebels could rally. He had played 25 times for Bucks with one day of glory in 1958 when he and Rex Avery had dismissed Berkshire for 39 at Slough. His return of six for 16 that day was the first of three six-wicket hauls. However, afflicted with back problems, he was now bowling very little, while the runs that flowed from his bat in club cricket – he had made over a thousand for High Wycombe in 1965 - had seldom done so for the county. He had never held down a regular place in the county side, and had made only two appearances in the previous two years.

Brian Janes

The Janes ticket was for more representation of club cricketers, whereas Stoddart epitomised the wandering player who favoured matches with such teams as the Eton Ramblers, the Butterflies or MCC. Moreover, he lived in the north of the county, adding fuel to his critics' complaint that he knew little of the ability of players in the south, where the strongest clubs competed. Stoddart was certainly well liked within his own team, but he was an easy target for the rebels and Janes was duly elected by 17 votes to 14.

Whatever the merits of the argument, after all he had done for Bucks cricket, it must have been deeply disappointing for Stoddart to lose the captaincy in this way. It was certainly no fault of his that Brian Janes had a difficult season. Several leading players – most notably Johns in his final season – underperformed, others were not available and the captain himself enjoyed little personal success. Without a win in ten matches, the team sank to twenty-second place in the table. Only once before, in 1910, had a season passed without a single championship success. To the secretary, writing in the yearbook, the county's fortunes were 'at their lowest ebb within living memory.'

The Slack years: another Championship

Brian Janes led the team for only one year. His successor, John Slack, remembers driving out of London with Tony Prince when the secretary popped the question: would he care to take up the challenge? Slack had made his mark by scoring a century for Cambridge on his first-class debut in 1954 and he had won a blue that year. His club cricket had been mainly for UCS Old Boys until he joined Beaconsfield on moving to Iver. He had played four matches for Bucks in 1964 and a couple more in 1966, though without any striking success. However, with long experience of captaincy, notably with the Club Cricket Conference, where he had had experience of the two-day game, he was a well-qualified choice - provided he could spare time from his law practice and the demands of a young family.

John Slack's decision that he would take his annual holidays in the cause of Bucks cricket had the happiest of outcomes. Widely regarded as one of the best of the county's post-war captains, it was testimony to his leadership skills that, by his third year in charge, Bucks were once again champions. Well attended net sessions in the indoor school at Finchley helped to build team spirit, and when the matches began Slack's highly perceptive cricket brain quickly got to grips with the tactics of minor counties cricket, in which the first day was typically spent jockeying for position while the second hinged on the timing of declarations. His first year saw a modest upturn in fortunes as Bucks ended in fourteenth place. It was another summer of rain-interrupted matches, with the only wins coming, home and away, against Suffolk, while there were four losses. But the new captain was quickly recognized as one who would keep a game open, and his generous approach would pay dividends in later years.

Colin Lever, playing in all the matches, scored well over twice as many runs as any other batsman. David Janes, an increasingly powerful striker of the ball as he grew stronger, topped the averages and useful runs also came from Clive Leach, though he could play in only half of the matches. A powerful leg-side player, Leach had been on Warwickshire's books for three years in the 1950s. He later earned a CBE after a distinguished career in television management with Tyne Tees and Yorkshire, before returning to cricket as the energetic present chairman of Durham. Fred Harris, with 42 wickets at only 12.52, had his best season, but the support he received from Tony Waite, once of Middlesex, who had been specially registered in 1965 and was now his regular opening partner, was disappointing.

Brian Poll

One who played in all matches was Brian Poll, the new wicket-keeper, who comfortably surpassed Ben Barnett's record of 19 catches in a season by holding 32. Never the most stylish of keepers, Poll had the advantage of being naturally left-handed, a great asset in taking balls passing down the leg side. "Yes, he was a bit untidy," says fast bowler Ray Bond, "but so efficient. From my point of view he didn't miss much." In 132 matches, 68 fewer than Walter Franklin, Poll held 68 more catches than the Bucks legend, and in ten separate seasons he exceeded Franklin's best of 16. But it neatly encapsulates the changes to the game in the intervening decades, and the style of Frank Edwards' bowling, that Franklin should have claimed 189 more stumpings than Poll.

In Slack's second year things began to click, despite Lever having now moved north. Addressing the need for a spin bowler of quality, the captain brought in Chris Parry.

Many years earlier Slack, as captain of UCS, had given the 14 year-old Parry his chance in the school team, and they had subsequently played together in club and Conference cricket. Parry was an off spinner, good enough to have played for Middlesex Second Eleven, who nevertheless soon earned a reputation as 'the phantom spinner.' "He did turn it, but not very often," says one member of the team remembering him as "one of those players who always look as though they are going to bowl off spin, but then the ball goes straight on." John Slack points out that Parry also bowled "a rather good gentle away swinger, which effectively accounted for people believing he bowled both leg breaks and off breaks. But he never bowled a leg break in his life!"

In his teenage years Parry had gone to Lord's for coaching sessions with Jack Hearne, who impressed upon him the importance of accuracy. He was encouraged to pitch every ball on a handkerchief and "towards the end of the session Jack just left the middle stump there. He put half a crown on top of it and I had six balls and if I could hit the handkerchief and the stump, the half crown was mine." An employee of the Bank of England, Parry was fortunate to be able to play whenever he was required. "I could have as much time off as I liked," he admits. "I was playing 70 or 80 days of cricket every summer. And I went on a Conference tour of Australia for eight weeks on full pay!" For the next seven seasons Parry played with great regularity for Bucks, finishing his career with 233 wickets at 18.58.

The seam attack benefited from the emergence of Beaconsfield's Ray Bond, whose fast bowling had been brought to the county's attention by Tom Orford after a string of successes for the Young Amateurs. Bond had played a couple of matches as a 20 year old in 1965 and he would soon be regarded as one of the county's finest post-war bowlers. He stamped his presence in the second match of the 1968 season with figures of 12 for 85 against Oxfordshire at Buckingham. After a poor first year with the bat, the captain enjoyed a productive summer, David Janes was also in good form, and in the opening match of the season 19-year-old John Turner made the first of his 151 appearances that would bring a record aggregate of 7,524 runs for the county.

Ray Bond and John Turner

There was the most unnerving of starts for young Turner, who opened the batting with his captain on the Newbury Grammar School ground against Berkshire, for as they went to the wicket they knew that there was almost no-one to follow. Ian Feasey, a High Wycombe player making his second appearance for the county, remembers the problems they all encountered. He had gone round to David Janes' parental home, having been promised a lift to the ground. He watched Janes eat a leisurely breakfast before they set off in his MG. Soon they discovered that all the roads around Newbury were clogged – the races were on! "When we got there Tony Waite was padded up to go in three, Clive Leach had just got there and was tearing about getting changed and the orders were: 'Bat in order of arrival!'" Making 44 in an opening stand of 78, Turner helped stave off the crisis. He would never have cause to look back, scoring 512 runs in his first season. For Parry, too, it was a successful debut; he claimed five victims in Berkshire's second innings as the home county survived with their last pair at the crease. Parry and Harris were the season's top wicket takers.

Bucks had chosen to play 12 matches this year, restoring Bedfordshire to the list of opponents. The weather again had a big say, restricting the county to four wins against a solitary loss. This came at Lakenham, where Turner had impressed all who saw it with a masterful 99 against exceptionally hostile Norfolk bowling. There was a dramatic win at Amersham in the penultimate match, a game that exemplified the best of Slack's captaincy. Determined to keep his opponents interested in the prospect of victory, he had brought Parry into the attack to ensure that more overs were bowled. His gamble paid off, Parry took vital wickets and Atkins, making one of only three appearances this year, threw down the stumps with four minutes left to give Bucks victory by 11 runs. This set up an exciting end to the season when Norfolk came to Beaconsfield. The visitors needed a win to challenge for the title, while victory for Bucks would mean qualification for the Gillette Cup. Rain restricted the game to a one-innings contest, in which Bucks owed their 40-run success to Chris Pickett, who took five for 45 on one of his rare appearances after years of absence.

David Janes, Fred Harris and John Slack watching the rain

The Gillette Cup draw for 1969 took Bucks back to Lord's. After a watery Saturday the teams re-assembled on Monday, and Bucks' bowlers did well to restrict a Middlesex side with eight past or future internationals to 87 from their first 40 overs, but, as the bowlers struggled with a wet ball, the batsmen eventually broke loose to finish on 232. As on their previous visit, the Bucks innings soon subsided as Middlesex ran out winners by 128 runs.

The team quickly put this disappointment behind them as they embarked on their championship programme. They began with comfortable wins against Oxfordshire and Bedfordshire. Rain spoilt the next match with Hertfordshire, but there was a fine victory against Norfolk at Lakenham with half an hour to spare, High Wycombe's Roy Huntley, who played the season primarily as an opening batsman, taking seven for 32 in the second innings. A six-wicket loss to Suffolk after Slack had declared twice was followed by a victory by the same margin against Berkshire. Rain on the second day ended hopes of a positive result in the return match with Oxfordshire at High Wycombe, after which Bucks moved on to Slough where, in the season's closest encounter, they just got the better of Berkshire by two wickets.

This was a low-scoring match played on a spiteful pitch. Turner grafted well in both innings, but after his dismissal Bucks, needing only 81 for victory, were soon in deep trouble at 60 for 8. With the home club's Barry Sidaway keeping an end up without scoring, Chris Parry took control to see Bucks home. There were 20 minutes to spare when Suffolk were beaten by 57 runs at Ernest Turner's, but victory over Hertfordshire at Chesham came in the last over, thanks to a splendid 105 not out from John Turner, his first century for the county.

Bucks were now assured of finishing at the top of the table. Only a successful challenge could deprive them of the title. A curiosity of the scoring system was that if Bucks *lost* the next match the Championship was theirs. This was because victory for Bedfordshire would lift that county into second place, and only a county that had not previously played the championship leaders could issue a challenge. But a Bucks win would take Cornwall into second place and give them the right to challenge. The match at Ascott Park duly ended with Bucks all out for just 72 in their second innings, the losers by 118 runs. "I think by the time we got to our second innings nobody was very interested," says John Slack. The season nevertheless ended on a more uplifting note at Beaconsfield when Norfolk's last man contrived to be run out off the final ball, giving Bucks victory by not one but two runs!

Only the captain played in all the matches, but Turner, the mainstay of the batting, missed only one. Though not related to the eponymous owners, he was one of the main beneficiaries of employment at Ernest Turner's. Scoring enough runs proved to be the main challenge, especially as Janes was out of form, but Roy Huntley and Tom Hickling from Chesham both played several useful innings, as did Atkins and Ken Young in their few appearances. The bowlers were the strength of the side with Lever heading the averages and Harris, Parry and Waite, another Ernest Turner employee, all taking at least 35 wickets at under 15 each.

John Slack and his team
Standing: **Chris Parry, Ray Bond, Roy Huntley, John Turner, Brian Poll, Tony Waite, Keith McAdam**
Seated: **Colin Lever, Chris Pickett, Sir John Aubrey-Fletcher** *(President)***, John Slack, David Janes**

The captain's 'positive and attacking spirit' was highlighted in the yearbook. Contemporaries have spoken of him as being in the Brearley mould. "He seemed to get the best out of people," says Ian Feasey, who also admired his tactical acumen: "I remember being sent out into the long field at Turner's against Suffolk. Fred Harris was bowling and one of their best batsmen came in, a chap called English. They'd obviously worked him out that he liked to pick the ball up off his legs in front of square. I was sent out into the deep and, sure enough, after a few overs he hit it straight to me."

The celebratory dinner at the Bellhouse, Beaconsfield, was marked by the presentation of a silver salver to the captain, whose last season this was to be. He had taken time away from his legal practice to serve Bucks and he now resumed a distinguished career that very soon saw him appointed a recorder and thereafter become one of the first solicitors to sit as a circuit judge. For many years he dispensed justice at Aylesbury and later brought courtroom discipline to the deliberations of the County Cricket Club committee as its chairman. "Meetings were always over by ten o'clock," says Jack Tomlin, manifesting his admiration.

There had been an important change off the field during John Slack's time in charge. In 1969 Tony Prince retired as secretary and was replaced by Paul Slatter. Slatter had been honorary treasurer since 1956 and was now to serve in both capacities for the next 16 years. He had been designated as team manager from 1961, and from 1964 he was assisted in this role by Horace Perrin as team secretary; but it was Slatter of whom so many who played over the next two decades would say that he *was* Bucks cricket, a man whose passion for the cause knew no bounds. "He wore his heart on his sleeve," says John Slack, and if the team were in a tight corner successive captains grew to expect Slatter to increase the tension. "He got incredibly emotional about games as they unfolded," David Mackintosh remembers. Stuart York, who

Paul Slatter

played in the 1970s, agrees: "He was very nervous. If it was a tight finish he was never watching – he was behind the pavilion."

As befitted a bank manager, Paul Slatter's careful husbandry of Bucks' finances was not the least of his assets, while the yearbooks bear witness to his command of language and reveal an exceptionally detailed record of the county's fluctuating fortunes. In all he did Slatter was the consummate professional; yet those who played in the team have no recollection that he had ever played the game, and several felt that his understanding of cricket's subtleties did not match his readiness to offer opinions.

There was a bit of a love/hate relationship between Slatter and Perrin, it has been suggested, with Perrin's organisation and punctuality not always matching Slatter's exacting standards. Perrin was principally responsible for team administration and for getting eleven men on the field. "He'd have anything between nine and thirteen when we got there," one captain quipped, while another remembered that Perrin, a keen compiler of statistics who did most of the scoring, could create panic by arriving at the eleventh hour just as someone else was preparing to deputise.

Gillette Cup excitement: Chris Parry & David Mackintosh

Under the leadership of Chris Parry, who succeeded John Slack in 1970, Bucks retained a place in the upper half of the table, twice qualifying for the Gillette Cup and reaching fourth spot in 1973, the last of his four years in charge. The 1970 Gillette campaign opened with a convincing win against Bedfordshire, followed by a chastening defeat at Chesham, where Barry Reed's undefeated 143 in a Hampshire total of 278 for 3 was at that time the highest individual score in the competition apart from Geoff Boycott's 146 in the 1965 final.

The Hampshire match had started on a disquieting note as the visitors complained that no towels had been provided in their dressing room, obliging Paul Slatter to rush off to the town centre to put matters right. "We minor counties players expected to bring our own towels," Chris Parry explains, and it was ironical that any aspect of the hospitality at Chesham should have been criticised because the warmth of welcome to visiting teams with Jack Mash around had always been legendary. "A wonderful man," says Robin Peppiatt of a colleague who served over 20 years with him on the county committee. "Jack used to captain them and he'd have been rolling the pitch in the morning then after the match he'd be the one packing everything away. Then it would be 'What are you all having to drink?' to his team, who'd done damn all to help!"

Somewhat disenchanted by the visitors' attitude, Bucks made no serious attempt at the target Hampshire had set, but the newly signed Ron Hooker, with 65, valiantly strove to bat out the overs as bouncers were fired at the tailenders. "Ten minutes after the match they were all gone," says Chris Parry, "and their captain didn't even say good-bye."

Only two championship matches were won in 1970, but first innings points were earned in each of the four games that were lost enabling Bucks to finish eighth, not quite good enough for another tilt at the Gillette.

The arrival of Ron Hooker, who had retired after a first-class career with 300 games for Middlesex, brought valuable experience to the Bucks team. Engaged as a professional for the county, he topped the averages in his first year and his solid batting, steady medium-pace bowling and friendly advice were to serve Bucks well for another six years. 1970 was also the one substantial season for Richard Bray, an Old Rugbeian later to become a circuit judge. His stylish batting brought 601 runs at 40.07 and he was also a valuable slip fielder. The captain had his most productive year with 47 wickets, while Colin Lever, playing in just five matches, was now at his peak as a bowler. "He was a far better bowler than his brother, who played for England," his captain insists. "He never bowled a bad ball and he attacked the batsman the whole time." Lever's 31 wickets at 8.52 earned him the honour of becoming the first holder of the Frank Edwards Trophy. Presented by Bucks in memory of their greatest bowler, who had died that year, the trophy is awarded each year to the minor counties bowler with the best average. Coming six years after Lever had taken the batting award, his achievement remains a unique double in the annals of minor counties cricket.

Ron Hooker

The following summer Ray Bond ensured that the Frank Edwards Trophy remained in local hands. An economical bowler with a fast arm action, he skidded the ball through at a good pace and could move it in either direction. His 34 wickets, taken at only 10.44, played a crucial part in ensuring that Bucks would be in the Gillette draw for 1972, but qualification only came after a dramatic victory at Amersham in the penultimate match of a season in which the team had been beset by injuries. After trailing Bedfordshire by 137 on first innings, Bucks hauled themselves back into the game thanks to fine bowling by John Mills, recalled after an absence of eight years. Needing 227 to win against the clock, the hero of the hour was Bill Atkins, whose 73 steered his side to a three wicket win in what had supposedly been his hundredth championship appearance for the county – it was actually his 104th match – for which he had been presented with a silver salver at the start of play.

Gillette Cup excitement: Chris Parry & David Mackintosh

The Gillette campaign in 1972 opened in style. Drawn to play Cambridgeshire at Fenner's, Bucks scored 224 for 7 with 95 from David Janes. The home team's batting then buckled in 75 minutes as Bucks' opening bowlers operated unchanged. Bond, with five for 17, and Harris, with four for 21, dismissed the home team for only 41. For 13 years this remained the lowest total in the competition, printed on the back of score cards across the country. The county's reward was a home tie at Amersham against Glamorgan.

Up to this point Bucks had always been as the proverbial lambs when facing first-class opponents. This was now due to change. Perhaps unwisely, Tony Lewis, on winning the toss for the visitors, chose to bat. By lunch his team, with a top four of Alan Jones, Roy Fredericks, Majid Khan and Lewis himself, were precariously placed at 80 for six. The tail then wagged, with Malcolm Nash leading the resistance, as Glamorgan were thankful to reach 174. "I made a bit of a cock of it," Chris Parry confesses years later. "Because Ron Hooker had pulled a muscle and was limping everywhere. With about five overs to go I suddenly realised that I'd ended up with one of my prime bowlers, Ray Bond, only going to bowl eleven overs. Something went radically wrong all because Ron had pulled up lame." In fact, the captain took the final wicket with the last ball of the fifty-eighth over, but by this time an over he had not initially planned to bowl had gone for 17 during a productive ninth wicket stand.

Despite this the Glamorgan total was starting to look too few as Bucks reached the drinks interval on 122 for two, Turner and Hooker having added 88. However, Hooker had started his innings with his muscle injury and had subsequently broken a knuckle. He now felt that he would serve the cause best by retiring. "He shouldn't have done," Chris Parry now reflects. Wickets tumbled, among them Turner for 66. Fred Harris, who had been the pick of the bowlers with four for 33, clouted a huge six before being held on the third man boundary. The final over came with 13 still needed. Could Bucks become the first of the minnows to beat a first-class county? The last pair were at the wicket, Hooker having returned with a bandaged hand, and by now the television cameras were on the ground. A place in history was still at stake as Solanky came up to bowl the final ball. It had to be hit for four, but Bond swung and missed so Glamorgan were the narrowest of victors. For Bucks there was some consolation as Jack Robertson named John Turner as his Man of the Match, while for the visitors there were celebrations into the night in the Amersham pavilion. "It was all quite different from Hampshire," Chris Parry remembers.

An indifferent championship performance meant that Bucks were not in the Gillette Cup for 1973, but Parry's legacy was to ensure that the team would be re-joining battle with first-class opponents the following year. The captain had played a full part with 39 wickets, but during his time in charge Parry had seen the potency of his side's attack diminishing. Lever, Bond and Waite all offered only spasmodic availability and Fred Harris, though he played his last match as late as 1976, had virtually called it a day.

As opportunities for new bowlers arose, a few were tried whose figures suggest that they fell short of the necessary standard, but one who briefly seized his chance was Nigel Rogers, a brisk outswing bowler from Tring Park. He began with five wickets in the first innings of his debut match, against Bedfordshire at Buckingham. There were only seven more victims in his next four games and he had gone wicketless in the first innings at Bray when Berkshire batted a second time with a lead of 46. Stuart York recollects that Rogers' first wicket came from a catch on the boundary and that, when Lever was replaced by leg spinner Laurie Champniss, the Berkshire captain Francis Neate was obsessed with taking all the bowling from the spinner, leaving Rogers to wreak havoc at the other end and set up a seven-wicket victory for Bucks. His final analysis of nine for 50 is second only to Frank Edwards as the best in the county's history. These two apart, the only other Bucks bowler to have taken more than eight wickets in an innings is Oliver Battcock. Rogers played on through the 1974 season but after his red-letter day he took only 19 more wickets for the county.

Laurie Champniss, the foil to Rogers at Bray, had begun his Bucks career in 1971, and he brought welcome variety to the attack. His leg breaks and googlies, delivered with a wheeling action off the wrong foot, commanded respect for their accuracy. Never as big a spinner of leg breaks as the preliminaries suggested, Champniss could turn his wrong 'un prodigiously. "A great character," Ian Feasey remembers, "he was a stickler for field placings. He would make sure everybody was in the right spot before he bowled. He'd shout to the three men in the covers to make sure they were in line. He'd even move the umpire six inches." Another Champniss idiosyncrasy was his practice of wearing three sweaters almost regardless of the weather. His 106 wickets for the county came at only a fraction over 20 apiece.

Parry had other spinners at his disposal in his final year. More orthodox leg breaks came from Michael Sant, an Australian who played at Amersham, while there was left-arm spin from Peter Plummer, a former Young Amateur who returned to Bucks cricket after four years with Nottinghamshire. He occasionally made useful runs, but his bowling suffered by comparison with that of Ray Hutchison, who played the first of his three seasons in 1973. Hutchison was a dentist from New Zealand, who arrived in England having played 31 matches for Otago and quickly made his presence felt at High Wycombe. Slightly built but ferociously competitive, his prior reputation was as a batsman, but his left-arm spinners soon started to bamboozle club batsmen in the nets at Wycombe and he quickly proved himself as an all-rounder in the truest sense. Never afraid to give the ball air, in the three years in which he played for Bucks Hutchison secured 118 wickets at 14.51 - no post-war bowler has taken so many at a lower cost. With the bat he averaged 31, and in the field he was in a class of his own at cover point with a wonderfully strong arm. "As good as Colin Bland," Chris Parry asserts, "and in overs cricket he was worth 15 or 20 runs."

Ray Hutchison

New batsmen emerged during the time of Parry's captaincy. Keith Edwards, who played for Amersham, is recalled as a beautiful striker of the ball. "On his day the best batsman in Bucks by far," says one who played with him "but he hit the ball in the air too much." "He looked such a good player," says another contemporary, "but he never made the runs he should have." Over a hundred matches without a century and an average of just below 25 suggest that this may be a fair assessment, though Edwards' fielding helped to assure his place in the side – he had a memorably strong flat throw from the boundary - while, like others who batted in the middle order, he often perished in the cause of quick runs, especially with the introduction in 1969 of a rule awarding first innings points to the side scoring most runs in their first 55 overs.

Another who had begun in 1971, David Mackintosh, had learnt his cricket in Scotland, where he had attended Paisley Grammar School and Glasgow University. When his work brought him south he joined the Amersham club, whose cause he was still espousing as chairman and captain of the third eleven in 2005. An effective rather than elegant batsman, he was possessed of an eye that allowed him to hit across the line, and he is recalled as a bustler at the crease, one who kept the fielders on their toes with quick running. Mackintosh had already been capped by Scotland before winning his Bucks cap in his first season.

The Bucks team under Chris Parry
Back row (l to r): **Ray Bond, Nigel Rogers, Gwynne Jones, David Smith, John Turner,
Ron Hooker**
Front row: **Brian Poll, Mike Sant, Chris Parry, Keith Edwards, David Mackintosh**

As a relatively young man – he was only 27 – and with limited knowledge of all the players on the local circuit, Mackintosh was seen by many as a surprising choice to succeed Parry at a time when a number of others fancied taking on the job. He soon found himself involved with a tricky selection decision for the Gillette Cup match against Kent at Canterbury: should he play Champniss or his own club colleague Sant? "We opted for Champniss," he now recalls. "We thought his novelty value might buy us a couple of wickets. I remember getting a personal visit from Mike Sant on that Sunday evening absolutely berating me about his omission. I can see him now!" With match figures of eleven for 116 Sant had played the major part in beating Suffolk at Marlow in 1973, but for all his Aussie aggression, the case for Champniss is supported by their end of career figures.

Mackintosh had already played in the Glamorgan cliff-hanger, and he recalls the lunch interval at Canterbury of his first match in charge. Bucks were again calling the tune against first-class opposition, and had reached 126 for no wicket against one of the most successful one-day sides: "I thought, 'Is there a possibility that we might be featuring on the back pages of the Sunday newspapers?'"

Once again John Turner was rising to the challenge of a big occasion. His opening partner was Gwynne Jones, a powerful Rhodesian, who had made his debut in 1972 and was to play 57 matches before the end of the decade. Jones perished shortly after the resumption, but Turner went on to 88 as Bucks posted a competitive 223 for 5 from their 60 overs. Derek Underwood, then at the peak of his powers, ended with no wicket for 52. Another England player, Brian Luckhurst, soon fell to Lever as Kent began their reply and, when Champniss limbered up in preparation to bowl, Ray Bond remembers that his preliminaries included a couple of cartwheels! Other team members recall that there was a notable ripple of noise around the ground. "Try a googly first up," David Smith suggested as Champniss prepared to bowl to Mike Denness. England's captain of the time failed to read it but survived an lbw appeal, and an unbeaten 120 from Graham Johnson saw Kent to a comfortable seven-wicket victory. Nevertheless it was John Turner whom Reg Simpson chose as his Man of the Match.

John Turner batting at Canterbury

Later in the season Turner played in what was to be his only first-class match, for the Minor Counties against the touring Pakistanis, marking the occasion with a fine 106 in the second innings. In John Slack's view Turner was a superb judge of when to leave the moving ball as an opener. "He had a simple approach to batting," says David Mackintosh. "If it was on the wicket he played straight and defended it. If it was off the wicket he thrashed it, and he was such a big chap that he could score his runs very quickly." Turner was also a marvellous close fielder on the leg side, his 197 catches an eloquent tribute to his ability and courage. Wicket-keepers apart, no other Bucks player has yet taken 100 catches. And those who played with him emphasise that, as a left-arm thrower, Turner posed an additional threat to batsmen with his shies at the stumps after intercepting a firmly played shot.

Hutchison, Hooker and Jones all hit hundreds in 1974, and Turner had six scores over fifty. Hutchison topped the bowling averages with 47 wickets, and Ray Bond recorded a career best for the county with eight for 34 against Berkshire. It was a measure of the Bucks' strength at this time that Turner, Hutchison and Bond, together with Keith Edwards, should all have been chosen to represent the Minor Counties South in the Benson and Hedges Cup this year. Yet only by winning three of the last four championship matches was the last minor county place in the 1975 Gillette Cup secured.

One of the best matches of the season was against Oxfordshire at Chesham, where Kevin Beaumont, now the county secretary, was standing as umpire in one of his first minor counties matches. He recalls arriving at the ground on the second day to find that the slight slope on the square had rendered the covers totally ineffective against heavy overnight rain. Knowing that only a change of pitch could save the match, he rang the TCCB to establish that no match regulations prevented the umpires from offering the two captains the chance to resume on a new pitch. After some deliberation at Lord's, the message came through that this would be in order and a fresh strip was cut. Set 159 in two hours and 20 minutes, Bucks reached the last over still needing 15. Lever hit the first two balls for four but fell to the third to give the visitors victory by six runs.

Bucks' third visit to Lord's witnessed another challenging total from Middlesex, Mike Brearley top scoring with 124 in their 268. Bucks' reply owed much to 73 not out from Stuart York, the present chairman of the club, who was establishing himself in the side around this time. He and Brian Poll added 56 undefeated for the eighth wicket, at the time a competition record, but Middlesex won by 99 runs. Later in the season York recorded his only championship century with 118 not out at Hertford. There were 802 runs for Gwynne Jones and 49 wickets for Hutchison, but Turner and Mackintosh had a thin time with the bat and injuries and lack of availability conspired to reduce a potentially strong side to a disappointing twelfth place in the table.

The North Circular team: Brian Poll and David Smith

1975 had been the first season without the steadiness of Chris Parry's off spin, but he continued to be involved with Bucks' affairs, serving on the committee for six years. One of the first to be recruited from London club cricket, he had been instrumental in enlisting a number of others such as Champniss, who played club cricket for Northwood but whose teams were listed in successive yearbooks as Privateers, Stoics, Harrow Wanderers and MCC, Gwynne Jones, who played for Wanstead and Stoics, and Ron Hooker, whose club cricket was for South Hampstead. All gave valuable service to Bucks, but others were called up whose credentials were less clear or who failed to live up to prior reputations. As the years passed an ever growing stream of such players, first called the North Circular Eleven and later dubbed 'the M25 lot', claimed places in the county team, few of them owing any allegiance to Bucks. "Paul and Horace were naughty, really," Chris Parry now feels, "there were far too many special registrations." Around the clubs in Bucks there were many who would have agreed. The fuse of discontent had already been lit, but the explosion was still more than ten years away.

After just two years David Mackintosh gave way to Brian Poll. Established as the wicket-keeper and a useful lower order batsman, Poll's career with Bucks had begun after he had joined the High Wycombe club while on the staff at the Royal Grammar School. Universally liked, Poll engendered a good spirit in the team, but by the time he had become captain he was teaching at Ellesmere College in Shropshire and had become a little remote from the local club circuit, and some players felt that he became over reliant on Perrin to assemble teams.

The 1976 season, Poll's first in charge, was a time of change. Hutchison had returned to New Zealand, Lever's fine career was drawing to a close, Jones, now a professional with Middleton, managed only four matches and was out of form and Hooker was fading out, but these losses were balanced by the arrival of new players. Ray Bailey, once of Northants, had played a few matches in 1975 and another opening bowler, Peter Gooch, briefly with Lancashire, now joined him. With Ray Bond still on hand there was a formidable pace attack, to which Gooch's aggressive demeanour gave a cutting edge. Gooch also had the ability to switch from pace to off cutters, while for just this one season the county could call on a class spinner. Eric Gillott, a slow left-armer, who had toured England with the New Zealanders in 1973, played in every match of a long, hot summer that belonged to batsmen and emerged as chief wicket taker. 'Rowdy' one colleague remembers Gillott being called – because he hardly spoke a word!

For some years the Slough batsman and future county captain David Smith had been unable to

Wilf Slack

command a regular place. Seen as a bits and pieces player, batting in the middle order and bowling a few overs of seam, he had not managed to translate his aggressive club runs into success in the minor counties game. The summer of 1976 was to prove a watershed, an average of 34 giving an indication of his true potential. But the star of the show this year was a 21-year-old left-hand batsman born in St Vincent, whose talent was first revealed in adult cricket for the village of Frieth and who had moved on to score heavily for High Wycombe, Wilf Slack. Still one of only two players to have graduated from the Bucks team to play Test cricket for England, Slack opened the batting in every match, scoring 748 runs. A product of the Young Amateurs, after just one season in the county side, he was engaged by Middlesex, going on to win the first of his three England caps when called up to reinforce David Gower's team on their tour of the Caribbean in the winter of 1985-86. It was a huge shock to his many friends when Wilf Slack collapsed and died while playing cricket in Gambia on 15 January 1989. He was only 34.

Poll's first season as captain was marked by a sequence of close finishes that characterised the best of minor counties cricket. Among the twelve matches eight were in the balance until the end:

- a four-wicket victory over Berkshire at Reading, reached thanks to an unbroken seventh wicket stand of 62 (Poll 51 not out) that enabled Bucks to reach a target of 194;
- a draw at Bedford with Bucks' last pair together, having lost only one wicket in the last 20 overs;
- victory at Hertford by one wicket after Gooch and Gillott had added 27, the future Indian Test spinner Dilip Doshi firing two boundary balls down the leg side to end the match;
- the last pair hanging on to earn Bucks a draw against Norfolk at Lakenham;
- losing by 28 runs at Ipswich when Suffolk took the last wicket with the final ball of the match;
- losing by six wickets to Oxfordshire at Marlow with seven balls remaining;
- surviving against Suffolk at Chesham with just one wicket intact;
- taking the last wicket with the first ball of the final over to register a second victory against Berkshire.

Eleventh in 1976 and sixth a year later, Bucks still failed to qualify for the Gillette Cup, missing out by a single point in 1977. 'It would be nice to see an off-spinner in the Bucks side again,' the captain had written in his report on the 1976 season, commenting that leg spinners had proved to be 'an expensive luxury'. No more was to be seen of Sant and little of Champniss, but the captain's prayers were answered by the arrival of Andy Lyon. A member of the High Wycombe club, in a county career that stretched from 1977 to 1987 he played 109 championship matches, claiming 367 wickets and ending seven of his eleven seasons as principal wicket-taker. Having started as a seam bowler, Lyon came to High Wycombe as an off spinner of brisk pace. Making full use of his height, he could be close to unplayable in helpful conditions, yet on other occasions he was said to be too keen to experiment. "He'd have his men in round the bat and then throw in a slow full toss on the leg side, which had everyone ducking and diving," said one who played with him.

Andy Lyon

There were also debuts for former Young Amateurs, Neil Hames, a fast-scoring left-hander and future county captain, and Paul Ashton of Amersham, who seldom did justice to his talent in Bucks colours. From within the North Circular came Terry Cordaroy, once briefly of Middlesex, whose painstakingly correct batting helped to give the innings a firm foundation for the next three years. There was another debutant who was destined to go further in the game than any of these, Gordon Parsons from Slough, later of Leicestershire and Warwickshire, whose two matches for Bucks yielded him a duck and three overs for 18 runs.

A more commercially oriented world lay round the corner. On the world stage Kerry Packer was flexing his muscles. Already Bucks, like all minor counties, relied heavily on TCCB handouts, but 1978 was the year in which a sponsor was first found for the county, Richard Zeidler of ACE Office Cleaners stepping forward with £2,500 for each of three years. There were also cash incentives to reward individual performances. The players agreed that the money earned should be pooled and in one dead match at Marlow the promise of an easy time at the bar persuaded the opposition to connive in ensuring that a Bucks bowler should take five wickets for the second time in the match!

In a wet summer the county team managed four wins and earned enough points to take fourth place in the table and with it qualification for the Gillette. This was assured with a six-wicket win against Norfolk in the final match of the season. The batting was strengthened this year by the enrolment of Richard Hayward, a left-hand batsman from Ickenham, who had played for Middlesex Second Eleven and who now headed the averages. In a career punctuated by spells on the staff with Hampshire and Somerset, Hayward's correct and forceful batting brought him 3,320 runs at the healthy average of 44.27. There was good support from Smith, Edwards, Feasey and Cordaroy.

Richard Hayward

Gooch, Bailey, Bond and Lyon constituted a powerful quartet of bowlers with Hedley Wright from High Wycombe coming in for the last four games. But there cannot have been too much in reserve with the county turning, for the Berkshire match at High Wycombe, to Alan Coxon, a left-armer from Chesham, who had earned his place in history by saving the 1952 Varsity Match for Oxford when, in a defiant last wicket stand, he had played a ball from the South African fast bowler Cuan McCarthy with his unprotected head. In those days he had been an opening bowler but, when he made his sole appearance for Bucks, Coxon was bowling a gentle brand of spinners that befitted one who had passed his forty-eighth birthday.

The last of Poll's four seasons, 1979, was a disappointment. After losing a crucial toss Bucks crashed at the first hurdle in the Gillette Cup losing by two wickets to Suffolk, while only two championship matches were won – with a bit of luck it might have been five - and the county could manage no better than twelfth in the table. The perennial problems with availability meant that Bond and Lyon missed the tour of Hertfordshire, Norfolk and Suffolk, and the opportunity was taken to introduce three new faces in the same match: Mike Milton, Sam Mehar and David J Smith.

Milton was to play off and on for ten seasons and score six centuries. An opening batsman strongly focused on his own success, he was nevertheless capable of scoring quickly. In 1981 he almost became the first Bucks player to score two centuries in a match, making 120 and 95 against Berkshire at Slough. Milton was also a useful left-arm spinner. Mehar was an accurate 'skiddy' bowler who moved his medium-pacers off the seam. For the next five years, appearing intermittently, he brought much needed experience to the attack and sometimes made handy runs. Off spinner Smith played only a couple of years, initially as a replacement for Lyon, but in eight matches he achieved relatively little. All three newcomers were from London, only Mehar having any form of local connection. His club, Harrow, played in the Thames Valley League, while Mehar himself worked for Bowyer's in Amersham. "Every match he would bring along a box of Scotch eggs for tea," David Smith remembers.

The emphasis in all this recruitment was on experience. Milton was 35 when he first played, while Dick Humphrey was brought in as a wicket-keeper the following season at the ripe old age of 44. By this time David Smith had taken over the captaincy. He had always felt that Brian Poll had been too reluctant to move up the batting order, and he saw Humphrey, whom he knew through Conference cricket, as a wicket-keeper/batsman whose selection would enable another bowler to be played. A keeper who had played a few games for Surrey in the 1960s, Humphrey was always prepared to stand up to bowlers of pace, and he quickly repaid his captain's faith in his batting with a fine century in his first match on a difficult pitch at Hertford against a particularly testing attack.

Sam Mehar

Dick Humphrey

The seemingly relentless policy of finding players from outside Bucks inevitably led to schisms within the committee and there was some discontent among the clubs, notably at Chesham, whose committee were soon to make their ground unavailable for county matches, High Wycombe and Amersham. The matter for debate was simple: should the county pursue playing success at all costs – and with it participation in the lucrative Gillette (soon to be NatWest) Cup – or should Bucks be represented by those with roots in the county or at least playing for Bucks' clubs? Slatter and Perrin were both consumed with achieving success on the field and Perrin was always a willing servant of those who wanted a good player signed up, but those concerned with developing young talent sought to limit his recruiting zeal.

Throughout the post-war decades the Young Amateurs had continued to thrive, the smooth running of a programme of some eight matches, preceded by trials, still owing much to Tom Orford's energy and devotion. If there had been elitism, it had melted away: the local grammar schools, especially the Royal Grammar School at High Wycombe, had produced many fine players. Orford could rely on Jim Etchells to help with the umpiring, and for several years Ken Drucquer had shared the administrative burden. Like Orford, he was a bachelor, who now proudly admits that the young cricketers were his 'family' and, with a passion for coaching, he devoted long hours to the development of

Tom Orford

the county's best youngsters. Years later Ken Drucquer would proudly recall Wilf Slack, as an established county cricketer, saying of his time with Bucks Young Amateurs: "I learnt not just about how to play cricket, but how to behave oneself and do things in a proper way."

With the ACE sponsorship and with support now coming from the Sports Council, the first of a series of residential coaching classes at Bisham Abbey had taken place in the Easter holidays in 1978, with 24 Young Amateurs earmarked for intensive sessions with a professional coach. Each year since the original inception of the Colts, caps had been awarded to outstanding players. They were not easily earned and, when Cardigan Connor received his in the summer of 1978, it was only the seventy-fourth to be presented since 1947. About half of those earning caps, and many others who did not, had progressed to the county side for a match or two and a few, like Norman Butler, Ray Bond, Bill Atkins, Keith Edwards and John Turner, had gone on to long and successful careers. A few others were catapulted into the first-class game without ever playing for the county senior team, most notably Ian Gould, of Middlesex and Sussex, who played limited overs matches for England, and David Thomas of Surrey, once in the twelve for a Test match. But other young cricketers who had shown promise were lost to the county, and this concerned Orford and Drucquer. It was Drucquer who conceived the idea that there should be an Under 25 side to which the Young Amateurs could graduate and continue to develop their game. While Orford looked after the Young Amateurs with others assisting, the Under 25s became Drucquer's prime responsibility. "There was no difficulty with fixtures," he says. "The Army, the RAF, the Civil Service and some of the counties - we had a good list." It all began modestly - three fixtures in 1981 but before long there was a festival with four counties competing for the Tom Orford Trophy.

With all this activity Drucquer, in particular, was understandably incensed that so many of his best players should be ignored by the county team. It was not easy for David Smith as captain. He had to rely on the word of others when the claims of promising school and university players were pressed, and he knew that the step up to minor counties cricket was harder than others recognised. Moreover, when he sought a lead from the committee, he found people expecting the best of both worlds: instant success but with home-grown players. He recalls one meeting: "I said to them, 'You can't have both things together. If you want to bring in youngsters, fine – but it'll take us two or three years, and I'm quite happy to go along with that – but if you want instant success we've got to bring some players in to do that.' This was the big argument and it was agreed by the committee that we should bring some players in."

The North Circular was not the only recruiting ground for outsiders. The county also chose to follow the fashion of the day by registering overseas players, though those signed up by Bucks were still of unproven quality. In 1980 an Australian, Ken MacLeay, played a full season. He scored a few runs but his wickets were rather expensive, while the 13 captured by the New Zealander Gary Robertson were exorbitantly so. Nor did another Australian, left-armer Sam Parkinson, who opened the bowling in 1981, seriously strengthen the attack, though his compatriot Greg Ritchie, who arrived in the same year, showed that he was already a batsman of the highest class, passing fifty six times in the four matches in which he was able to play.

Ritchie went on to represent Australia in 30 Tests, MacLeay played 16 limited overs matches for his country before returning to play for two seasons with Somerset in 1991, while Robertson played ten ODIs and one Test match for New Zealand. Parkinson alone of the quartet never tasted international cricket, but enjoyed moments of success with South Australia. Yet their combined performances for Bucks were arguably little better than the home-grown youngsters who might have been given their chance.

When he first took over, David Smith had inherited a team that was breaking up. Gooch and Bond had both played their last match and Bailey was soon to follow them into retirement. Of the batsmen Cordaroy had given up and the best player, Hayward, had obtained a contract with Hampshire. So, even with the imported players, Bucks were starved of success in the new captain's first three years: fifteenth, eleventh and nineteenth in the table – with only Cornwall and Cumberland below Bucks in 1982 - represented years of struggle in which the principal problem lay with the bowling, where there was an increasing burden on the shoulders of Lyon.

Of bowlers nurtured within the county, Cardigan Connor, born in Anguilla, was first blooded as an 18 year-old in 1979. He played his club cricket at Slough with David Smith, who championed his cause against those who argued that selection was premature. Connor served five years' apprenticeship with Bucks, carefully nursed in his early seasons then spearheading the attack in his last two summers; but it was only after he had moved into the first-class game that he revealed his true worth with more than 600 first-class wickets for Hampshire. Another whose time with Bucks was brief was Philip Newport, a product of the Royal Grammar School at High Wycombe. He had distinguished himself in junior cricket, but he was still learning his trade when he made his Bucks debut as an 18 year-old in 1981. The next year Worcestershire had snapped him up and by 1988 he was to become the second Young Amateur to win a Test cap, taking the Man of the Match award on debut against Sri Lanka at Lord's.

David Smith

Ian Hodgson

Ian Hodgson, a three year blue at Cambridge, was earmarked for greater things than he achieved as a quick bowler. An arduous university season and a troublesome knee combined to reduce his effectiveness, though he made useful runs including one century, against Hertfordshire at High Wycombe in 1982. Another youngster to take the new ball around this time was Jon Coles. Like Hodgson, he played for Gerrards Cross and he is currently the highly regarded team manager of the senior county side. Eleven matches and 14 expensive wickets tell their own story of his struggle to make the grade as a minor counties player.

In 1982, the most unsuccessful of Smith's years in charge, 18 of the 25 players chosen for Bucks had been Young Amateurs. The principal pace bowlers, Connor, Coles and Hodgson were among them, as was Stuart Ridge, who had opposed Hodgson in the Varsity Match, and who played three games for Bucks. Alumni of the Royal Grammar School were prominent and some did well: Paul Dolphin played in all the matches as an opening batsman, scoring a fine century in the season's only victory against Suffolk at Ipswich; Peter Harvey, who played with Dolphin at Beaconsfield, hit a century in the return match against Suffolk at Chesham, and Tim Russell, wicket-keeper and batsman, started out on a county career that would stretch to 2000.

Vincent Flynn, a product of Aylesbury Grammar School and former YA captain, who had spent three seasons on the books of Northants, was given games as a wicket-keeper. High Wycombe's Bob Dell, better known for his skills on the football field, played several matches, Aylesbury's Nigel Farrow made his first appearance and opportunities were given to Andrew Herrington of Gerrards Cross, Stuart Renshaw and Jon Potter, later to earn fame as an Olympic hockey player.

The captain played in every match. He could usually call on the experience of Turner and Lyon while Milton, Mehar and Humphrey all played in a few matches, as did Hames, but too often places were taken by youngsters still to find out if they could cope. Though scoring runs was seldom a serious problem, wickets were taken more expensively than ever before. Moreover, there were problems in getting a balanced side onto the field with the finger pointed at Perrin for occasionally grabbing the first man he could find to fill a vacancy without reference to others on the selection committee. David Smith recalls arriving at the Morris Motors ground in Oxford for the first championship match and finding a total stranger sitting in the dressing room. Perrin had signed up a new opening bowler – and agreed that he should be paid – without any reference to the captain. The team were unimpressed and the newcomer played just two matches.

Was it fair to blame the captain for the lack of success? David Smith found himself under pressure to resign. He chose not to do so and those who played in his team ensured that he was re-elected. In 1983 his luck would change.

Regional Divisions for the Minor Counties

Success again

For some time the Minor Counties Cricket Association had been grappling with ideas for creating a more competitive structure for their game. In 1983, empowered by sponsorship from the United Friendly Insurance Company, the Association was able to introduce the concept of a championship with two regionally separated divisions of ten counties all of whom would play each other once, with a one-day play-off match between the winners of the two divisions. Gone for ever was the notion of counties choosing their own opponents, and with it went the old home and away arrangement that had helped to foster so many friendships - and some bitter rivalries. There was also recognition of the growing popularity of limited-overs cricket with the introduction of the English Industrial Estates knockout competition.

Assigned to the Western Division of the new Championship, Bucks lost all their traditionally established opponents except Oxfordshire and Berkshire. Instead, they found themselves embarking on a tour to Devon and Cornwall, renewing acquaintance with Wiltshire and, for the first time since the spats with Franklin, Dorset. They were also to be playing at Taunton against Somerset Second Eleven, the only remaining representative of the first-class counties, soon to be replaced by Wales. Completing the list of new opponents were Shropshire and Cheshire.

There was a splendid start to the season with wins by emphatic margins against Shropshire and Somerset, albeit the latter was only achieved when the last wicket was captured with eleven balls to spare. The Dorset match was lost, but there were then three victories on the trot against Oxfordshire, Cornwall and Devon. Next came the season's only drawn game, with Bucks still needing two wickets to beat Cheshire. The divisional title was already safe before the penultimate match was lost to Wiltshire by 84 runs at High Wycombe, but the programme ended on a more fitting note with a ten-wicket defeat of Berkshire at Amersham.

The strength of the side was its batting. A county record was set with an average of over 36 runs scored per wicket lost. Richard Hayward, back in the side after trying his luck with Hampshire, led the way with 853 runs at 77.55 – only Colin Lever had ever scored more, Dick Humphrey averaged 53.22, Mike Milton weighed in with 558 runs at nearly 43, and newly registered Mickey Gear, a former Bedfordshire player, also averaged over 38. Those making all the runs were the imported players. One local boy who made his county debut in 1983 was Andrew Harwood, who had been scoring prolifically for the Young Amateurs and the Under 25 side. In four matches he averaged 31, but was still denied a regular place. His fielding was comparatively weak and, in common with other young players like Dolphin, his innings tended to be one-paced when the shape of a typical minor counties game put a premium on dominating the bowling to set up or chase totals.

The bowling, meanwhile, remained heavily reliant on Andy Lyon, who ended with 42 wickets, while Milton, who had by far his best season as a bowler, claimed 32 with his left-arm spinners. Of the other bowlers only Connor, taking his wickets more economically than hitherto, had much success. However, there were seven cheap wickets for Martin Jean-Jacques, when he made his debut in the final divisional match. Soon he would be lost to Derbyshire.

Bucks' opponents in the final at Worcester were old rivals Hertfordshire. For almost the first time the weather intervened, reducing a match planned for 55 overs to 35 a side. Winning the toss and choosing to bat, Bucks reached 190 for four with Hayward making 60 not out. The pace attack, Jean-Jacques, Connor and Hodgson, now reinforced by Phil Newport, kept a tight rein on the scoring. As his fifth bowler Smith turned to Milton, in preference to the season's most successful, Lyon, who bowled not a single ball. It fell to Milton to deliver the last over with Herts, eight wickets down, still needing 15. The runs came off the first four balls and included two sixes. "Paul Slatter was incandescent," one witness remembers.

Earlier in the season there had been a bizarre start to the knockout competition when Slatter had met his opposite number from Cornwall at the Bernard Arms at Kimble, where the visiting team had planned to stay before their match on the Molins ground at nearby Monks Risborough. The match having been called off due to the weather the previous afternoon, the result was determined by the toss of a coin in the pub car park. Cornwall's secretary called incorrectly and Bucks were into the next round and a match with Devon at Torquay. A three-wicket win brought a place in the quarter-final, where Bucks met their match, losing to Bedfordshire by 42 runs.

The upturn in Bucks' fortunes took the team back into what had now become the NatWest Trophy for 1984 and with it came the chance to play on a third Test match ground, Old Trafford. A century by Graeme Fowler ensured a Lancashire total of 272 for 7 that was always likely to be beyond Bucks, but Milton and Hayward made a spirited initial bid and Smith and Humphrey hit out well enabling Bucks to reach 199 for 8, though the victory margin was still a comfortable 73 runs. It was a less successful season in the Championship. Three victories took Bucks to second place in the Western Division, but with 36 points they were 31 behind Cheshire, who won six of their nine matches.

Nevertheless another NatWest tie was assured. This entailed a trip to Taunton to meet a star-studded Somerset side with Ian Botham, Viv Richards and Joel Garner in their pomp. Put in to bat, there was a brave opening partnership of 58 between Milton and Russell, but the pace of the West Indian Garner proved too much for the lower order and Somerset ran out comfortable winners by seven wickets.

The policy of looking outside the county's boundaries for new talent was continuing. Two important newcomers in 1984 were all-rounder Steve Burrow, who had asked to join from Berkshire, and Gary Black, a swing bowler and useful batsman later to captain the county. "A one hundred per cent trier," says David Smith of Black, whose 22 wickets at 11.45 won him the Frank Edwards Trophy in his second season. Burrow, after starting with seven for 55 in his first match against Shropshire, played on until 1996 proving himself one of the very finest all-rounders in Bucks' history. Bowling medium pace or, especially later in his career, fast off breaks, his first captain describes him as 'a bit like a right arm Underwood.' With the bat Burrow was always busy at the crease with a reputation as a fast runner between the wickets. He was also a top class fielder whom David

Steve Burrow

90

Smith liked to keep at cover point whether there was a right- or left-hander at the wicket.

With the popular Cardigan Connor winning a contract with Hampshire, a top priority was to get more bite into the opening attack. Horace Perrin's answer was to recruit Hartley Alleyne, a Bajan who had played for Worcestershire from 1980 to 1982. For a couple of seasons Perrin would take on the task of bringing his new fast bowler to the county's matches in his own car. "And for one of the matches up north," Tim Russell recalls, "there were transport difficulties and Hartley had to catch a plane. Horace had to leave the scoring to pick him up at the airport." "Hartley was *rapid*," wicket-keeper Russell remembers, and Smith ruefully recalls that opposing counties took fright and did their best to prepare docile pitches to thwart him. In eight matches, spread across two seasons, Alleyne managed only 29 wickets, seven of them on his penultimate appearance, against Wiltshire at High Wycombe.

The problems of availability hit hard in 1985, a summer in which, for only the second time since World War I, not a single championship match was won. The season had opened on an optimistic note with Richard Hayward elected as the new captain. Apart from his outstanding batsmanship, it was felt that his personal qualities would make for a successful time as county skipper. Moreover, he had experience of first-class captaincy with Central Districts in New Zealand. However, the season had hardly begun when a plea was received from Somerset, beset with injuries to their batsmen, seeking Hayward's services as cover. Thus the captain could play in only four championship matches. David Smith was persuaded to help out and Dick Humphrey also took a turn as skipper.

Even without Hayward there was a magnificent win at Longton in the English Estates Knockout Cup when Bucks, with centuries from Harwood and Burrow, amassed 306 for 2 in their 55 overs against Staffordshire to set up a 116-run win. However, the end of the campaign came in the next round, when a score of only 144 against Dorset proved inadequate and thereafter, in a miserably wet summer, the batting was a constant problem. John Turner had retired and moved to live in Wiltshire two years earlier. Gear had also moved on and, just when he was needed most, Milton missed all but two of the matches through injury and achieved little when he did play, while Humphrey's form with the bat deserted him. Moreover, Harwood, who had been denied opportunities earlier, also missed matches through injury. There was a recall after an absence of two years for Keith Edwards, and Paul Dolphin, another who had been edged out, also played a few matches.

Inevitably there was little consistency of selection, but one young man who made his debut was still stamping his presence on Bucks' cricket in 2006 – the current captain, Paul Atkins. Atkins had already shown evidence of his exceptional talent with the Young Amateurs, but it was a strange twist of fate that brought him forcefully to the attention of the county selectors. Bucks were playing Oxfordshire at St Edward's School and found another match taking place on an adjacent ground. The Southern Schools were playing the Northern Schools and a young man in the Southern team had the good fortune to make 150. "They wondered who this guy was," Atkins now recalls. "If I hadn't got that score that day I wouldn't have played as early as I did."

After making another fifty against the Western Schools and going on to play for the English Schools at Lord's, 19-year-old Atkins had already begun to make national headlines when he played his first match for Bucks on the Molins ground against Cheshire. It wasn't the friendliest of starts. He had to open against Pakistani Test cricketer Mudassar Nazar, and he did so without the words of encouragement he might have expected from some senior players. There were modest returns in the first few matches, but 54 against Berkshire at Amersham was seen at close quarters by the former Surrey and England player Graham Roope, who was in the Berkshire team. He made sure that his former county took note of the young Atkins.

The following year, 1986, Atkins averaged 61, with a top score of 160 not out against Shropshire at Bridgnorth, to earn the Wilfred Rhodes Trophy. For this season the captaincy remained a problem. Richard Hayward was not around and the nominal skipper, David Smith, could play in only the last five matches, Ian Hodgson deputising in the knockout matches, Neil Hames taking over in the Championship and Steve Burrow also captaining on one occasion.

There were two tight games in the knockout, victory against Staffordshire coming with one wicket and two balls to spare, then failure, by just five runs, to overhaul Berkshire's total of 194. Paul Atkins was at the centre of the action in both games, partnering Burrow in a recovery stand of 116 for the sixth wicket in the first match and watching the late order wickets tumble at Bracknell as he stood undefeated on 85 with victory tantalisingly close.

The hero of the last wicket stand against Staffordshire had been Steve Edwards, who had first appeared for the county the previous summer. A useful batsman, his principal role was as a tight left-arm seam bowler. He came to Bucks in his mid-thirties, another from London club cricket but one whose work would take him to Milton Keynes and membership of the Wolverton club. In 1986 he was Bucks' leading wicket-taker in the Championship, and he was regarded as an ideal bowler in the limited overs game. Opening the attack with Edwards this year was Chris Booden, briefly with Northants, who would become a pillar of Bucks sides into the 1990s, playing 66 matches. He had the first of two outstanding analyses, taking seven for 19 in the defeat of Devon at Marlow, figures he improved upon with seven for 17 against Wales MC in 1988, but at the end of the day the price of his 124 wickets, 32.48, illustrates the growing domination of the bat in minor counties cricket.

Jack Tomlin

Jack Tomlin had succeeded Paul Slatter as secretary in 1985. Another destined to serve a long term as secretary, Tomlin had played 14 matches for the county as a middle order batsman, but he had found greater sporting fame as a footballer with Wycombe Wanderers, for whom he played in front of a crowd of 90,000 in an Amateur Cup Final at Wembley. Sixth place in the Championship in 1986 was enough to ensure Bucks qualification for the NatWest Trophy but, with the only wins coming at the expense of Devon and Cornwall, the team's performance was a disappointment to the new secretary, who wrote in his report of the season: 'It is perhaps a pity that qualifying for the NatWest seems to be the primary objective in competing for the Minor County Championship and actually winning the Championship seems to be of secondary importance.' Perhaps these words goaded the team on to greater things.

The greatest day: defeat of Somerset

The time had come for David Smith to hand the captaincy on to Neil Hames. Smith's last match, in 1988, was his 141st and when he retired only John Turner and Walter Franklin had scored more than his 4,922 runs for Bucks and only Turner had exceeded his 99 catches. Smith had enjoyed mixed fortunes as county skipper and he would share the assessment of others that he was not always the most aggressive of leaders. "Neil was more adventurous than I was," he now says of his successor, "and whatever he tried it would always work!"

In 1987 there was the regular schedule of one-day warm-up matches against Oxford University, the OU Harlequins and, this year, Wales CA before the first championship match, against Somerset Second Eleven at Taunton. Here the Bucks cause was frustrated first by the weather then by the batting of Amersham-born Richard Baigent, whose patient innings brought his side first innings points. Little did the Somerset players guess what lay in store for their senior team, who were due to be at High Wycombe three weeks later for the first round of the NatWest Trophy.

Neil Hames

A damp June had hampered preparations for the match, but sunshine greeted the teams as Somerset won the toss and asked Bucks to bat. In the absence of Atkins, now with Surrey, Harwood opened with Trevor Butler of Wolverton. The pair began solidly but after Butler's dismissal at 31 the first-class bowlers imposed a tight grip on the game. 89 for 3 at lunch soon became 98 for 6 with the dismissal of Harwood, who had grafted through 47 of the 60 overs to make 47. It took some brave blows from Steve Edwards in the closing overs to enable Bucks to reach 154 for 9.

Andy Harwood

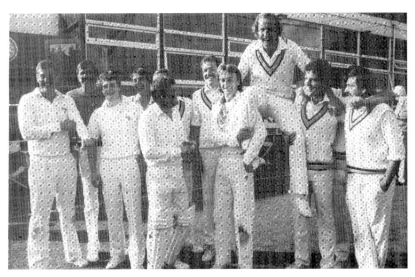

Neil Hames and his team celebrate victory over Somerset

David Smith remembers that the Wycombe club had a reputation for fine, true pitches, but after all the rain "the ball was never quite coming on." There had been thoughts that the professionals might struggle, but this was before Bucks had posted such a paltry score. Yet as Booden and Edwards got to work, the target began to look more imposing. So tightly did the openers bowl that Neil Hames decided to keep them going through their full 12 overs, and when they finally rested their figures were:

Booden	12	5	12	2
Edwards	12	5	14	2

Not only had Somerset fallen behind the asking rate of little more than two and a half an over, but they had also lost wickets, among them their captain, Peter Roebuck, and the New Zealand Test star Martin Crowe, who had never looked comfortable. At one stage 21 for 4, Somerset began a recovery led by Richard Bartlett first with Vic Marks then Graham Rose, but Lyon, Burrow and Black all ensured that scoring was difficult so that, when Black came to bowl the last over, ten runs were still required. Wicket-keeper Neil Burns, destined to become a Bucks player eight years later, carried Somerset's receding hopes with number eleven Adrian Jones for company. Singles off the first two balls brought Burns back on strike. Going for glory he swung the ball to midwicket, where Smith held the catch.

Steve Edwards receives the Man of the Match award from Trevor Bailey

For Somerset it was a body blow after a winter of discontent that had seen Richards, Botham and Garner leave the club. Admitting that his team had batted too timidly, Peter Roebuck acknowledged that Bucks had bowled and batted better than his men. For the home county it was a fairy story come true as they became only the fifth county to overcome first-class opposition. Trevor Bailey nominated Steve Edwards as his Man of the Match and, reviewing an encounter where Bucks had fielded splendidly, he made special mention of the standard of the wicket-keeping. Behind the stumps for Bucks was David Goldsmith, another mature cricketer brought in from London cricket, and widely agreed to have been a keeper of the highest class.

Any thoughts of further progress in the NatWest quickly evaporated at Edgbaston, where a century from Andy Moles paved the way to a Warwickshire total of 329 for 5. A dogged 57 from Harwood was clearly in a lost cause as Bucks amassed only 128, but returning to the Championship it soon became clear that the success against Somerset had brought a new confidence to the team's play. There were four wins, all of them closely fought, against a single loss, by three wickets against Devon at Exmouth with only two balls left. Three of the victories came in consecutive matches. Set to make 225 in 124 minutes plus 20 overs, Bucks beat Shropshire by three wickets at Slough. Then, after the first day had been washed out, Oxfordshire were defeated by six wickets in a single innings match at Aston Rowant. Finally, at Wadebridge, Steve Edwards uprooted the stumps of the Cornwall number eleven with the fourth ball of the final over as Bucks triumphed by just one run. After the Devon defeat the fourth victory came at Dorchester where the home team, requiring 186 to win, were dismissed for 99 with Lyon taking a career best of six for 12.

The team benefited from having a more settled side. Hames, Burrow, Edwards and Harwood played in every match, Hayward returned to play in all but one, as did Lyon, whilst the most significant newcomer was Malcolm Roberts, the man who was destined to re-write the county's batting records. A London policeman who was able to fill his summers on the cricket field, he played in the second match and was a regular thereafter, hitting five fifties.

Curiously, for a team that ended the season as divisional winners, no-one hit a championship century, though Roberts made an undefeated 132 in the one-day final against Eastern Division winners Cambridgeshire at Worcester. This innings took Bucks to 235 for five in their 55 overs, a score which looked impregnable after Edwards, with three for 20 from his eleven overs, and Booden had contained the early batsmen. However, the match took a dramatic turn as Julian Benson, later to enjoy brief success with Leicestershire, took command, scoring 121 before he was eighth out, bowled by Burrow with the first ball of the 52nd over, at 216. The ninth wicket fell at the same score, but Cambridgeshire were still not done and, as Gary Black prepared to bowl the final over in gathering gloom, only four were required. A single off the first delivery was followed by three dot balls then another single. Needing two from the last ball, the batsman could only drive to wide mid on, where Malcolm Roberts fielded and raced to the stumps to prevent a second run. The scores were tied, but having lost fewer wickets Bucks were champions for a record-breaking ninth time.

It could have been an even more stunning first year for Neil Hames had Bucks not faltered after reaching the last four in the knockout competition. Wins against Shropshire and Berkshire brought a semi-final against Cheshire at Marlow, where Bucks were unable to defend a total of 184 on a difficult pitch, eventually losing by two wickets.

It was not all rejoicing as the season came to a close. Just five days after the triumph at Worcester came the death of the ebullient David Janes. Always full of cheery banter in the dressing room, he died at the sadly early age of 43.

Restrictions on the M25 players

The following year was markedly less successful. There was a swift exit from the NatWest Trophy at the hands of Kent, and a first round defeat by Hertfordshire in the knockout competition. Only Hames was able to play in every championship match, though Booden, Butler and Goldsmith missed only one each. Crucially, there was no Hayward, Edwards sustained a knee injury and was ruled out for the season, while Roberts was able to play only four times and Burrow and Harwood in just five of the matches. Atkins was tasting success with Surrey – a century on first-class debut against Cambridge University and 99 in his first championship match - whilst Lyon, in his last season, was miserably ineffective in the six matches in which he played. So the county recorded only one win and fell to eighth place in the table, above only Wales and Cornwall.

The availability problems at least opened doors for some locally nurtured talent. Trevor Butler enjoyed an extended run as an opener and acquitted himself well, Tim Scriven, once of the Royal Grammar School, who had had three years on the staff with Northants, showed promise as a left-arm spinner, taking 26 wickets, opportunities were given to Richard Tredwell, an off spinner from the north of the county, and there was a chance to see the forceful batting and brilliant fielding of Bruce Percy, a former YA captain. Colin Tungate, keeping wicket in the only match that Goldsmith missed, set a county record with seven catches in an innings against Wales MC – all off Booden en route to his career-best analysis.

In January 1989, a Bucks team embarked on its first winter tour. Seventeen players, with Stuart York as manager, played 15 limited overs matches in Australia, winning nine. Some strong opponents were met, notably the Australian Academy side who were the party's second opponents at the Adelaide Oval, where the team included future Test players Stuart Law and Greg Blewett.

**Wolverton trio off to Australia:
Chris Booden, Steve Edwards
and Trevor Butler**

Back in England, notwithstanding the opportunities given to local players the previous summer, there were still rumblings about the number of players whose connections with the county were tenuous, of whom Malcolm Roberts was the most recent and conspicuous. Black, Burrow, Edwards, Goldsmith, Roberts – here were five 'outsiders' claiming regular places in the county team whenever they were available, and there were others like Milton still hovering in the wings. They were all fine players who gave of their best for Bucks, several involving themselves off the field, Goldsmith, for instance, years after his playing days were over coming back to manage a tour to South Africa. But Ken Drucquer, by now chairman of the committee, had had enough. "I said to Tom Orford, 'You and I are working our guts out to bring along young players. For what reason? To play for Bucks. We've got lots of lads who would do very well, but they seldom get invited'" Drucquer enlisted the support of a few Young Amateurs of recent vintage and, in particular, he turned to John Swain, a member of the Chesham club and recently qualified as a barrister, who was now on the committee.

Together they prepared a new clause to the rules of the County Club pertaining to selection. There was a stormy AGM at Chesham at which it was successfully proposed that any player chosen to represent the county should meet one of four criteria: to be playing regularly for a Bucks club; or to satisfy the committee that he had done so for a minimum of three consecutive years; or to have been born in the county; or to have been a bona fide resident in the county for at least 12 months.

The team was allowed a single player who did not conform to these requirements, making it possible for a professional to be signed up if this were needed, whilst one further way of qualifying was initially permitted – to have been registered for the county before 1st April 1989, the date at which the new rule came into force. So none of those already in the side was immediately at risk. Nevertheless this was a pivotal moment for Bucks cricket. From this point on there would have to be a more conscious effort to fill gaps in the team from home-grown talent.

In welcome sunshine Bucks' fortunes looked up in 1989. Though there was a first round defeat by Hertfordshire in the knockout, the team pressed for honours in the Championship with four wins and only a single loss. The counties were tightly bunched at the top of the table and, though in fourth place, Bucks were only five points behind the divisional winners, Oxfordshire. The team went into the final match against Wiltshire at Amersham needing one point to ensure qualification for the NatWest, but looking for a win to take the divisional title.

Wiltshire won the toss and may have regretted their decision to ask Bucks to bat. Malcolm Roberts, who had already enjoyed a magnificent season, took the opportunity to post a record fourth century, going on to reach 193 not out and taking David Johns' record for the highest score by a Bucks batsman. Sadly for Bucks, the Wiltshire batsmen also enjoyed the free-scoring conditions, posting 310 in reply to the home side's 337 for 5. Bucks then hit 153 for 5 in 16 overs, but could not tempt the visitors into a run chase.

Malcolm Roberts' career stretched on to 1997, by which time he had amassed 5,989 runs at an average of 45.37 and hit 15 centuries in the Championship, a figure that discounts his hundred in the one-day final. Second to Roberts is David Johns with eight centuries. What made Roberts such a prolific run scorer? Contemporaries stress his hunger for runs. Though he was a team player, it was scoring runs that made him happy. Few will have played more games with him than Tim Scriven, who saw Roberts' great strength as the ability to play off either front or back foot. "He played quick bowling fantastically well. If someone dropped it short he'd pull it for four. If it was pitched up he'd drive you for four. He had a lot of time and lots of options where to hit the ball." Paul Atkins also points out that Roberts was lucky to play as much cricket as he did, so he always had his eye in: "I shared a house with him. He possibly played more cricket than I did, and I was on the staff at Surrey!"

Malcolm Roberts

Roberts apart, there were useful runs from Burrow, Black and Harwood, while Richard Hayward played his last two matches for the county and scored a century in each of them. There was also an outstanding season for Steve Lynch of Beaconsfield, who was second in both the batting and bowling averages. He was already a mature cricketer when he had made his first appearance in 1984, and he would make his last as late as 2001, by which time he had taken on the role of team manager and still took the field in moments of emergency, playing on one occasion alongside his own son, as Neil Hames once did. His highest score for Bucks, 91 against Wales MC, was followed shortly after by his best bowling analysis, six for 28, when his left-arm spinners proved the undoing of Cornwall and earned Lynch his county cap.

A shadow cast across the season was the sudden death of Horace Perrin at the age of 66. He died following a meeting shortly after he had accompanied the team on their tour of Devon and Cornwall. An assistant secretary of the National Union of Teachers, he was approaching retirement, having for 25 years devoted his holidays to the service of Bucks cricket. Few have given so much to the county over such a prolonged period.

Horace Perrin

Another glorious summer in 1990 meant that runs flowed and bowlers' successes were hard earned. There were 921 championship runs for Roberts, who also won a Man of the Match award playing for the Minor Counties against Sussex in the Benson & Hedges Cup and marked his first-class debut by scoring 85 against the Indians. There were fine all-round seasons for Burrow and Scriven, who now complemented his left-arm spin with purposeful batting and was awarded his cap. Though they could manage only two wins, Bucks went undefeated in the Championship and did enough to finish equal third. There was a comprehensive 192-run defeat by Nottinghamshire in the NatWest Trophy, but the performance in the one-day Holt Cup was the highlight of the season. The campaign began against Berkshire at Wellington College, where heavy rain caused the abandonment of the first match after nine overs. When a fresh 25-over match started at 4.30, Bucks' total of 145 proved sufficient for an 18-run win. 262 for 4 set up a 20-run win against Bedfordshire and, when Bucks again batted first at Christ Church, 217 for 8 was too much for Oxfordshire, who went down by 31 runs.

Tim Scriven

In a knockout final for the first time, Bucks travelled to Lord's to meet Lincolnshire but suffered the disappointment of seeing play washed out on the Sunday. Returning next day, they won the toss and a splendid 97 not out from Paul Atkins was the centre-piece of their total of 227 for 7. Tight bowling from Booden and Tim Barry created early pressure, but the decisive moment came when a throw from Atkins on the long on boundary achieved a direct hit to run out the danger man Jim Love, once of Yorkshire and a one-day England international. Thereafter Bucks retained control to take the match by 16 runs.

Neil Hames' last season as captain marked the centenary of the County Club, an event that was celebrated with a dinner at the Bellhouse Hotel and a one-day match against MCC at Marlow, where Bucks' opponents included the former Young Amateur Ian Gould, who had gone on to keep wicket for England's one-day team in Australia. The NatWest Trophy took the Bucks team to Bath, where a total of 159 for eight never looked like unseating Somerset for a second time. Hopes of retaining the Holt Cup had also perished by this time, a comfortable win against Bedfordshire being followed by defeat at Bishops Stortford, where Hertfordshire got home by five wickets with seven balls to spare.

In the Championship Bucks were once again in contention, leading the division for most of the season but slipping up in the penultimate match against Shropshire at Beaconsfield to finish in second place just two points behind Oxfordshire with three wins and a tied match against only the one loss. The tie, the third in the county's history, came at Truro, where Cornwall, needing 210 for victory, had reached 153 for no wicket before Tim Scriven broke through. The match went down to the final ball with the last wicket claimed when Cornwall made an attempt at a third run which would have brought them victory. This was an outstanding match for Scriven with 60 in the first innings, top score of 41 in the second and then five for 66 in the last innings.

Throughout the season runs came as usual from Roberts, Harwood, Burrow and Scriven, but there also a first century from Bruce Percy and promising contributions from another locally developed player Simon Shearman. Another to make his debut was High Wycombe's Jason Harrison, a prodigious run-maker for the Young Amateurs, who began modestly for the senior side but would soon become a heavyweight with the bat. An Australian, Paul Roshier, who had played a few games for Kent Second Eleven, came into the side as an opening bowler but cut little ice.

This was the last year in which Paul Slatter was to watch his beloved Bucks teams in action. He had known that time was not on his side as he had bravely produced an estimable short history of the club for the centenary, and his death came on 16 March 1992. His contribution to Bucks' cricket, appreciated best by those who represented the teams, still stands second to none, and his parting was equally mourned by local dramatic and operatic groups, for whom he had produced 25 shows. Always a hard taskmaster, his obituary notice in the yearbook quoted his son: "He had a professional attitude and found it difficult to accept anything less in other people. Not everyone found him easy to get on with, but he enriched many people's lives."

Switch to Eastern Division

When Gary Black took over the captaincy in 1992 he was immediately presented with a more demanding challenge in the Championship. To accommodate newcomers Herefordshire, Bucks were moved to the Eastern Division, where there was general agreement that playing standards were higher. There was no shortage of drama in the opening match as Bucks set out to make 135 for victory against Hertfordshire. Fifteen were still needed when last man Booden joined Roshier. They edged closer to the target until Booden succumbed to the third ball of the final over, giving Herts victory by just one run. Thereafter there was a two-wicket win against Cumberland and a disappointing loss to Cambridgeshire, sandwiched between draws, before Bucks entered the final match, against Bedfordshire at Amersham, needing a win to secure qualification for the NatWest Trophy. Set to score 200 in 95 minutes plus 20 overs, Bucks' middle order seemed to have lost their way so that, with only 20 balls remaining, 39 were still needed. The clean hitting of Bruce Percy and Tim Barry met the challenge with just one ball to spare.

With comprehensive defeats in the knockout competitions, by 201 runs to Sussex in the NatWest and by 148 runs to Staffordshire in the semi-final of the Holt Cup, it was not an easy first season for the new captain, who had had to cope with the loss of several players to injury and other calls. That winter Gary Black managed the second Bucks tour overseas, with Neil Hames resuming as captain, on this occasion visiting Zimbabwe, still a tourist haven, where there was time to see Victoria Falls and to visit game parks while enjoying a competitive programme of eleven 50-over games, of which six were won.

Gary Black

Black's second year was beset with similar problems to his first and the team had little luck. There was a decent performance before losing to Leicestershire in the NatWest, but participation in the knockout, now styled the MCC Trophy, ended in the first round. The Championship brought only one win and Bucks sank to ninth place in the table. Despite these difficulties the captain earned nothing but praise from his successor, Tim Scriven, who saw him as an aggressive leader who was always looking to be positive and win games. By this time he was making less of a contribution as a player but, Scriven stresses, "Gary was always interested in trying to bring Bucks cricket forward."

It was a time of transition for the county when Tim Scriven took over as captain in 1994, and there was now an increasing reliance on local players. David Goldsmith had not played again after the 1991 season, Steve Edwards' already infrequent appearances ended the following summer and Gary Black retired when his term as captain came to an end in 1993. In his first year in charge Scriven could still call on Burrow but, in what was to be his last season, he played only five matches, retiring with 3,446 runs and 195 wickets to his name. The new captain would enjoy the services of Roberts throughout his four years in charge, but the rest of the M25 brigade were now gone. As with many a minor county, Bucks also suffered the loss of leading youngsters to the first-class game, James Bovill, a promising pace bowler, joining Hampshire in 1992 and Jason Harrison signing for Middlesex the following year.

Among local players given their chance, Tim Russell had been restored as wicket-keeper – for three summers he missed not a match after playing only once in the previous five years. Bruce Percy played with more frequency when not assailed by knee or back problems, Simon Shearman briefly became a regular as a middle order batsman, Richard Baigent, once with Somerset, returned to the county of his birth and won his cap as an opening batsman, and Graeme Paskins of Marlow, who had captained the Under 25 team, was also given opportunities as a stroke-playing batsman. New opening bowlers, Denzil Owen and Simon Stanway, established themselves.

Denzil Owen

Owen, born in Jamaica, was already a mature bowler when he was persuaded by Steve Lynch to join Beaconsfield. Immediately identified by his characteristic headgear – he seems happy that it should be called a giant tea cosy – he first played for the county in 1993 at the age of 37, making his mark as a bowler of awesome accuracy but no great pace, who was able to nip the ball off the seam in both directions. Stanway, from Tring Park, had first played in 1989. By 1995 he had made just five appearances, but thereafter he soon became a regular. Tall and with the sparest of frames, he has become a watchword for accuracy, maintaining a measure of control for more than a decade when times have been at their hardest.

An engaging character and a tactically astute captain, Tim Scriven came to the job as a Bucks boy and the son of one who had played five games for the county in the early 1960s. His greatest success in his first season came in the MCC Trophy, where there were solid wins against Hertfordshire and Berkshire before succumbing in the semi-final to Lincolnshire. After rain spoilt the opening game at Hertford matches in the Championship were characterised by close finishes. Challenging declarations brought a loss with eight balls to spare against Northumberland, followed by a victory with a similar number of balls in hand when Bucks captured the last Cumberland wicket. Staffordshire then prevailed with only three deliveries to spare. In the next match a misfield by Lincolnshire enabled Bucks to level the scores off the last ball. Three more draws and a one wicket loss to Cambridgeshire completed an exhilarating championship season in which Bucks were unfortunate to finish no higher than seventh.

The man on strike for the final delivery of the Lincolnshire match at Slough was the newly signed professional Andy Clarke. He had needed to hit a four for victory but managed only three. Hired as a leg spinner after four years with Sussex, Clarke had also been at the centre of the drama at Penrith when he had captured two Cumberland wickets in three balls in his final over. Wicket-keeper Tim Russell remembers the dismissal that brought victory: "He suddenly bowled a bouncer off four or five paces that the batsman tried to fend off his helmet. It flicked his glove and went for a catch to slip."

In his first season Clarke captured 48 of the 102 wickets to fall to bowlers. His heyday came in the narrow loss to Cambridgeshire at Fenner's where his match figures of 14 for 189 were to remain the best of his Bucks career. He was helped on his way by Tim Russell whose six stumpings in the match included five off his bowling. Though Walter Franklin stumped five batsmen in a match on three different occasions, only once has Russell's performance been exceeded for Bucks, by Ben Barnett against Norfolk in 1954.

For the next ten summers, with a brief respite when he had a single season with Norfolk, Andy Clarke became an integral member of the Bucks side, as popular in the bar after the match as in the heat of battle. Captains have praised his ability to give them a measure of control as well as the chance of running through a side in the fourth innings. Some of those who played with him have said that he was not a big spinner of the ball, but Tim Russell has no doubts about the difficulties of keeping to him: "He had a large variety of balls pace wise, a stock in-dipping thing rather than a leg spinner, but he had a devilish leg spinner as well – he bowled it very slowly and it turned a lot."

Neil Burns, who will have kept most often to Clarke, sees him as an old-fashioned slow bowler of the kind who flourished between the wars, Bomber Wells being a more recent

Andy Clarke

example. Astute and with bags of stamina, he was adept at exploiting slow pitches on which the run-of-the-mill minor county player who was not good enough to work him around would get bogged down or hit out in desperation. In every season in which he played for Bucks Clarke was the leading wicket-taker. Only eight bowlers have exceeded his 284 wickets for the county, but so much reliance was placed upon him that no-one in post-war years has conceded more runs.

In March 1995, the year following his triumphant display at Fenner's, Tim Russell was awaiting the new season with keen anticipation when the telephone rang. It was his friend Tim Scriven: "Tim, I know that you always book your holidays for the county matches. Well you needn't bother!" Thus was the captain imparting the news of Bucks' new signing, Neil Burns. Russell would still play a few matches – it helps to be self-employed when the captain is looking for an eleventh man on a Saturday evening – but the arrival of Burns, after spells with Essex and Somerset, was to make a bigger impact on Bucks' cricket than a mere change of keeper. In five seasons he hit 2,684 runs at an average of 47.93, higher even than Roberts, and he was yet another in the long list of fine Bucks keepers. But what he had to offer went much further.

The consummate professional, Burns had not initially warmed to what he saw as the more relaxed and leisurely notion of minor counties cricket. He had been contemplating a life in South Africa and it was there that the seed of an idea was sown in conversations with Jason Harrison, then with Middlesex. But the crucial person in

Neil Burns

bringing Burns to Bucks was Tim Scriven. Their paths had first crossed in second eleven cricket and they had got to know each other better when Scriven had briefly assisted Somerset. Burns held the Bucks skipper in high regard and, after he had dipped his toe in the water, made it clear that he could be of greatest value to Bucks if he were allowed to help the captain by operating as a player/coach. By 1998 Burns' wider contribution was recognised with his appointment as the county's Director of Cricket, and he played an increasing part in bridging the gulf between the County Club and the members' clubs competing in their different leagues across the county. He reached into the Asian communities, where talent had not hitherto been well tapped and, as he got to work, his impact was felt more widely across the better players in all age groups.

Despite the new signing, 1995 was destined to be another summer of disappointment with seventh place in the Championship once again offset by reaching the semi-final of the knockout through good wins against Bedfordshire, Cheshire and Dorset. But there was a middle order batting collapse against Cambridgeshire just when a final at Lord's was beckoning. Problems with availability cost points in the Championship, but qualification for the NatWest looked assured until a curious sequence of results by other counties just denied Bucks. The best match of the year was at Lakenham where Bucks declared to set Norfolk 293 to win. Needing eight from the final over with two wickets in hand, Norfolk lost their ninth wicket to a run out off the last ball as their batsmen strove in vain for the winning run. This match was notable for the debut of Charlie Jaggard, who hit a fifty in each innings.

There was yet another semi-final in the MCC Trophy in 1996 but one more failure to reach Lord's as Cheshire won by 23 runs at New Brighton. However, things looked up in the Championship, third place assuring a return to the NatWest for the following season. Roberts again enjoyed spectacular success, becoming the first Bucks player to score two centuries in a match when he hit 177 and 101, both undefeated, against Northumberland at Jesmond. Sadly, it was to no avail as rain caused the match to be abandoned on the second afternoon shortly after Roberts had reached his target. Neil Burns also averaged over 50, as did Bruce Percy, for the second year in succession, though he was now able to play in only three matches. There was also a maiden century for Richard Hurd of Beaconsfield, against Cambridgeshire at Kimbolton School. The attack, moreover, had a new potency, with the speed of Anatole Thomas bringing him 35 wickets, the same number as Clarke. Sadly, his temperament, occasionally too fiery even for a fast bowler, denied Tolly Thomas the further successes his talent could have brought him.

Participating in the NatWest Trophy for the first time in three years, Bucks entertained Essex at Beaconsfield in front of a good crowd on 24 June 1997. Allowed one overseas player, the selectors enlisted the West Indian Test batsman Keith Arthurton, who was engaged as professional at High Wycombe. His principal contribution was with the ball. In his 12 overs he took four for 54 as Essex, mainly thanks to a whirlwind 67 not out at the end of the innings from Robert Rollins, amassed 327 for 7. Undaunted by the target, Neil Burns and Tring Park's Matt Bowyer at one point took eight fours from two overs in reaching 117 for one. But the asking rate was well above Bucks' reasonable capabilities and the innings petered out at a creditable 238 for 7.

Earlier in the month there had been a chastening encounter at Jesmond in the MCC Trophy. Put in to bat, Bucks scored the second highest total in the 14-year history of the knockout competition. An opening stand of 257 between centurions Harrison and

Roberts paved the way to 334 for 5, a total which Northumberland eclipsed with a boundary off the final ball. With two wins and two losses, Bucks took fifth place in the Eastern Division of the Championship, sufficient to ensure another tilt at first-class opposition in the NatWest. Once again there were several close matches. Northumberland inflicted further pain with a two-run win at Amersham after Bucks had needed only 112. At Ipswich 23-year-old Russell Lane from Slough, still striving to clinch a place in the side, bravely faced up to the last over with 13 required for victory. Four, two, four, four and it was all over. The Bedfordshire match also went to the wire before a two off the final ball spelt defeat by two wickets.

The return of Harrison after his time with Middlesex and the engagement of Neil Mallender, a pace bowler with two Test caps, had boded well for a better season, but Mallender pulled up lame early in his fourth match and never played again, soon going on to become one of the country's leading umpires. With none of the other bowlers performing particularly well, this left an uncomfortable burden on Clarke. There were few problems with the batting. Harrison was in prime form, averaging 56, Hurd, Burns and Jaggard made good runs and Bowyer showed rich promise, as did 17- year-old Paul Sawyer, a left-hand batsman from High Wycombe, who played a full season. But it was a disappointing and uncharacteristic end to Malcolm Roberts' fine career that his season's average should drop to just below 20.

Into the Modern Age

Changing structures

As Tim Scriven passed the baton on to Jason Harrison in 1998, there had been changes off the field as well. Tom Orford had died on 12 January 1996 at the age of 90. He had been president since taking over from Sir John Aubrey-Fletcher in 1983. His services to Bucks cricket, and especially the Young Amateurs, had been recognised in 1992 when he won Buckinghamshire's 'Service to Sport' award, receiving a certificate and cup from Sir Peter Yarranton, the chairman of the Sports Council. His successor as president of the County Club was Robin Peppiatt. Though both Sir John Aubrey-Fletcher and his father, whom Sir John had succeeded in 1960, had resigned

Ken Drucquer

through poor health, Orford was not the first president to die in office and Peppiatt accepted with the declared intention of serving for a maximum of five years and creating a pattern whereby the presidency would pass around more freely. True to his word, Peppiatt made way for Ken Drucquer in 2001 and he, in turn, was succeeded by Jack Tomlin in 2006.

A change of chairman was also in the offing at the time of Robin Peppiatt's accession to the presidency. This had now become a post to which the holder was elected by the membership as opposed to the committee. There had been pressure for change at the AGM in 1996, but the members were persuaded that it was wise for Ken Drucquer to continue for one more year with his understanding of what was involved in the setting up of the new Bucks Cricket Board. With this body, replacing the Bucks Cricket Association and representing the county arm of the about-to-be-formed ECB, would come a new mechanism for the distribution of funds to grass roots cricket, and it would bring with it a stronger structure for the organisation of junior cricket and the identification of talent. Hitherto Bucks had run teams at Under 25, Under 19 and Under 17 levels; now county sides stretch down to Under 10s and girls also play representative matches at different age levels.

The new structure meant that the Board's paid official was reporting to the ECB, while the County Club's officers remained concerned with the success of the county team and the welfare of individual members, so there were bound to be differing agendas. Additional problems came for those counties who had significant assets, of which Bucks was one. For some years there had been a watchful eye on the county's funds, which later benefited from the substantial bequest in the will of Graham Skinner, the last survivor of the great 1932 side. In Bucks it took a little time for roles to be fully understood but, under the chairmanship of Cliff Pocock, relationships with the Board have become increasingly harmonious with the passage of time, while the Board's two

Development Officers, Stephen Goldthorpe, a former teacher at the RGS, and his successor Steve Ayres, a prominent Young Amateur, were both local men with the best interests of Bucks close to their heart.

At the 1997 AGM the chairmanship passed on from Ken Drucquer to Stuart York. At the same time a new secretary was identified who would succeed Jack Tomlin the following year. In office since 1985, Tomlin had battled on through ill health, but he had made it clear that he was no longer able to fulfil his duties as he would have wished and that a replacement would have to be found. It was a fortunate turn of fate that the ever enthusiastic and efficient Kevin Beaumont should just have negotiated early retirement, and he was attracted by the possibility of shadowing Tomlin for one year and taking over at the next AGM. Beaumont had first made his mark in the county as an umpire, reaching the minor counties' panel at the age of only 25. Now he was about to embark on his greatest contribution to the county's cricket.

Kevin Beaumont

With changes in the wind for the first-class game, minor counties competition also adopted new structures in 1998. The one-day competition was expanded to include 38 teams, the 20 minor counties now being joined by Board teams representing each of the 18 first-class counties. The competition began with groups of round robin matches, from which the winners qualified for the quarter-finals of a knockout. In the Championship, meanwhile, the concern was to address the problem of contrived two-day matches, the outcome of which all too often hinged on a third innings declaration after a relatively pointless first day. An initial solution was to adopt, for three of the nine matches, the Australian 'grade rules' format with a points structure whereby each side would be encouraged to bat for a whole day, providing a chance for batsmen to build the long innings that are the key to success in the upper reaches of the game.

Thus a new set of challenges faced Jason Harrison, but he had at his side Neil Burns, who had spent an active winter, in his new role of Director of Cricket, setting up monthly sessions at Lord's with particular emphasis on team-building and weekly technical sessions in the nets at Finchley. A pre-season training weekend at Stowe School was also arranged. A newly formed Academy, which was to replace the Under 25 team, joined up with members of the county team to provide a stronger, more focused squad, in which Burns was quick to support the selection of younger players for the county side. "I pushed for a policy of playing the ten best players plus one outstanding young player," he said. Those to gain experience from holding a regular place without being too hastily judged on short-term performance were Paul Sawyer, Kelvin Locke, Greg Hames, son of former captain Neil, Matt Eyles and Jamie Benning.

As soon as he had arrived Burns had identified senior players like Harwood, Owen and Stanway, who had the commitment to be part of his plan and the will to succeed, but for some others it was all too intense, too much of an imposition on their working and family lives – and they melted away. One who had always admired what Burns was striving to achieve was the ex-captain Tim Scriven, who also praises his technical ability: "His coaching skills were second to none, probably the best I've ever worked with. He was always positive, a proper professional cricketer."

Once regarded as potentially headstrong, by the time he took on the captaincy, Jason Harrison had matured as a person and a player, but he was still a strong and determined personality. "He was his own man," says Paul Atkins, back in the fold after a seven year absence, "He did seek advice, but he liked to do it his own way. He was hardworking and thorough. And the determination that he put into everything he did rubbed off on the rest of the team."

For the round robin stage of the re-vamped one-day competition Bucks assigned players special roles. In batting Harrison was to be the anchor man while the more expansive left-handers, Lane, Burns and Sawyer, were to play their shots, allowing Atkins' experience to be applied as necessary, while Mark Sullivan of Beaconsfield, an experienced off-spinner though rarely a championship player, was brought in to open the bowling and deny the early batsmen pace. After a comfortable win against Berkshire, it was Sullivan who saved the day with the bat as he dispatched the final ball over third man to earn a one wicket win against Hampshire Board Eleven. Rain then conspired to make life difficult for the bowlers at Ashford as Kent CB managed to overhaul a challenging Bucks total of 259 for 8, to which Burns had contributed 109. This spelt the end of the road for Bucks, a win against Sussex CB being academic, though it was always likely to be remembered by the Wycombe seamer Adam Cole, whose six overs brought him figures of six for 2. A promising cricketer who had made a useful contribution in championship matches, Cole was to be another youngster lost to Bucks when his career took him to a job at Lord's.

Despite the disappointing outcome for Bucks, the new competition had ensured that the team received useful practice ahead of their NatWest match with Surrey at The Oval, the fourth Test ground to entertain a Bucks side, where their opponents lined up with seven Test players. The captain soon had to adjust his tactics as 31 came from the bats of Alec Stewart and Jason Ratcliffe in the first three overs. Harrison's own off-spinners restored some order, but Surrey closed on 315 for 9, a total which Bucks never threatened despite a top-scoring 46 from the special import, South African Mike Rindel.

Paul Sawyer and Jason Harrison

Rain made a horrid mess of the championship matches but Bucks still managed four victories without a loss to take second place in the divisional table. A highlight of the season was the 'grade rules' match against Norfolk at Slough in which Jason Harrison and 18-year-old Paul Sawyer added 322 for the third wicket, the highest Bucks partnership for any wicket. Sawyer fell for 181, just as he was threatening Malcolm Roberts' record. He still awaits a second century for the county. For Harrison, who made 147 that day, there was much with which to be satisfied in his first season as captain. For those involved in running Bucks cricket it was a surprise and disappointment that he should resign during the winter and throw in his lot with Lincolnshire.

Harrison himself was still motivated by unfulfilled ambition. He had found a comfort zone in playing for his home county, and the possibility of a move to Lincolnshire, where he would be taken on as a professional and judged on performance, was a challenge that appealed. With his new county he had the satisfaction of winning the minor counties title. Harrison returned to play for Bucks in 2005.

Atkins takes up the challenge

Harrison's successor as captain was Paul Atkins. He had enjoyed several seasons with Surrey without being able to command a regular place in that very strong team. Personal hopes that he might have been allowed to join Somerset were thwarted by Surrey's need to cover the demands of representative calls on their players. After his first-class days were over there had been several years in which Atkins might have played a few games for Bucks, but he had become disenchanted at seeing how some of those with whom he had played for the Young Amateurs had been treated by the senior team selectors. Now 32, he still had much that he wished to prove in the game and Bucks were to become the beneficiary from one whose birth, education and residence all made the county his undisputed home.

Paul Atkins

As he enters his eighth season in charge in 2006, Paul Atkins has experienced the full roller coaster of experiences and emotions. It all began when he inherited a team that, notwithstanding the loss of one of its premier batsmen, had players of quality on whom he could call. Yet there were disappointing batting performances in the ECB 38 County Trophy in 1999 and a feeling that more might have been achieved in the Championship, where Bucks ended fourth with the most frustrating loss, by two wickets to Norfolk in the penultimate over at Lakenham, coming after undefeated innings of 86 and 138 from Neil Burns and match figures of ten for 153 from Andy Clarke.

As so often, there were problems with availability, most conspicuously with James Bovill, now back with Bucks after his first-class career with Hampshire had ended in 1997. Potentially one of the best pace bowlers on the minor counties circuit, he managed to play in only three championship matches. There were signs of promise from several younger players, but the side relied heavily on Burns, Clarke and Scriven. In what he had made clear would be his last season, Tim Scriven turned in splendid all-round figures – 23 wickets at 14.13 and a batting average of 56.33. With 3,574 runs and 265 wickets his all-round contribution to Bucks in 98 matches (legend has it that he played 99!) has been bettered only by Mat Wright and Colin Lever.

With Scriven's retirement and Clarke's defection to Norfolk, Atkins faced the next summer without both his spin bowlers, and before the season began he had also lost Burns, invited back to the first-class game by Leicestershire, for whom he enjoyed three successful years with bat and gloves. For Bucks there were three successive losses in the 38 County Trophy and a defeat by Wales in the NatWest, where an important lbw decision denied against West Indies Test batsman Phil Simmons proved crucial in a match lost by only 11 runs.

In the Championship the grade rules experiment was abandoned after just two seasons. After rain had brought a premature end to the Staffordshire match, the Bucks' campaign made an encouraging start with wins against Norfolk and Hertfordshire, the latter despite manager Steve Lynch being obliged to play and bring in two teenage debutants, one of them his own son. None of the three fill-in players batted or bowled as Bucks scored 278 for 4 to set up victory by an innings and 66 runs, the county's most emphatic win for more than 30 years. The prospect of heading the division was blown away with a loss to Bedfordshire and two more defeats on the northern tour, by just one wicket against Northumberland at Jesmond and by five wickets after another Bucks declaration against Cumberland. The Jesmond match was a memorable one for the captain, who became only the third Bucks player, after Charles Gresson and John Aubrey-Fletcher, to carry his bat through an innings. At Carlisle Simon Stanway confirmed his reputation as a bowler to answer a captain's prayers when the going is tough. He bowled unchanged through the two Cumberland innings, a total of 50 overs, at a time when circumstances had again conspired to leave Bucks struggling with an unbalanced side.

Atkins' bat-carrying 86 not out at Jesmond was one several fine innings in a season where he had had to shoulder extra responsibility as younger players strove to make their mark. Among those who began to fulfil promise were Graeme Paskins, who also kept wicket in several of the matches, and the free-scoring left-hander Russell Lane, but others of known ability in whom Burns had pinned faith, Matt Eyles of High Wycombe and Kelvin Locke of Bletchley, were still struggling to come to terms with the demands of batting at this level. A notable debutant was Jamie Benning, who made his first appearance shortly after his seventeenth birthday and averaged over 30. This was to be his only season for Bucks before joining the staff at Surrey, for whom he has made his greatest impact as a batsman in the one-day game.

Top of the bowling averages was Steve Naylor, whose 20 wickets included a match-winning spell of seven for 22 against Hertfordshire. Jamie Bovill was able to play six matches and performed well, while the experienced Paul Woodroffe brought steadiness to the attack. Replacing Clarke as the main spinner was Jeremy Batty, older brother of the England bowler Gareth Batty. Like his brother, he bowled off breaks and brought the experience of 84 first-class matches for Yorkshire and Somerset. Batty's 16 wickets were expensive and he achieved little with the bat.

The advent of three-day cricket

The 2001 season brought three-day cricket to the minor counties. Two days had once provided plenty of time to bowl sides out twice. But the quality of pitches had steadily improved, so the average wicket in Bucks games (whether batting or bowling) was now going for over 70% more than it had in Franklin's day and it was worth a third more than in the 1970s. So matches had become increasingly contrived with the first innings having less and less relevance to the run chase that had to be set up on the second day. "The game dictated itself," says Paul Atkins, "the art of captaincy wasn't there. I found it very negative cricket. It wasn't about bowling the other team out; it was more stopping them getting runs."

Playing three-day matches nevertheless brought problems to counties like Bucks, where players often found it difficult to take a Tuesday off as well as a Monday, and where employers were not keen on holidays aggregated in odd days. To compound the problem knockout competitions involving the major clubs were scheduled for Sundays, and at High Wycombe, by some way the strongest club in the county, there was always a real prospect of success. The club won the Evening Standard Challenge Trophy in 2002 and has reached two semi-finals of the National Club Championship. With the prospect of a final at Lord's or The Oval, players' loyalties were divided and the club tended to win at the county's expense.

For Paul Atkins these were testing times. His strike bowler, Bovill, was posted overseas and Bruce Percy had also played his last game for the county; but it was some compensation that Andy Clarke had returned after only one year away. The new championship programme was, rather unsatisfactorily, cut down to six matches – yet only Atkins and Naylor were able to play in all of them. In a season where no matches were won, the greatest problems lay with the bowling. Of the batsmen Paskins and Lane performed well and both were capped, while a newcomer, Danny Drepaul from Beaconsfield, topped the averages. At his home club he shared a partnership of 229 with Paskins, as both scored centuries, to give Bucks the prospect of an improbable win after following on against Cumberland. Set 251 in 66 overs the visitors had only just begun their chase when the onset of rain ended the match. Though he could not repeat his success in his second season, it was a sad loss for Bucks that Drepaul, also a useful wicket-keeper, should decide to emigrate to New Zealand at the end of the next season.

Though the championship sides often included too many unproven youngsters, performances in the Cheltenham and Gloucester Trophy showed what a full-strength team could achieve. There had been an early departure from the 2001 competition, when Bucks, with New Zealand Test opener Mark Richardson in the side, lost to Kent CB, but the county enjoyed greater success at the end of the season. Under a new arrangement whereby qualifiers for the next season's matches were determined the previous summer, Bucks first beat Worcestershire CB at Dinton and then Durham CB at Beaconsfield. For both these matches the county were able to field strong teams that included Jamie Benning.

These late summer successes brought Bucks a home tie in the C & G Trophy for 2002. Entertaining Sussex at Beaconsfield, Bucks looked the underdogs throughout, the first-class county winning in comfort by 125 runs. In the 38 County Trophy there were two abandoned matches and two defeats. In the Championship two matches were lost, two drawn and one won with the last game of the season, against Suffolk at Mildenhall, never starting because of the weather. Paul Atkins alone enjoyed much success with the bat. Against Staffordshire at Beaconsfield, he became the first Bucks player to carry his bat twice in a career. His 70 not out that day was the only crumb of comfort in a comprehensive defeat. Against Cumberland at Barrow an Atkins century led a recovery from an unpromising start, nine wickets for Clarke bringing victory by 53 runs against the only team to finish below Bucks in the table.

Again the C & G Trophy provided some end of season cheer. Against Suffolk at Dinton David Taylor, a left-hander from High Wycombe, hit 140 from 77 balls. With 110 from Atkins, Bucks reached 424 for 5 in their 50 overs. Only twice in the history of the competition had higher totals been achieved – both in the same match at The Oval ten weeks earlier when Surrey and Glamorgan had amassed 867 runs. It was no surprise that the Suffolk reply at Dinton should fall short by 230 runs. This success was followed by a closer-run battle with Shropshire before Bucks got home by 11 runs.

Taylor, the hero at Dinton, was destined never to appear in championship cricket for Bucks. His whirlwind display against Suffolk brought him to the attention of

Worcestershire, for whom he appeared in their Twenty20 side when this novel form of cricket began in 2003. Taylor started with a bang - 46 in 20 balls in his first innings to win the Man of the Match award, but thereafter he had little success, and the story was the same when he was briefly signed to inject fireworks into the Derbyshire National League side.

Before the next season there was time for another overseas tour, this time a return visit to South Africa. Gary Black had come out of retirement to lead a large party in 1996. Now there were 13 players under manager Jon Coles in a party of 27. Once again it was the holiday of a lifetime for those who went to support the team, while four wins against three defeats was a heartening record in a country where no visiting team expects easy successes.

Bucks' reward for their one-day successes at the end of the previous summer was a home tie against Gloucestershire, the ultimate winners of the C & G Trophy in 2003. Ascott Park was at its most beautiful as the visitors elected to bat first in early spring sunshine. Soon the ball was flying to all parts with former Test players Craig Spearman and Jonty Rhodes supporting Man of the Match Tim Hancock's 135 as Gloucestershire posted 401 for 7. Hancock later commented that minor counties usually provide a dodgy pitch to make the first-class batsmen struggle, but that Bucks had prepared a belter. It didn't stop the Gloucestershire bowlers, led by Mike Smith and James Averis, from dispatching the home batsmen for only 77.

A century by the captain set up a 76-run victory over Wiltshire in the Minor Counties Knockout, which had now replaced the 38 County competition, and Atkins stood alone in the next round with 88, but a total of 188 was never a stiff enough target for Shropshire, who won by five wickets. Meanwhile there was the most dispiriting of seasons in the Championship. With not one win – there had now been only one in three years - Bucks were rooted to the bottom of Eastern Division. It was at Stone that chairman Stuart York sat with the captain to reflect on what might be done. "It was the closest I got to jacking it in," Atkins reflects. He had taken the field still one man short, and had then seen one of his few experienced players, Russell Lane, laid low with illness and replaced in the field by the 52-year-old manager, Steve Lynch. He had been powerless to stop Staffordshire piling up 450 for 5. Not since 1948 had a higher score been made against Bucks. The batsmen then managed just 89 in 37 overs, the lowest Bucks total for 15 years. It was less embarrassing in the follow-on, but reaching 213 could not prevent this being one of the heaviest defeats in the county's history.

Stuart York

At least there were no squabbles in the dressing room. "We had disappointment rather than discontent," says Atkins. But the harsh truth was that the team comprised five or six genuine minor county players if no stars but, with the difficulties in getting High Wycombe players to play, the balance was made up with those who were at best unproven and at worst unlikely ever to make the grade. In the very next match Northumberland rattled up 426 for 3 at Jesmond, the second highest score off Bucks bowling in over 50 years. Despite the shaft of light in Matt Eyles' 89 not out before rain came, it was clear that something had to change if the county was ever to move forward again. It was decided that time was up for Andy Clarke. Now 41, he still earned his keep as a bowler, but there his contribution ended. He was no batsman and a pedestrian fielder. Off the field he was a great character, but he was not an ideal role model for a young side looking for guidance and inspiration. A change of manager also presented itself with the resignation of Steve Lynch. At a time when relations with High Wycombe were at their most difficult, he had often had to battle against the odds to keep the show on the road, but in six years his dedication to the task never wavered.

Coles and Medlycott lead a revival

Ahead of the 2004 season Jon Coles was installed as team manager and Keith Medlycott was taken on as player/coach. Coles, who had briefly opened the bowling for the county in the 1980s, was still playing at Gerrards Cross and proved to have an ideal rapport with the players. An excellent unflamboyant administrator and a good communicator, he developed and implemented the ideas first floated by Stuart York to produce a more effective squad system. "He got everyone working together," says Paul Atkins.

Another matter was addressed - ensuring that the players were not out of pocket in playing for the county. A plan was drawn up that offered mutual commitment: there would be compensation for loss of earnings provided the players, having declared their availability, did not subsequently drop out when chosen for matches.

It was Atkins' idea that Keith Medlycott should come to Bucks. The two had become good friends in their time at Surrey and had played together in South Africa. Medlycott had had an unfulfilled playing career as a left-arm spinner. Picked to tour the West Indies in 1989-90 under Graham Gooch, he later suffered the special brand of lost confidence that occasionally afflicts spin bowlers. Commonly called 'the yips', in Medlycott's case it proved terminal for his playing career, but he had developed his coaching skills and enjoyed great success in that role with Surrey. Atkins guessed that, with his Surrey contract now at an end, Medlycott would still fancy a return to the game as a player, and he felt sure that he was a good enough batsman to succeed in minor counties cricket. "I didn't have to persuade him, he jumped at it," says Atkins.

Keith Medlycott receives his cap from Paul Atkins

The new package soon began to work, and for the 2004 Championship only 20 players were called up, whereas in 2003 no fewer than 29 had played in the six matches. There was a new spirit in the dressing room, for which Paul Atkins and the long-serving Simon Stanway give great credit to Keith Medlycott. Less intense than Burns had been, Medlycott has restored the feeling of fun in playing cricket. He has striven to stop players being afraid of failure and has encouraged them to express themselves. So, for instance, Russell Lane can give it a whack at the start of the innings, and each team member knows his role.

Atkins, too, has taken care to ensure that all his players feel included. He abhors the senior player cliques that characterised the team when he first played. Once said to be over-concerned about his personal performance - a common and necessary characteristic of those who seek to make their living from the game – his focus is now clearly set on the performance of his team, his own position in the batting order adjusted to the wider need. There is a new keenness. "I've got the buzz back," says Jason Harrison, who had at one time retired from minor counties cricket but now regrets the clash of commitments that can make it difficult to play regularly for Bucks at a time when he feels everything is right on the field and off. As Harrison now sees it, Atkins is a fantastic captain tactically, Medlycott excels at man management and Coles provides brilliant administrative support.

Sadly, there was no C & G Trophy match to set the 2004 season under way, Bucks having lost a bowl-out to Dorset the previous August, when rain prevented any play on the reserve day at Bournemouth after the county had been well placed on 272 for six from 48 overs. For this match Bucks had called on the services of the Marshall twins, Jamie and Hamish, from New Zealand. Jamie was playing for Gerrards Cross, while his brother, who was already a Test player, was with a club in the north. Hamish made 66 not out in what was to be his only appearance for the county, but Jamie, who was also subsequently capped by his country, played in a total of four one-day matches for Bucks, though with little success.

There was a swift exit from the Minor Counties Knockout competition, Suffolk gaining a comfortable nine-wicket win at Copdock. However, once the championship matches got under way, it was soon evident that the new regime was working well and Bucks rose to third in the table. Two of the six matches were won. The first came against Cumberland when county cricket was brought to Gerrards Cross for the first time. Russell Lane, with 112, gave Bucks the initiative and Bobby Sher, from the Slough club, with match figures of nine for 88, was the decisive bowler as the visitors fell 84 short of their target. The only loss came when a strong Northumberland batting line-up successfully chased a target of 293 to win by five wickets at Beaconsfield. The hero of the second win was Simon Stanway, whose five for 40 in Norfolk's second innings came in a match in which the bat had been dominant and Bucks had trailed by 53 on first innings. An opening stand of 104 between Medlycott and Lane led to a nine-wicket victory.

The gods of the weather had been unkind in the three drawn matches, in all of which Bucks appeared to have had the upper hand. The game against Bedfordshire at Luton was notable for the all-round performance of Bobby Sher, who followed his unbeaten 108 with six for 83 in Bedfordshire's only innings. Sher's 20 wickets at 19.25 brought him the Frank Edwards Trophy, the third Bucks player to win it after Colin Lever and Ray Bond. An experienced and wholehearted cricketer, Sher's appearances are sadly rationed by the demands of his business.

With 508 runs Medlycott was the season's most prolific scorer, but there were good contributions from Sawyer, Atkins and Lane and a second season of solid returns from David Barr of Reading. Barr had played a series of good innings and averaged 74 after being drafted in for the last three matches of the disastrous 2003 season, and now averaged 49 in his second year. He is one of the two outsiders now permitted for championship matches under the county's rules, which also stipulate that one of the outsiders must coach within the county.

The 2005 season started with the home tie that had now become the automatic right of the minor county in the C & G Trophy. Bucks' opponents were among the most attractive in the land, Lancashire with Andrew Flintoff. The venue was Wormsley, where Bucks had already played a championship match in 1999. Set in the parkland of the Getty family home, the Wormsley ground was first laid out with no expense spared by the late Sir Paul Getty, cricket's leading modern philanthropist. With gently sloping grass banks above a manicured outfield, and with red kite circling majestically above, it must be doubtful if cricket is played in a more beautiful setting anywhere in the world. For ten years it has always been a very special privilege for Academy teams and others to be allowed to play at Wormsley.

Wormsley

Sadly for spectators and players, the spring idyll was compromised by a bitter wind and finally destroyed by squally showers. Sent in to bat, Lancashire made 370 for 4, the principal contribution of 162 not out coming from the unsung Andrew Crook before a phenomenal burst of hitting by Glen Chapple, whose 55 not out came off only 16 balls. Before the rain set in for good Bucks reached 39 for 2 in what was, for the time being at least, the swansong for all minor counties' participation in the only competition in which they have been able to rub shoulders with first-class opposition. For those who believe that money is the root of all evil, here is powerful evidence to support their case as swathes of the country are denied any possibility of seeing Test stars in action.

Bucks' hopes for the Minor Counties Knockout ended in the first match with a 33-run loss to Wiltshire, while the Championship was a curious mix of disappointment and superlative individual performances. Two wins, two losses and two draws meant slipping down the table to sixth. A five-wicket loss to Cumberland in a low-scoring game at Barrow was followed by a heartening 65-run win, set up by Russell Lane's second innings century, against Staffordshire at Beaconsfield. There were six first innings wickets for Simon Stanway and six in the second for Jonathan Newell, a spin bowler from Gerrards Cross making his county debut. Following a draw against Cambridgeshire, Lincolnshire were beaten by 103 runs in a high-scoring game where a Medlycott hundred gave Bucks a splendid start and Chris Batt of Taplow secured the win with five second innings wickets. At Ipswich, Suffolk, the ultimate winners of the division, declared their first innings at 392 for 8 to pave the way for a comfortable nine-wicket victory. The season's final match brought county cricket to the Slough Club's well appointed new ground at Upton Court Road for the first time, the game ending with the Bucks fielders crowding round an injured Trevor Ward in a vain effort to capture the final Norfolk wicket, which would have brought the summer's third win. Earlier Matt Eyles had hit 119 and it was Jonathan Newell's seven for 99 in the second innings that had taken Bucks to the brink of victory.

**Bobby Sher
displays his County Cap**

It was the earlier draw, against Cambridgeshire at Gerrards Cross, that made the greatest impact on the record books. Entering at 100 for 4, Bobby Sher displaced Malcolm Roberts' highest individual score when he struck Bucks' first ever double century. With skipper Paul Atkins he added 241 for the seventh wicket, comfortably surpassing the record set 51 years earlier by John Cockett and Brian Lucas. The match was also notable for a return of five for 19, including a hat trick, from Chris Batt on debut. Sadly for Bucks, rain and an undefeated 193 by Michael Sutliff in the follow on denied Bucks victory.

Earlier in the season there had been signs of a new direction that minor counties' competition might take when Bedfordshire, Hertfordshire and Oxfordshire joined Bucks for a Twenty20 tournament at Burnham. Fielding a weakened side due to an Academy match clash, Bucks lost all three of their matches, but plans are afoot to repeat the venture.

As he looks to the future Paul Atkins can take heart from knowing that cricket in Bucks has come a long way from the dark days of 2003. The county of the swan has bounced back before, and respectability has now returned, if not yet the success of the 1920s. The captain no longer takes the field with players in whom he does not believe. He looks to the future with several goals still unfulfilled, but he talks enthusiastically of the likes of Tom Brooks and Kieran Price, who have come through the Bucks youth system and started to make their presence felt in his team.

The Academy side, meanwhile, is playing a full part in preparing players for the step up to minor counties cricket. They have all benefited from intensive coaching sessions involving Paul Atkins and Steve Ayres, with Keith Medlycott brought in to stimulate their thinking about their game. The Tom Orford Trophy is still keenly contested, but five counties are involved rather than four and the matches, now played over two days on the 'grade rules' principle, are spread through the season instead of being concentrated into a festival week. The days when the county captain might have known little of the talent pressing for places in the senior team are past.

The future will always be uncertain and many aspects of the game may have changed beyond recognition from the amateur pastime it was when the gentry of Bucks met at the Charing Cross Hotel in 1891. But their meeting was not in vain. Were they to look down on those who take the field for Bucks today, all age groups and both sexes, they would surely feel that the hundred pounds they needed to get a county club started was money wisely invested.

2005 Team
Back row (l to r): **Jon Coles** *(team manager)*, **Andy B Ward, Jonathan Newell, David Barr, Chris Batt, Tom Brooks, Matt Eyles, Lesley Hawkins** *(scorer)*, **Stuart York** *(chairman)*
Front row: **Simon Stanway, Bobby Sher, Russell Lane, Paul Atkins, Keith Medlycott, Graeme Paskins**

Postscript

A task that has taken several years to complete is over. Inevitably the story set out in these pages has been selective and incomplete. Many heroic deeds on the field and many a devoted labour off it will have gone unrecorded. To those who should have been mentioned but haven't I can only apologise.

There is a certain sadness when a self-imposed task of this kind comes to an end. It has been a privilege to talk to so many of different generations who have played the greatest of all games and done their best for Bucks. As I have written this short history I have often wondered who might play in an all-time Bucks team. One former captain encouraged me to include such a team. I shall take him up. The career statistics, set in the context of the era in which the candidates played, will guide me, but I shall also be mindful of the testimony of their peers.

The likes of Greg Ritchie are not going to be eligible. It is what the players did for Bucks over a sustained period that will be my criteria. Are there any who claim a place without argument or debate? I offer only three: Mat Wright, Frank Edwards and Malcolm Roberts. Let their figures do the talking. We need a captain. I can hardly envisage Franklin watching the team without wanting to take charge, and his record suggests that he should be allowed to do so. Franklin will keep wicket. He has powerful competition from Charles Cobb from the 1890s - like Franklin he stumped more than one batsman a match across his career - and from Test keeper Ben Barnett, another who could have been captain. From more modern times Neil Burns can stake a claim and, like Barnett, he would expect to make more runs than Franklin. But so long as Edwards is there Franklin must be our wicket-keeper.

As opening partner for Roberts, I shall go for Charles Gresson, who was averaging over 35 before he left for the Boer War, excellent figures for those early days. Then RHJ Brooke must play, the only regular player to average over 30 before 1939. Until Malcolm Roberts came along the batting records belonged to David Johns, whose career figures undervalue his true worth. He seems not to have been a man for cheap runs, often sacrificing his wicket before a declaration. A useful bowler too, though with Edwards around his left-arm spin may be redundant.

Mat Wright will bowl all day if the captain wishes, so will Edwards, but we need some pace. Hazelton, Jack Whiting, Vic Lund, Oliver Battcock, Fred Harris, Ray Bond...a case could be made for any of these as strike bowler, but I fancy that what I have heard of Ronnie Rutter, with his classical action, just tips the balance in his favour. Despite the claims of Steve Burrow and Tim Scriven, Colin Lever must also play as an all-rounder, and we will hope that his batting and bowling will both be on song together. We can do with a spinner who will offer a contrast to Edwards, and Alf Hughes' record gives him the berth ahead of Andy Lyon.

We have one place left to fill. There is plenty of bowling so let us find another batsman, preferably one who is a good fielder. A left-hander would be useful, and there have been plenty of them over the years. Bill Atkins springs to mind because of his fielding, but a case can be made for Norman Butler or Richard Hayward. Ray Hutchison, too, would give us a left-hander and another stunning fielder, but as with

Johns we shall not need his bowling. Or we could play Neil Burns as a batsman. Then there is John Turner, left-handed only with his throwing arm. Should his sheer weight of runs win a place? Paul Atkins, batting on better pitches, can point to a more impressive average. But we may need someone to crouch under the helmet and Turner set new pinnacles of bravery without one. But Turner is an opening batsman and I have preferred Gresson. Then there is Claude Taylor, the only man to average over 50 for more than a handful of innings. But he only played for two seasons and I harbour worries that he may plague Franklin with his theories and his determination to see the game played 'properly', when Franklin will be flat out to win.

In the end I have gone for none of these. Especially in a strong team, there is a place in the middle of the order for someone who can belt the living daylights out of the ball and turn the course of a match. No-one has done it more dramatically for Bucks than Philip Le Gros, the leading batsman of the early 1920s, the period when scoring runs was at its very hardest. He won't be swooping on the ball in the covers – twelfth man Bill Atkins will do that if he can get on the field – but Le Gros will bring safe hands to the slip cordon.

The team, then, is:

1.	Malcolm Roberts
2.	Charles Gresson
3.	David Johns
4.	Hubert Brooke
5.	Philip Le Gros
6.	Colin Lever
7.	Mat Wright
8.	Walter Franklin
9.	Ronnie Rutter
10.	Frank Edwards
11.	Alf Hughes
12th man	Bill Atkins

How many, I wonder, will keep their places when the history is next written?

OFFICERS OF THE COUNTY CLUB

Presidents

1891	Lord Rothschild
1892	Lord Carrington
1893	Captain FJ Penton
1894	Leopold de Rothschild
1895	Baron F de Rothschild MP
1896	Lord Curzon
1897	AJ Robarts
1898	Lord Addington
1899	Lord Chesham
1900	H Leon
1901	WH Grenfell MP
1902	Colonel A Gilbey
1903	W Tyrwhitt Drake
1904	Hon W Rothschild
1905	Lord Burnham
1906	A Finlay
1907	FC Carr-Gomm
1908	Lord Desborough
1909	Lionel de Rothschild
1910	Sir Samuel Scott Bart
1911	HS Leon
1912-13	Anthony de Rothschild
1914-19	PJ de Paravicini
1920-21	Lord Chesham
1922-46	The Rt Rev PH Eliot, Bishop of Buckingham
1947-59	Sir Henry Aubrey-Fletcher Bart
1960-82	Sir John Aubrey-Fletcher Bart
1983-95	TC Orford
1996-2000	DR Peppiatt
2001-2005	K Drucquer
2006-	SJ Tomlin

Chairmen

1990-96	K Drucquer
1997-	SE York

Captains

1891-92	CW Parry
1893-1907	PJ de Paravicini
1908-12	WF Lowndes
1913-14	EHD Sewell
1919-46	WB Franklin
1947	CH Taylor
1948-51	OG Battcock
1952-54	BA Barnett
1955	G Reynolds
1956-58	DFV Johns
1959-65	PLB Stoddart
1966	BC Janes
1967-69	JKE Slack
1970-73	CJ Parry
1974-75	DS Mackintosh
1976-79	BW Poll
1980-83	DE Smith
1984	RE Hayward/DE Smith
1985	DE Smith
1986-91	NG Hames
1992-93	GR Black
1994-97	TJA Scriven
1998	JC Harrison
1999-	PD Atkins

Team Secretaries/Managers

1928-31	OG Battcock
1932-36	RH Rutter
1937-46	JHL Aubrey-Fletcher
1959-62	HW Johnson
1963	TJ Plumridge
1964-89	HE Perrin
1990-96	GE Thompson
1997	JD David
1998-2003	SG Lynch
2004-	JM Coles

Hon Secretaries

1891-1903	GR Ward
1903-07	HE Bull jnr
1908	Dr B Abrahams
1909-10	HG Hogarth
1911-18	EHD Sewell
1919-22	Captain SL Trevor
1923-24	OP Horlick
1925-26	Major HL Aubrey-Fletcher
1927-34	GH Brocklehurst
1935	RH Rutter
1936-45	GH Brocklehurst
1946-51	H Tyson Chambers
1952-53	H Bayley
1954-68	CA Prince
1969-84	PMM Slatter
1985-97	SJ Tomlin
1998-	KA Beaumont

Hon Treasurers

1891-94	CM Woodbridge
1895-1902	CE Cobb
1903-07	ENN Bartlett
1908-11	Colonel FTH Bernard
1912-19	HE Bull jnr
1920-22	OP Horlick
1923-27	WH Lavington
1928	EF Robson
1928-36	H Baker
1937-45	W Bliss
1946-51	W Crowther
1952-53	FJ Holmes
1956-83	PMM Slatter
1984-86	BEF Bennett
1987-93	M Raymond
1993-95	CJ Hayfield
1996-	NA Relph

THE RECORDS

Bucks Record in the Minor Counties Championship

	Captain	P	W	L	D	T	A	Posn	Bat	Bowl	Diff
									Average per wicket		
1895	PJ de Paravicini	4	3	1	0			NA	12.11	10.00	2.11
1896	PJ de Paravicini	8	4	1	3			2	17.29	11.14	6.15
1897	PJ de Paravicini	8	5	2	1			4	19.88	14.28	5.60
1898	PJ de Paravicini	8	1	2	5			2	22.88	23.32	-0.44
1899	PJ de Paravicini	8	1	0	7			1	30.61	22.71	7.90
1900	PJ de Paravicini	8	3	1	4			4	21.15	16.41	4.74
1901	PJ de Paravicini	8	5	1	2			3	17.86	15.13	2.73
1902	PJ de Paravicini	8	3	3	2			6	19.10	15.45	3.65
1903	PJ de Paravicini	8	2	2	4			10	14.12	17.27	-3.15
1904	PJ de Paravicini	10	3	2	5			10	18.68	19.54	-0.86
1905	PJ de Paravicini	8	2	3	3			8	21.95	19.33	2.62
1906	PJ de Paravicini	8	2	5	1			15	18.18	24.19	-6.01
1907	PJ de Paravicini	8	2	2	4			18	19.32	20.52	-1.20
1908	WHF Lowndes	8	2	6	0			16	14.18	22.87	-8.69
1909	WHF Lowndes	8	2	5	1			17	14.83	22.63	-7.80
1910	WHF Lowndes	8	0	6	2			21	14.76	28.70	-13.94
1911	WHF Lowndes	10	2	5	3			15	21.57	29.26	-7.69
1912	WHF Lowndes	6	3	1	2		2	4	21.00	17.09	3.91
1913	EHD Sewell	8	2	5	1			16	20.54	23.93	-3.39
1914	EHD Sewell	2	1	1	0		6	8	20.53	19.06	1.47
1920	WB Franklin	8	5	1	2			4	20.32	14.82	5.50
1921	WB Franklin	8	4	2	2			8	19.53	20.64	-1.11
1922†	WB Franklin	9	6	1	2			1	15.74	13.32	2.42
1923†	WB Franklin	9	7	0	2			1	18.63	12.78	5.85
1924	WB Franklin	8	3	1	4			4	16.72	11.11	5.61
1925†	WB Franklin	8	5	0	3	1		1	16.64	10.40	6.24
1926	WB Franklin	8	5	1	2			2	18.70	14.23	4.47
1927	WB Franklin	8	5	1	1	1		3	17.70	10.37	7.33
1928	WB Franklin	8	4	2	2			5	22.18	16.16	6.02
1929‡	WB Franklin	11	4	2	5			2	21.95	19.34	2.61
1930	WB Franklin	10	5	2	3			4	17.86	11.15	6.71
1931	WB Franklin	10	4	1	5			3	17.16	12.02	5.14
1932†	WB Franklin	11	10	0	1			1	23.93	11.11	12.82
1933	WB Franklin	10	3	3	4			15	19.61	18.02	1.59
1934	WB Franklin	8	1	3	4			16	19.38	20.94	-1.56
1935	WB Franklin	8	3	2	3			9	23.62	23.16	0.46
1936	WB Franklin	8	1	4	3			20	12.93	17.46	-4.53
1937	WB Franklin	8	3	1	4			7	19.73	17.89	1.84
1938†	WB Franklin	9	7	0	2			1	24.69	13.25	11.44
1939	WB Franklin	8	4	1	3			4	16.79	14.05	2.74
1946‡	WB Franklin	9	2	1	6			2	24.33	11.28	13.05
1947	CH Taylor	10	1	2	7			13	31.59	31.22	0.37
1948	OG Battcock	10	2	5	3			23	15.99	19.14	-3.15
1949	OG Battcock	10	6	2	2			6	21.09	18.55	2.54
1950	OG Battcock	10	2	2	6			12	19.24	16.69	2.55
1951	OG Battcock	10	2	1	7			9	29.22	22.49	6.73
1952†	BA Barnett	11	7	0	4			1	29.64	18.01	11.63
1953	BA Barnett	10	5	2	3			2	24.72	20.38	4.34
1954	BA Barnett	10	4	1	5			2	26.06	18.24	7.82

	Captain	P	W	L	D	T	A	Posn	Bat	Bowl	Diff
1955	G Reynolds	10	3	4	3			12	22.21	22.87	-0.66
1956	DFV Johns	10	3	2	5			7	18.03	18.61	-0.58
1957	DFV Johns	10	2	3	5			19	21.63	21.32	0.31
1958	DFV Johns	10	2	1	7			12	20.74	20.98	-0.24
1959	PLB Stoddart	10	3	3	4			13	23.73	23.91	-0.18
1960	PLB Stoddart	10	5	2	3			3	19.96	22.02	-2.06
1961	PLB Stoddart	10	5	2	3			4	26.74	21.14	5.60
1962	PLB Stoddart	10	3	2	5			9	21.78	18.45	3.33
1963	PLB Stoddart	10	2	2	6			16	21.07	27.81	-6.74
1964	PLB Stoddart	10	3	2	5			7	29.78	26.98	2.80
1965	PLB Stoddart	9	2	0	7		1	11	24.40	20.67	3.73
1966	BC Janes	10	0	3	7			22	15.83	22.11	-6.28
1967	JKE Slack	10	2	4	4			14	19.64	20.54	-0.90
1968	JKE Slack	12	4	1	7			3	19.70	18.05	1.65
1969φ	JKE Slack	12	8	2	2			1	20.96	15.83	5.13
1970	CJ Parry	12	2	4	6			8	25.18	22.78	2.40
1971	CJ Parry	12	3	1	8			7	22.47	17.72	4.75
1972	CJ Parry	12	3	2	7			10	23.17	22.70	0.47
1973	CJ Parry	12	5	1	6			4	26.33	19.99	6.34
1974	DS Mackintosh	12	4	3	5			7	22.18	18.84	3.34
1975	DS Mackintosh	12	3	4	5			12	22.93	23.05	-0.12
1976	BW Poll	12	4	3	5			11	23.34	23.98	-0.64
1977	BW Poll	11	4	3	4		1	6	18.59	18.75	-0.16
1978	BW Poll	12	4	1	7			4	26.46	18.31	8.15
1979	BW Poll	12	2	4	6			12	22.36	23.56	-1.20
1980	DE Smith	12	1	4	6	1		15	25.76	29.20	-3.44
1981	DE Smith	12	4	6	2			11	24.86	29.27	-4.41
1982	DE Smith	12	1	5	6			19	23.80	32.76	-8.96

NEW DIVISIONAL STRUCTURE INTRODUCED

	Captain	P	W	L	D	T	A	Posn	Bat	Bowl	Diff
a 1983	DE Smith	9	6	2	1			1	36.31	24.65	11.66
1984	DE Smith	9	3	2	4			2	27.12	26.35	0.77
1985	RE Hayward/										
	DE Smith	9	0	2	7			8	19.27	19.12	0.15
1986	DE Smith	9	2	1	6			6	28.93	27.89	1.04
b 1987	NG Hames	9	4	1	4			1	26.97	24.99	1.98
1988	NG Hames	9	1	3	5			8	24.53	27.63	-3.10
1989	NG Hames	9	4	1	4			4	34.23	30.33	3.90
1990	NG Hames	9	2	0	7			3	32.22	33.73	-1.51
1991	NG Hames	8	3	1	3	1	1	2	26.97	25.55	1.42
1992	GR Black	9	2	2	5			5	24.73	30.70	-5.97
1993	GR Black	9	1	2	6			9	33.28	33.82	-0.54
1994	TJA Scriven	9	1	3	5			7	32.02	33.47	-1.45
1995	TJA Scriven	9	2	3	4			7	29.08	29.98	-0.90
1996	TJA Scriven	9	3	4	2			3	29.83	28.68	1.15
1997	TJA Scriven	9	2	2	5			5	29.17	27.52	1.65
*1998	JC Harrison	8	4	0	4		1	2	38.91	30.40	8.51
*1999	PD Atkins	9	3	3	3			4	28.55	24.79	3.76
*2000	PD Atkins	9	2	3	4			6	27.35	26.27	1.08
2001	PD Atkins	6	0	2	4			8	26.77	34.60	-7.83
2002	PD Atkins	5	1	2	2		1	9	22.66	26.20	-3.54
2003	PD Atkins	6	0	4	2			10	24.94	40.32	-15.38
2004	PD Atkins	6	2	1	3			3	36.60	29.14	7.46
2005	PD Atkins	6	2	2	2			6	27.50	28.89	-1.39
TOTAL		914	305	218	388	3 (14)					

Notes:
†   Challenge Match won included in figures
‡   Challenge Match lost included in figures
φ   No Challenge Match required
(a) One-day play off match lost not included in figures
(b) One-day play off match won not included in figures
*   Results include some grade rules matches, usually shown separately in Championship tables. Under these rules, unfinished matches where a side has a first innings lead have been treated as matches won Abandoned matches, where no ball was bowled, are excluded from totals.

Championship Performance against Other Teams

	P	W	L	D	T
Bedfordshire	108	31	28	49	
Berkshire	124	42	26	56	
Cambridgeshire	18	7	3	8	
Carmarthenshire	2	2	0	0	
Cheshire	9	2	4	3	
Cornwall	9	6	0	2	1
Cumberland	12	6	4	2	
Devon	11	3	3	5	
Dorset	18	4	4	10	
Glamorgan	2	0	1	1	
Hertfordshire	152	48	37	66	1
Kent 2nd XI	27	11	7	9	
Lancashire 2nd XI	1	1	0	0	
Leicestershire 2nd XI	2	1	0	1	
Lincolnshire	16	6	3	7	
Monmouthshire	2	0	0	2	
Norfolk	113	43	23	46	1
Northamptonshire	2	1	0	1	
Northumberland	13	4	4	5	
Nottinghamshire 2nd XI	2	0	0	2	
Oxfordshire	109	43	18	48	
Shropshire	9	3	1	5	
Somerset 2nd XI	5	1	0	4	
Staffordshire	18	2	8	8	
Suffolk	61	20	16	25	
Surrey 2nd XI	19	5	9	5	
Wales Minor Counties	4	1	0	3	
Wiltshire	40	11	16	13	
Worcestershire	4	0	3	1	
Worcestershire 2nd XI	2	1	0	1	
TOTAL	914	305	218	388	3

Abandoned matches in which no play took place are excluded.

Grounds Used for Championship Matches

	First Match	Last Match	Total Played
Amersham CC, Shardeloes Estate	1968	1997	28
Ascott Park, Wing	1905	2003	48
Aspro Sports Ground, Slough	1951	1954	4
Aylesbury CC	1896	1998	42
Beaconsfield CC	1967	2005	25
Bletchley Park	1899	1933	33
Bletchley Town CC	1986	1988	2
Buckingham Town CC	1968	1990	12
Chesham CC	1907	1982	33
Ernest Turner's Sports Ground, High Wycombe	1965	1969	3
Eton College (Agar's Plough)	1946	1950	5
Gerrards Cross CC	2004	2005	2
High Wycombe CC	1895	2001	116
Marlow CC	1909	2004	30
Milton Keynes (Campbell Park)	1999	2000	2
Molins Sports Club, Monks Risborough	1982	1985	3
Slough CC, Calvey Road	1904	1998	58
Slough CC, Upton Court Road	2005	2005	1
Stoke Poges CC	1911	1911	1
Stowe School	1947	1982	4
Wolverton CC, Osborne Street	1904	1921	7
Wolverton (The Big Field)	1895	1895	1
Wormsley (Sir Paul Getty's Ground)	1999	1999	1

Team Records

Highest for Bucks
505	v Bedforshire at Bedford	1912
459	v Hertfordshire at Watford	1897
439	v Notts 2nd XI at Eton College	1947
435-8	v Carmarthenshire at Slough	1911
432-8	v Cambridgeshire at Gerrads Cross	
		2005

Highest against Bucks
505-9	by Hertfordshire at High Wycombe	
		1913
505-6	by Staffordshire at Stone	1948
490	by Surrey 2nd XI at The Oval	1907
469	by Surrey 2nd XI at Reigate	1908
453-8	by Hertfordshire at High Wycombe	
		1922

Lowest for Bucks
20	v Hertfordshire at Aylesbury	1903
24	v Leicestershire 2nd XI	
	at High Wycombe	1924
26	v Kent 2nd XI at High Wycombe	
		1930
30	v Oxfordshire at Banbury	1896
34	v Surrey 2nd XI atWolverton	1909

Lowest against Bucks
15	by Kent 2nd XI at Bletchley Park	
		1925
31	by Hertfordshire at High Wycombe	
		1930
31	by Bedfordshire at High Wycombe	
		1946
33	by Leicestershire 2nd XI	
	at High Wycombe	1924
33	by Oxfordshire at High Wycombe	
		1925

Close Matches

Tied matches
1927	Bucks tied with Hertfordshire at Ascott Park
1980	Bucks tied with Norfolk at Amersham
1991	Bucks tied with Cornwall at Truro

Matches won
1981	Beat Bedfordshire by 1 run at Stowe School
1987	Beat Cornwall by 1 run at Wadebridge
1923	Beat Oxfordshire by by 2 runs at HighWycombe
1969	Beat Norfolk by 2 runs at Beaconsfield
1906	Beat Wiltshire by one wicket at Swindon
1957	Beat Oxfordshire by one wicket at High Wycombe
1976	Beat Hertfordshire by one wicket at Hertford

Matches lost
1979	Lost to Norfolk at by 1 run at Amersham
1992	Lost to Hertfordshire by 1 run at St Albans
1997	Lost to Northumberland by 2 runs at Amersham
1908	Lost to Berkshire by 3 runs at Wolverton
1896	Lost to Hertfordshire by one wicket at Watford
1994	Lost to Cambridgeshire by one wicket at Fenner's
2000	Lost to Northumberland by one wicket at Jesmond

Appearance Records

100 Championship appearances

WB Franklin	1911-46	200	LG Baker	1924-47	114
F Edwards	1914-46	166	OG Battcock	1925-51	114
JB Turner	1968-83	151	NV Butler	1950-68	109
MW Wright	1895-1913	143	JKS Edwards	1971-86	109
DE Smith	1967-88	141	NG Hames	1977-93	109
BW Poll	1966-80	132	AW Lyon	1977-88	109
			G Atkins	1957-72	107

Batting Records

3000 runs in a career

		M	I	NO	R	Ave
JB Turner	1968-83	151	286	16	7524	27.87
MJ Roberts	1987-97	75	145	13	5989	45.37
WB Franklin	1911-46	200	301	22	5191	18.61
DE Smith	1967-88	141	246	44	4922	24.37
MW Wright	1895-1913	143	241	27	4762	22.25
NV Butler	1950-68	109	184	11	4735	27.37
G Atkins	1957-72	107	194	26	4689	27.91
DFV Johns	1950-66	83	126	10	4270	36.81
C Lever	1962-78	92	155	19	4074	29.96
JKS Edwards	1971-86	109	191	27	4041	24.64
DA Janes	1960-76	94	161	19	3805	26.80
NG Hames	1977-93	109	197	27	3800	22.35
PD Atkins	1985-	73	119	27	3750	40.76
LG Baker	1924-47	114	172	14	3744	23.70
TJA Scriven	1986-99	98	149	29	3574	29.78
AR Harwood	1983-95	65	119	6	3458	30.60
S Burrow	1984-96	80	136	25	3446	31.05
RE Hayward	1978-89	50	92	17	3320	44.27
BA Barnett	1951-64	80	125	15	3222	29.29
PLB Stoddart	1955-67	77	124	14	3097	28.15
PW Le Gros	1911-30	80	132	11	3050	25.21

Highest career averages with at least 1500 runs

		M	I	NO	R	Ave
ND Burns	1995-99	39	68	12	2684	47.93
JC Harrison	1991-	30	51	9	1960	46.67
MJ Roberts	1987-97	75	145	13	5989	45.37
RE Hayward	1978-89	50	92	17	3320	44.27
PD Atkins	1985-	73	119	27	3750	40.76
DFV Johns	1950-66	83	126	10	4270	36.81
BS Percy	1986-2000	50	79	17	2229	35.95
ME Milton	1979-89	45	88	7	2845	35.12
RHJ Brooke	1929-35	51	80	6	2471	33.39
TE Busby	1936-51	40	61	8	1677	31.64

Most runs in a season

		M	I	NO	R	Ave
C Lever	1964	10	19	4	1011	67.40
MJ Roberts	1990	9	18	1	921	54.18
RE Hayward	1983	8	16	5	853	77.55
DFV Johns	1952	9	13	1	846	70.50

RHJ Brooke	1929	8	19	1	822	45.67
MJ Roberts	1989	8	16	2	818	58.43
GA Jones	1975	11	22	1	802	38.19
ND Burns	1999	9	15	4	761	69.18
WN Slack	1976	12	24	0	748	31.17
S Burrow	1990	9	17	1	743	46.44

Highest individual scores
200	ZA Sher	v Cambridgeshire at Gerrards Cross in 2005
193*	MJ Roberts	v Wiltshire at Amersham in 1989
191	DFV Johns	v Bedfordshire at Bedford in 1952
181	PR Sawyer	v Norfolk at Slough in 1998
178	ND Burns	v Staffordshire at Beaconsfield in 1997
177*	MJ Roberts	v Northumberland at Jesmond in 1996
165*	J O'Connor	v Bedfordshire at Bedford in 1947
164*	RHJ Brooke	v Bedfordshire at Bedford in 1932
162	Dr E Weaver Adams	v Berkshire at Reading in 1909
160*	PD Atkins	v Shropshire at Bridgnorth in 1986
158*	C Lever	v Berkshire at High Wycombe in 1964
157	NV Butler	v Bedfordshire at Aspro Sports Ground, Slough in 1953
155*	MJ Roberts	v Cornwall at Marlow in 1988
155	PW Le Gros	v Hertfordshire at Watford in 1923
152*	ND Burns	v Bedfordshire at Luton in 1999
150*	H Taylor	v Norfolk at Aspro Sports Ground, Slough in 1954

Most centuries in a career
15	MJ Roberts
8	DFV Johns
6	NV Butler, RE Hayward, C Lever, ME Milton
5	BA Barnett, ND Burns
4	G Atkins, LG Baker, CRH Gresson, WB Franklin, P Isherwood, JB Turner, MW Wright
3	PD Atkins, RHJ Brooke, PJ de Paravicini, JC Harrison, RW Hooker, DA Janes, BS Percy, SS Peters, G Reynolds, CH Taylor

Two centuries in a match
1996   MJ Roberts: 177* and 101* v Northumberland at Beaconsfield

Carrying bat through an innings
111*	CRH Gresson	v Northants at Northampton in 1896
106*	JHL Aubrey-Fletcher	v Bedfordshire at Ascott Park in 1938
88*	PD Atkins	v Northumberland at Jesmond in 2000
70*	PD Atkins	v Staffordshire at Beaconsfield in 2002

Highest wicket partnerships
1st	217	TR Kent (123) and EHD Sewell (106) v Hertfordshire at High Wycombe in 1913
	217	TE Busby (94) and A Campbell (130) v Norfolk at Lakenham in 1950
2nd	263*	C Lever (135*) and DA Janes (133*) v Hertfordshire at Tring in 1964
3rd	322	JC Harrison (147) and PR Sawyer (181) v Norfolk at Slough in 1998
4th	205	MW Wright (85) and FH Mitchell (96) v Wiltshire at Trowbridge in 1899
5th	223	LG Baker (131*) and RT Campbvell (117) v Bedfordshire at Wing in 1937
6th	241	ZA Sher (200) and PD Atkins (84) v Cambridgeshire at Gerrards Cross in 2005
7th	172	PJ de Paravicini (120) and FT Higgins-Bernard (53) v Hertfordshire at Watford in 1897
8th	111	RJ Plested (57) and E Clifford (60) v Norfolk at Slough in 1959
9th	141	WB Franklin (119*) and MW Wright (34) v Hertfordshire at High Wycombe in 1913
10th	108	WE Hazelton (124*) and F Edwards (30) v Surrey 2nd XI at The Oval in 1929

Bowling Records

200 wickets in a career

		O	M	R	W	Ave
F Edwards	1914-46	5404.4	1739	11708	1059	11.06
MW Wright	1895-1913	6184	2480	11584	811	14.28
AJ Hughes	1948-58	2749.5	756	5966	391	15.26
OG Battcock	1925-51	2829.2	1034	5701	379	15.04
AW Lyon	1977-88	3021.2	832	7846	367	21.38
RH Rutter	1928-47	2104.2	594	5347	366	14.61
WE Hazelton	1912-30	1925	504	4916	333	14.76
FW Harris	1957-76	2556.5	784	6002	323	18.58
AR Clarke	1994-2003	2254.1	505	7190	284	25.32
RE Bond	1965-79	1863.3	494	4836	266	18.18
TJA Scriven	1986-99	2076.2	482	6886	265	25.98
G Nash	1895-1903	1519.2	471	3427	259	13.23
C Lever	1962-78	2046.1	652	4660	234	19.91
CJ Parry	1968-77	1803	622	4329	233	18.58
CA Pickett	1949-70	1780.2	557	4023	219	18.37
CW Smith	1954-67	1768.3	551	4381	202	21.69

Best average: 100 wickets or more

		O	M	R	W	Ave
F Edwards	1914-46	5404.4	1739	11708	1059	11.06
G Nash	1895-1903	1519.2	471	3427	259	13.23
VE Lund	1929-47	924.3	297	2148	159	13.51
MW Wright	1895-1913	6184	2480	11584	811	14.28
RW Hutchison	1973-75	718.1	253	1712	118	14.51
RH Rutter	1928-47	2104.2	594	5347	366	14.61
WE Hazelton	1912-30	1925	504	4916	333	14.76
OG Battcock	1925-51	2829.2	1034	5701	379	15.04
AJ Hughes	1948-58	2749.5	756	5966	391	15.26
RE Bond	1965-79	1863.3	494	4836	266	18.18

Most wickets in a season

		O	M	R	W	Ave
F Edwards	1923	401.5	108	987	96	10.28
F Edwards	1922	356.4	107	801	79	10.14
F Edwards	1932	305.4	99	606	79	7.67
F Edwards	1926	414.3	163	741	74	10.01
MW Wright	1904	440.4	157	986	72	13.69
F Edwards	1929	412.4	123	874	72	12.14
F Edwards	1924	335.1	121	623	69	9.03
F Edwards	1927	358	145	591	69	8.57
RH Rutter	1933	368	100	901	67	13.45
G Nash	1996	405.1	148	716	65	11.02

Best bowling analyses

9-29	F Edwards	v Oxfordshire at Oxford in 1930
9-50	ND Rogers	v Berkshire at Bray in 1973
9-63	OG Battcock	v Bedfordshire at Bedford in 1948
9-80	F Edwards	v Bedfordshire at Bedford in 1923
8-13	F Edwards	v Oxfordshire at High Wycombe in 1925
8-13	F Edwards	v Kent 2nd XI at High Wycombe in 1930
8-15	F Edwards	v Oxfordshire at Oxford in 1925
8-18	F Edwards	v Cambridgeshire at Bletchley Park in 1923
8-22	JWC Mills	v Hertfordshire at Watford in 1960

8-23	JBG Whiting	v Wiltshire at Bletchley Park in 1923
8-25	VHD Cannings	v Oxfordshire at Morris Motors Ground, Oxford in 1962
8-27	MW Wright	v Carmarthenshire at Llanelly in 1911
8-28	G Nash	v Oxfordshire at Thame in 1897
8-30	MW Wright	v Norfolk at Lakenham in 1904
8-32	WE Hazelton	v Bedfordshire at Wolverton in 1920
8-33	G Nash	v Bedfordshire at High Wycombe in 1895
8-34	RE Bond	v Berkshire at Reading in 1974

VE Lund twice took 7 for 9
The best match analysis is 16 for 74 by G Nash against Oxfordshire at Thame in 1897

All-Round Records

2,000 runs and 100 wickets in a career

		Runs	Ave	Wkts	Ave
MW Wright	1895-1913	4762	22.25	811	14.28
C Lever	1962-78	4074	29.96	234	19.91
TJA Scriven	1986-99	3574	29.78	265	25.98
S Burrow	1984-96	3446	31.05	195	25.10
DFV Johns	1950-66	4270	36.81	168	19.81

Wicket-Keeping Records

Most dismissals in a career

WB Franklin	1911-46	442
BW Poll	1966-80	321
BA Barnett	1951-64	160
CE Cobb	1895-1903	127
ND Burns	1995-99	109
TP Russell	1981-2000	83
DJ Goldsmith	1986-91	67
RG Humphrey	1980-85	60
TE Perkins	1969-80	54
DJS Taylor	1961-63	35

Most dismissals in a season

BW Poll	1969	37	(32c, 5st)
BW Poll	1967	34	(32c, 2 st)
WB Franklin	1923	33	(16c, 17st)
BW Poll	1975	30	(27c, 3st)
BW Poll	1976	29	(25c, 4st)
ND Burns	1997	29	(20c, 9st)
WB Franklin	1924	28	(6c, 22 st)
BA Barnett	1952	27	(15c, 12st)
WB Franklin	1929	25	(12c, 13st)
WB Franklin	1939	25	(15c, 10st)
BA Barnett	1959	25	(19c, 6st)
ND Burns	1996	25	(19c, 6st)

Most wicket-keeping catches in a career

BW Poll	1966-80	288
WB Franklin	1911-46	220
BA Barnett	1951-64	103
ND Burns	1995-99	81

CE Cobb	1895-1903	78
TP Russell	1981-2000	62
RG Humphrey	1980-85	47
DJ Goldsmith	1986-91	42
TE Perkins	1969-80	42
DJS Taylor	1961-63	31

Most wicket-keeping catches in a season

BW Poll	1967 & 1969	32
BW Poll	1975	27
BW Poll	1976	25
BW Poll	1979	24
BW Poll	1978	22
BW Poll	1970 & 1972	20
ND Burns	1997	20
BA Barnett	1959	19
BW Poll	1971	19
ND Burns	1996	19

Most wicket-keeping catches in a match

7	WB Franklin	v Hertfordshire at High Wycombe in 1939
7	BW Poll	v Norfolk at Beaconsfield in 1967
7	BW Poll	v Oxfordshire at Banbury in 1971
7	CJ Tungate	v Wales MC at Bletchley in 1988

Note: Tungate's catches were all held in the same innings

Most stumpings in a career

WB Franklin	222
BA Barnett	57
CE Cobb	49
BW Poll	33
ND Burns	28
DJ Goldsmith	25
TP Russell	21

Most stumpings in a season

WB Franklin in 1924	22
WB Franklin in 1923	17
WB Franklin in 1922	13
BA Barnett in 1952	12
WB Franklin (5 occasions)	11

Most stumpings in a match

7	BA Barnett	v Norfolk at Lakenham in 1954
6	TP Russell	v Cambridgeshire at Fenner's in 1994
5	WB Franklin	on three occasions

Four stumpings in an innings

WB Franklin	v Surrey 2nd XI at The Oval in 1924
WB Franklin	v Surrey 2nd XI at High Wycombe in 1924
BA Barnett	v Norfolk at Aspro Sports ground, Slough in 1952
BA Barnett	v Norfolk at Lakenham in 1954
DJ Goldsmith	v Wales MC at Colwyn Bay in 1991

Fielding Records

Most catches in a career

JB Turner	1968-83	197
DE Smith	1967-88	99
F Edwards	1914-46	90
NG Hames	1977-93	82
MW Wright	1895-1913	75
LG Baker	1924-47	71
NV Butler	1950-68	64
PW Le Gros	1911-30	64
CA Pickett	1949-70	61
FW Harris	1957-76	60
CJ Parry	1968-77	60

Most catches in a season

JB Turner	1971 & 1974	19
J Saunders	1897	18
EC Hobbs	1902	18
CJ Parry	1970	17
JB Turner	1968	16

Six catches in a match

JJ Birrell	v Norfolk at Lakenham in 1949
JB Turner	v Berkshire at Ascott Parkin 1974
JB Turner	v Bedfordshire at Luton in 1977
JB Turner	v Bedfordshire at Ascott Park In 1978
JB Turner	v Berkshire at Reading in 1979
JB Turner	v Oxfordshire at Marlow in 1981

Five catches in an innings

JJ Birrell	v Norfolk at Lakenham in 1949
NV Butler	v Hertfordshire at Tring in 1964
JB Turner	v Bedfordshire at Luton in 1977

Championship Centuries for Bucks

1896	J Saunders	114	v Northants at Aylesbury
	PJ de Paravicini	108*	v Oxfordshire at Aylesbury
	CRH Gresson	111*	v Northants at Northampton
1897	PJ de Paravicini	120	v Hertfordshire at Watford
1898	CRH Gresson	122*	v Hertfordshire at Watford
	PJ de Paravicini	105	v Oxfordshire at Thame
	CE Cobb	111	v Berkshire at Aylesbury
1899	CRH Gresson	103	v Berkshire at Aylesbury
	MW Wright	100	v Hertfordshire at Aylesbury
1900	ES Boddy	113	v Wiltshire at Trowbridge
	MW Wright	148	v Hertfordshire at Aylesbury
1901	MW Wright	102*	v Berkshire at Aylesbury
1904	Dr E Weaver-Adams	106	v Hertfordshire at St Albans
	CRH Gresson	100*	v Hertfordshire at St Albans
	MW Wright	123	v Berkshire at Reading
1905	FN Bird	133	v Berkshire at Slough
1906	FN Bird	104	v Berkshire at Reading

1908	WF Lowndes	139*	v Berkshire at Reading
1909	Dr E Weaver-Adams	162	v Berkshire at Reading
1911	NDC Ross	144	v Carmarthen at Slough
1912	DH Field	103	v Bedfordshire at Bedford
1913	PL Frith	102	v Hertfordshire at Broxbourne
	WB Franklin	119*	v Hertfordshire at High Wycombe
	EHD Sewell	106	v Hertfordshire at High Wycombe
	TR Kent	123	v Hertfordshire at High Wycombe
	EHD Sewell	109	v Bedfordshire at Aylesbury
1914	EA Shaw	117	v Dorset at Aylesbury
1920	PW Le Gros	117	v Wiltshire at Bletchley Park
1923	PW Le Gros	155	v Hertfordshire at Watford
1924	WN Roe	115	v Bedfordshire at Bedford
1925	WE Hazelton	102	v Surrey 2nd XI at The Oval
1926	WB Franklin	138	v Hertfordshire at Watford
1928	WB Franklin	135	v Kent 2nd XI at Folkestone
	WB Franklin	105	v Norfolk at Ascott Park
1929	WE Hazelton	124*	v Surrey 2nd XI at The Oval
	AG Skinner	104*	v Norfolk at Ascott Park
	RHJ Brooke	105	v Hertfordshire at Broxbourne
1930	RHJ Brooke	101*	v Oxfordshire at High Wycombe
1932	RHJ Brooke	164*	v Bedfordshire at Bedford
	LG Baker	105	v Oxfordshire at High Wycombe
	RH Rutter	106	v Oxfordshire at High Wycombe
	SS Peters	131	v Oxfordshire at High Wycombe
1933	AP Powell	100	v Oxfordshire at Merton College
1934	SS Peters	120	v Bedfordshire at Bedford
1935	LG Baker	131*	v Bedfordshire at Ascott Park
	RT Campbell	117	v Bedfordshire at Ascott Park
1937	JHL Aubrey-Fletcher	112	v Hertfordshire at St Albans
1938	AG Skinner	100	v Berkshire at High Wycombe
	JHL Aubrey-Fletcher	106*	v Bedfordshire at Ascott Park
	SS Peters	110	v Norfolk at High Wycombe
1939	LG Baker	100	v Norfolk at Lakenham
1946	W Yates	117*	v Bedfordshire at Bedford
	J O'Connor	112	v Berkshire at Eton College
	CA Prince	105*	v Berkshire at Eton College
	P Isherwood	102	v Dorset at High Wycombe
	LG Baker	131	v Bedfordshire at High Wycombe
1947	TE Busby	136*	v Bedfordshire at Bedford
	J O'Connor	165*	v Bedfordshire at Bedford
	DG Bousfield	129	v Notts 2nd XI at Eton College
	CH Taylor	131	v Notts 2nd XI at Eton College
	P Isherwood	116	v Hertfordshire at Stevenage
	CH Taylor	106	v Hertfordshire at Stevenage
	CH Taylor	114	v Bedfordshire at High Wycombe
1949	P Isherwood	111*	v Bedfordshire at Bedford
	TE Busby	145	v Hertfordshire at Ascott Park
1950	A Campbell	130	v Norfolk at Lakenham
	JH Hastie	102*	v Hertfordshire at St Albans
	DFV Johns	100	v Oxfordshire at High Wycombe
1951	BA Barnett	141	v Hertfordshire at Slough
1952	RE Clements	100*	v Berkshire at High Wycombe
	DFV Johns	191	v Bedfordshire at Bedford
	DFV Johns	126	v Hertfordshire at Hitchin
	DFV Johns	124	v Oxfordshire at Witney
	NV Butler	130	v Bedfordshire at Ascott Park
	P Isherwood	107	v Kent 2nd XI at High Wycombe

1953	BA Barnett	138	v Norfolk at Lakenham
	NV Butler	117	v Bedfordshire at Bedford
	BA Barnett	116*	v Berkshire at High Wycombe
	BA Barnett	123	v Hertfordshire at St Albans
	NV Butler	157	v Bedfordshire at Aspro Sports Ground, Slough
	DFV Johns	119	v Bedfordshire at Aspro Sports Ground, Slough
1954	JMH Tilbury	113	v Norfolk at Lakenham
	J Parton	113	v Oxfordshire at Cowley
	H Taylor	124	v Berkshire at High Wycombe
	JA Cockett	109	v Bedfordshire at Bedford
	BJ Lucas	100*	v Bedfordshire at Bedford
	H Taylor	150*	v Norfolk at Aspro Sports Ground, Slough
1955	G Reynolds	119	v Norfolk at Lakenham
	BA Barnett	146	v Hertfordshire at Slough
1957	NV Butler	132*	v Norfolk at Lakenham
	DFV Johns	103	v Oxfordshire at Cowley
	DFV Johns	122	v Hertfordshire at High Wycombe
	PLB Stoddart	100*	v Kent 2nd XI at Canterbury
1958	DFV Johns	137	v Norfolk at Lakenham
	G Reynolds	107	v Berkshire at Newbury
1959	NV Butler	121	v Norfolk at Lakenham
	PLB Stoddart	104	v Norfolk at Lakenham
	MJ Hardy	102*	v Berkshire at Reading
	G Reynolds	109	v Berkshire at High Wycombe
	G Atkins	101*	v Oxfordshire at Cowley
	LE Hitchings	108*	v Oxfordshire at Cowley
1961	G Atkins	127	v Hertfordshire at Slough
1962	DA Janes	105	v Suffolk at Ipswich
1963	G Atkins	101	v Norfolk at Slough
1964	C Lever	135*	v Hertfordshire at Tring
	DA Janes	133*	v Hertfordshire at Tring
	C Lever	158*	v Berkshire at High Wycombe
	C Lever	136*	v Berkshire at Home Park, Windsor
	LE Hitchings	100*	v Oxfordshire at Ernest Turner's Ground, High Wycombe
1965	C Lever	123*	v Oxfordshire at Chesham
	NV Butler	118*	v Berkshire at High Wycombe
1966	G Atkins	101	v Oxfordshire at Ernest Turner's Ground, High Wycombe
1967	C Lever	112*	v Suffolk at Ascott Park
1969	JB Turner	105*	v Hertfordshire at Chesham
1970	RW Hooker	112*	v Norfolk at Beaconsfield
1971	RW Hooker	125	v Suffolk at Buckingham
	JB Turner	104*	v Norfolk at Lakenham
1972	DA Janes	100*	v Norfolk at Lakenham
1974	RW Hutchison	102*	v Berkshire at Reading
	GA Jones	105	v Bedfordshire at Amersham
	RW Hooker	110	v Suffolk at High Wycombe
1975	SE York	118*	v Hertfordshire at Hertford
	C Lever	106*	v Hertfordshire at Hertford
	GA Jones	114	v Norfolk at Lakenham
1979	RE Hayward	108*	v Berkshire at Reading
	JB Turner	116	v Bedfordshire at Henlow
	ME Milton	106*	v Norfolk at Lakenham
1980	RG Humphrey	106	v Hertfordshire at Hertford
	JB Turner	117	v Suffolk at Chesham

1981	ME Milton	120*	v Berkshire at Slough
	DE Smith	101*	v Oxfordshire at Marlow
1982	ME Milton	128*	v Berkshire at Finchampstead
	P Dolphin	100	v Suffolk at Ipswich
	DE Smith	108*	v Suffolk at Ipswich
	PGC Harvey	102	v Suffolk at Chesham
	KI Hodgson	109	v Hertfordshire at High Wycombe
	ME Milton	108*	v Hertfordshire at High Wycombe
1983	ME Milton	109*	v Somerset 2nd XI at Taunton
	RE Hayward	101	v Somerset 2nd XI at Taunton
	RE Hayward	108*	v Dorset at Bournemouth
	ME Milton	128*	v Devon at Torquay
	RG Humphrey	129	v Cheshire at Buckingham
1984	RE Hayward	102*	v Cornwall at High Wycombe
1986	PD Atkins	160*	v Shropshire at Bridgnorth
	AR Harwood	127*	v Cornwall at High Wycombe
1988	AR Harwood	142*	v Dorset at High Wycombe
	MJ Roberts	155*	v Cornwall at Marlow
1989	MJ Roberts	121	v Wales MC at Ammanford
	MJ Roberts	103	v Cornwall at Falmouth
	MJ Roberts	149*	v Devon at Exmouth
	RE Hayward	144*	v Cheshire at Slough
	RE Hayward	101	v Shropshire at Marlow
	S Burrow	100*	v Shropshire at Marlow
	MJ Roberts	193*	v Wiltshire at Amersham
1990	MJ Roberts	106*	v Cheshire at Warrington
	MJ Roberts	124	v Wiltshire at Marlborough College
1991	BS Percy	123	v Cheshire at Slough
	MJ Roberts	111	v Devon at Sidmouth
	MJ Roberts	131	v Wiltshire at Amersham
1993	MJ Roberts	112*	v Lincolnshire at Stamford
	GDT Paskins	111	v Cumberland at Marlow
	JC Harrison	111*	v Cambridgeshire at Slough
1994	BS Percy	105	v Cumberland at Penrith
	MJ Roberts	111*	v Norfolk at Marlow
	RR Baigent	100	v Suffolk at Beaconsfield
1995	MJ Roberts	140	v Northumberland at Beaconsfield
1996	MJ Roberts	177*	v Northumberland at Jesmond
	MJ Roberts	101*	v Northumberland at Jesmond
	MJ Roberts	119*	v Hertfordshire at Shenley Park
	ND Burns	100*	v Hertfordshire at Shenley Park
	RB Hurd	105*	v Cambridgeshire at Kimbolton School
1997	ND Burns	178	v Staffordshire at Beaconsfield
	JC Harrison	107	v Cambridgeshire at Slough
1998	JC Harrison	147	v Norfolk at Slough
	PR Sawyer	181	v Norfolk at Slough
	ND Burns	140*	v Hertfordshire at Long Marston
1999	ND Burns	152*	v Bedfordshire at Luton
	ND Burns	138*	v Norfolk at Lakenham
2000	BS Percy	106	v Suffolk at Milton Keynes
	PD Atkins	102*	v Suffolk at Milton Keynes
2001	DR Drepaul	135	v Cumberland at Beaconsfield
	GDT Paskins	122	v Cumberland at Beaconsfield
2002	PD Atkins	113*	v Cumberland at Barrow
2003	MJ Eyles	126	v Bedfordshire at Ascott Park
	DJ Barr	103	v Bedfordshire at Ascott Park

2004	RP Lane	112	v Cumberland at Gerrards Cross
	KT Medlycott	111	v Northumberland at Beaconsfield
	ZA Sher	108*	v Bedfordshire at Luton
2005	RP Lane	106	v Staffordshire at Beaconsfield
	ZA Sher	200	v Cambridgeshire at Gerrards Cross
	KT Medlycott	136	v Lincolnshire at Grantham
	MJ Eyles	119	v Norfolk at Slough

Seven or More Wickets in a Championship Innings

1895	G Nash	7-42	v Oxfordshire at Thame
	G Nash	7-57	v Bedfordshire at High Wycombe
	G Nash	8-33	v Bedfordshire at High Wycombe
1896	G Nash	7-64	v Northants at Aylesbury
	G Nash	7-36	v Northants at Aylesbury
	G Nash	7-54	v Oxfordshire at Banbury
	G Nash	7-65	v Northants at Northampton
1897	G Nash	8-46	v Oxfordshire at Thame
	G Nash	8-28	v Oxfordshire at Thame
1898	MW Wright	8-47	v Berkshire at Reading
1900	JW Stratton	7-54	v Hertfordshire at Aylesbury
	MW Wright	7-21	v Oxfordshire at Aylesbury
1901	MW Wright	7-91	v Berkshire at Reading
1902	MW Wright	7-38	v Berkshire at Aylesbury
1904	MW Wright	8-59	v Wiltshire at Chippenham
	MW Wright	7-68	v Hertfordshire at Aylesbury
	MW Wright	8-75	v Berkshire at Slough
	MW Wright	8-30	v Norfolk at Lakenham
1905	MW Wright	8-36	v Hertfordshire at Ascott Park
	SJA Vickerstaff	7-86	v Bedfordshire at Bedford
1907	GA Wilson	8-125	v Surrey at Wolverton
1908	MW Wright	8-45	v Surrey 2nd XI at Aylesbury
	GA Wilson	8-109	v Dorset at Slough
1909	SJA Vickerstaff	8-54	v Berkshire at Aylesbury
1910	MW Wright	7-120	v Berkshire at Aylesbury
1911	MW Wright	8-27	v Carmarthenshire at Llanelly
1912	EHD Sewell	7-80	v Bedfordshire at Bedford
1913	WE Hazelton	7-77	v Berkshire at Marlow
1920	JBE Whiting	8-23	v Wiltshire at Bletchley Park
	WE Hazelton	8-32	v Bedfordshire at Wolverton
	JBE Whiting	7-42	v Wiltshire at Trowbridge
	JBE Whiting	7-39	v Berkshire at Slough
1921	F Edwards	8-60	v Bedfordshire at Wolverton
1922	F Edwards	7-40	v Hertfordshire at Bletchley Park
	F Edwards	7-26	v Hertfordshire at Bletchley Park
	F Edwards	7-52	v Oxfordshire at Blenheim Park
1923	F Edwards	8-18	v Cambridgeshire at Bletchley Park
	F Edwards	9-80	v Bedfordshire at Bedford
	F Edwards	8-41	v Cambridgeshire at Fenner's
	WE Hazelton	7-53	v Oxford at Trinity College, Oxford
1924	F Edwards	7-46	v Surrey 2nd XI at The Oval
	AU Payne	7-41	v Hertfordshire at Bletchley Park
	F Edwards	8-60	v Bedfordshire at Ascott Park

1925	F Edwards	7-8	v Kent 2nd XI at Bletchley Park
	F Edwards	8-15	v Oxfordshire at Oxford
	F Edwards	8-13	v Oxfordshire at High Wycombe
	WT Brindley	7-20	v Kent 2nd XI at Bickley Park
1926	F Edwards	7-17	v Lincolnshire at Frodingham
	F Edwards	7-28	v Lincolnshire at High Wycombe
	F Edwards	7-36	v Surrey 2nd XI at High Wycombe
1927	F Edwards	7-25	v Kent 2nd XI at Bletchley Park
	H Pitchford	7-45	v Hertfordshire at Ascott Park
1928	F Edwards	7-41	v Kent 2nd XI at Folkestone
1929	F Edwards	7-91	v Hertfordshire at High Wycombe
	F Edwards	7-22	v Hertfordshire at Broxbourne
1930	F Edwards	7-74	v Bedfordshire at Bedford
	F Edwards	9-29	v Oxfordshire at Oxford
	F Edwards	8-13	v Kent 2nd XI at High Wycombe
	F Edwards	7-31	v Kent 2nd XI at High Wycombe
1932	F Edwards	7-33	v Hertfordshire at St Albans
	F Edwards	7-52	v Hertfordshire at High Wycombe
	RH Rutter	7-22	v Norfolk at Lakenham
1933	RH Rutter	7-44	v Bedfordshire at Bletchley Park
	F Edwards	8-55	v Bedfordshire at Bedford
	RH Rutter	7-57	v Oxfordshire at High Wycombe
1934	AJ Birtwell	7-98	v Bedfordshire at Bedford
1935	F Edwards	8-42	v Oxfordshire at Oxford
1937	VE Lund	7-9	v Lincolnshire at Grantham
1938	CH Boddy	7-22	v Berkshire at Reading
	OG Battcock	7-20	v Bedfordshire at Bedford
1939	RH Rutter	7-55	v Berkshire at Reading
	VE Lund	7-24	v Norfolk at Ascott Park
1946	VE Lund	7-34	v Berkshire at Reading
	VE Lund	7-9	v Bedfordshire at High Wycombe
	OG Battcock	7-37	v Suffolk at High Wycombe
1948	OG Battcock	9-63	v Bedfordshire at Bedford
	OG Battcock	7-47	v Hertfordshire at Stevenage
	SJ Cook	7-63	v Norfolk at Slough
1949	OG Battcock	7-51	v Berkshire at Reading
	AJ Hughes	7-14	v Hertfordshire at St Albans
	AJ Hughes	7-44	v Norfolk at Lakenham
1951	AJ Hughes	7-65	v Norfolk at Lakenham
	OG Battcock	7-23	v Berkshire at Aspro Sports Ground, Slough
	AJ Hughes	7-40	v Oxfordshire at Chesham
1953	AJ Hughes	8-49	v Oxfordshire at Slough
	AJ Hughes	7-62	v Hertfordshire at Chesham
1955	AJ Hughes	7-30	v Hertfordshire at Slough
1957	AJ Hughes	7-50	v Norfolk at Ascott Park
1960	JWC Mills	8-22	v Hertfordshire at Watford
1961	EC Clifford	7-49	v Norfolk at High Wycombe
1962	DFV Johns	7-48	v Berkshire at Newbury
	VHD Cannings	7-54	v Suffolk at Chesham
	VHD Cannings	8-25	v Oxfordshire at Morris Motors Ground, Oxford
1963	CW Smith	7-18	v Norfolk at Slough
1967	FW Harris	7-79	v Hertfordshire at Chesham
1968	RE Bond	7-54	v Oxfordshire at Buckingham
	RH Huntley	8-50	v Hertfordshire at Letchworth
1969	C Lever	7-30	v Norfolk at Lakenham
	RH Huntley	7-32	v Norfolk at Lakenham
1970	CJ Parry	7-57	v Berkshire at Chesham

1971	RE Bond	7-84	v Suffolk at Buckingham
	CJ Parry	7-98	v Norfolk at Lakenham
1973	ND Rogers	9-50	v Berkshire at Bray
1974	RE Bond	8-34	v Berkshire at Reading
	RW Hutchison	7-45	v Berkshire at Ascott Park
1975	RW Hutchison	7-55	v Hertfordshire at High Wycombe
1977	RE Bond	8-36	v Norfolk at Amersham
1980	SA Mehar	7-17	v Hertfordshire at High Wycombe
1984	S Burrow	7-55	v Shropshire at Bridgnorth
1985	HL Alleyne	7-61	v Wiltshire at High Wycombe
	GR Black	8-47	v Wiltshire at High Wycombe
1986	SJ Edwatds	8-60	v Shropshire at Bridgnorth
	CD Booden	7-19	v Devon at Marlow
1988	CD Booden	7-17	v Wales MC at Bletchley
	TJA Scriven	7-68	v Wiltshire at Devizes
1994	AR Clarke	8-68	v Cambridgeshire at Fenner's
1995	AR Clarke	7-80	v Suffolk at Bury St Edmunds
1997	AR Clarke	8-60	v Lincolnshire at Bourne
	AW Thomas	8-83	v Suffolk at Ipswich
	AR Clarke	8-94	v Norfolk at Lakenham
1999	AR Clarke	7-66	v Northumberland at Beaconsfield
2000	SP Naylor	7-22	v Hertfordshire at Bishops Stortford
2005	JJ Newell	7-99	v Norfolk at Slough

Ten or More Wickets in a Championship Match

1895	G Nash	12-95	v Oxfordshire at Thame
	MW Wright	10-52	v Oxfordshire at Wolverton
	G Nash	11-118	v Bedfordshire at Leighton Buzzard
	G Nash	15-90	v Bedfordshire at High Wycombe
1896	G Nash	14-100	v Northants at Aylesbury
	G Nash	11-108	v Oxfordshire at Aylesbury
	G Nash	12-102	v Oxfordshire at Banbury
1897	G Nash	10-116	v Worcestershire at Aylesbury
	G Nash	10-71	v Oxfordshire at Aylesbury
	MW Wright	10-58	v Hertfordshire at Aylesbury
	MW Wright	10-89	v Berkshire at Aylesbury
	G Nash	16-74	v Oxfordshire at Thame
1898	MW Wright	14-116	v Berkshire at Reading
1900	MW Wright	11-105	v Wiltshire at Bletchley Park
	G Nash	12-68	v Berkshire at Aylesbury
	MW Wright	11-75	v Oxfordshire at Aylesbury
1901	MW Wright	10-108	v Berkshire at Aylesbury
	Houchin	10-56	v Norfolk at Lakenham
1902	MW Wright	11-84	v Wiltshire at Bletchley Park
	G Nash	11-45	v Bedfordshire at Aylesbury
	G Nash	10-116	v Hertfordshire at Aylesbury
	MW Wright	10-59	v Berkshire at Aylesbury
1903	MW Wright	11-40	v Bedfordshire at Aylesbury
	MW Wright	10-51	v Hertfordshire at Aylesbury
1904	MW Wright	13-109	v Wiltshire at Chippenham
	MW Wright	11-123	v Berkshire at Slough
	MW Wright	13-67	v Norfolk at Lakenham
1905	MW Wright	11-71	v Hertfordshire at Ascott Park
1906	MW Wright	11-140	v Berkshire at High Wycombe

1907	GA Wilson	12-78	v Berkshire at Aylesbury
	GA Wilson	11-88	v Worcestershire 2nd XI at Chesham
	GA Wilson	13-202	v Surrey 2nd XI at Wolverton
1908	GA Wilson	15-244	v Dorset at Slough
1911	MW Wright	10-103	v Carmarthenshire at Llanelly
1912	EHD Sewell	12-169	v Bedfordshire at Bedford
	EHD Sewell	10-175	v Berkshire at Reading
	MW Wright	11-66	v Wiltshire at Melksham
1913	WE Hazelton	12-140	v Berkshire at Marlow
1920	WE Hazelton	13-97	v Bedfordshire at Wolverton
	WE Hazelton	10-67	v Bedfordshire at Bedford
1922	F Edwards	14-66	v Hertfordshire at Bletchley Park
	F Edwards	12-73	v Oxfordshire at Blenheim Park
	F Edwards	10-83	v Oxfordshire at High Wycombe
	F Edwards	12-79	v Bedfordshire at High Wycombe
	F Edwards	11-114	v Norfolk at Lakenham
1923	F Edwards	11-48	v Bedfordshire at Bletchley Park
	F Edwards	14-38	v Cambridgeshire at Bletchley Park
	F Edwards	13-138	v Oxfordshire at High Wycombe
	F Edwards	15-196	v Bedfordshire at Bedford
	F Edwards	14-143	v Cambridgeshire at Fenner's
	WE Hazelton	11-125	v Hertfordshire at Watford
	WE Hazelton	11-112	v Oxfordshire at Trinity College Ground, Oxford
1924	F Edwards	11-28	v Leicestershire 2nd XI at Hinckley
	F Edwards	11-51	v Bedfordshire at Bedford
	F Edwards	13-132	v Bedfordshire at Ascott Park
1925	F Edwards	12-23	v Kent 2nd XI at Bletchley Park
	F Edwards	14-41	v Oxfordshire at Oxford
	WT Brindley	12-85	v Kent 2nd XI at Bickley Park
	F Edwards	13-24	v Oxfordshire at High Wycombe
	F Edwards	10-64	v Northumberland at Jesmond
1926	F Edwards	13-50	v Lincolnshire at Frodingham
	F Edwards	10-137	v Hertfordshire at Watford
	F Edwards	10-49	v Lincolnshire at High Wycombe
	F Edwards	11-80	v Surrey 2nd XI at High Wycombe
1927	F Edwards	12-50	v Kent 2nd XI at Bletchley Park
	F Edwards	12-68	v Norfolk at High Wycombe
1928	F Edwards	11-61	v Kent 2nd XI at Folkestone
	F Edwards	10-60	v Kent 2nd XI at Bletchley Park
1929	F Edwards	13-91	v Hertfordshire at Broxbourne
1930	F Edwards	10-125	v Bedfordshire at Bedford
	F Edwards	13-69	v Oxfordshire at Oxford
	RH Rutter	12-95	v Norfolk at Ascott Park
	F Edwards	10-37	v Hertfordshire at High Wycombe
	F Edwards	15-44	v Kent 2nd XI at High Wycombe
1931	RH Rutter	10-52	v Norfolk at Lakenham
1932	F Edwards	13-70	v Hertfordshire at St Albans
	RH Rutter	11-63	v Bedfordshire at Bedford
	F Edwards	12-96	v Hertfordshire at High Wycombe
	RH Rutter	11-58	v Oxfordshire at Merton College Ground, Oxford
	F Edwards	11-84	v Kent 2nd XI at Tunbridge Wells
1933	RH Rutter	10-81	v Oxfordshire at High Wycombe
1934	AJ Birtwell	12-113	v Bedfordshire at Bedford
1935	F Edwards	12-92	v Oxfordshire at Oxford
	F Edwards	10-123	v Norfolk at High Wycombe

1937	VE Lund	12-76	v Lincolnshire at Grantham
	VE Lund	10-101	v Norfolk at High Wycombe
1938	CH Boddy	12-57	v Berkshire at Reading
	OG Battcock	12-75	v Bedfordshire at Bedford
	OG Battcock	12-65	v Lancashire 2nd XI at High Wycombe
1939	RH Rutter	13-78	v Berkshire at Reading
	VE Lund	10-76	v Norfolk at Ascott Park
1946	J O'Connor	11-55	v Hertfordshire at Slough
	OG Battcock	11-85	v Suffolk at High Wycombe
1947	OG Battcock	12-175	v Hertfordshire at Stevenage
1948	OG Battcock	12-65	v Hertfordshire at Stevenage
	SJ Cook	11-161	v Norfolk at Slough
1949	AJ Hughes	10-36	v Hertfordshire at St Albans
1950	OG Battcock	12-70	v Oxfordshire at Witney
1951	AJ Hughes	12-124	v Norfolk at Lakenham
	AJ Hughes	13-65	v Oxfordshire at Chesham
	OG Battcock	10-47	v Norfolk at High Wycombe
1952	AJ Hughes	10-109	v Oxfordshire at Slough
1953	AJ Hughes	14-81	v Oxfordshire at Slough
1955	AJ Hughes	10-44	v Hertfordshire at Slough
1957	AJ Hughes	10-87	v Hertfordshire at Watford
	AJ Hughes	12-72	v Norfolk at Ascott Park
1962	VHD Cannings	12-64	v Oxfordshire at Morris Motors Ground, Oxford
1967	FW Harris	10-61	v Suffolk at Ipswich School
1968	RE Bond	12-85	v Oxfordshire at Buckingham
	RH Huntley	12-71	v Hertfordshire at Letchworth
1969	C Lever	11-64	v Oxfordshire at Henley
	FW Harris	10-55	v Berkshire at Boyne Hill
	AC Waite	11-115	v Suffolk at Ernest Turner's Ground, High Wycombe
	CJ Parry	10-84	v Hertfordshire at Chesham
1973	MR Sant	11-116	v Suffolk at Marlow
1974	RW Hutchison	12-64	v Berkshire at Ascott Park
1975	RW Hutchison	12-113	v Hertfordshire at High Wycombe
1977	RE Bond	13-75	v Norfolk at Amersham
	PA Gooch	11-73	v Bedfordshire at Southill Park
1978	RR Bailey	11-77	v Oxfordshire at Marlow
1979	AW Lyon	10-102	v Oxfordshire at Marlow
1980	SA Mehar	12-58	v Hertfordshire at High Wycombe
1981	AW Lyon	10-48	v Oxfordshire at Marlow
1985	GR Black	10-62	v Wiltshire at High Wycombe
1986	SJ Edwards	11-117	v Shropshire at Bridgnorth
1987	AW Lyon	10-58	v Dorset at Dorchester
1988	TJA Scriven	10-149	v Shropshire at Bridgnorth
	TJA Scriven	12-164	v Wiltshire at Devizes
1989	GR Black	10-84	v Cheshire at Slough
1991	TJA Scriven	10-137	v Wiltshire at Amersham
1994	AR Clarke	14-189	v Cambridgeshire at Fenner's
1997	AR Clarke	10-164	v Norfolk at Lakenham
1999	AR Clarke	11-163	v Northumberland at Besconsfield
	AR Clarke	10-153	v Norfolk at Lakenham
2000	SP Naylor	10-38	v Hertfordshire at Bishops Stortford
2001	AR Clarke	11-163	v Hertfordshire at Bishops Stortford

Bucks Performance in Minor Counties Knockout

English Estates Trophy
1983   beat Cornwall on toss of coin
beat Devon by three wickets
lost to Bedfordshire by 142 runs
1984   lost to Berkshire by seven wickets
1985   beat Staffordshire by 116 runs
lost to Dorset by five wickets

Minor Counties Knockout Competition
1986   beat Staffordshire by one wicket
lost to Berkshire by 5 runs
1987   beat Shropshire by three wickets
beat Berkshire by eight wickets
lost to Cheshire by two wickets

Holt Cup
1988   lost to Hertfordshire by 4 runs
1989   lost to Hertfordshire by four wickets
1990   beat Berkshire by 18 runs
beat Bedfordshire by 20 runs
beat Oxfordshire by 31 runs
beat Lincolnshire by 16 runs (final)
1991   lost to Hertfordshire by five wickets
1992   beat Berkshire by six wickets
beat Oxfordshire by seven wickets
lost to Staffordshire by 148 runs

MCC Trophy
1993   lost to Oxfordshire by five wickets
1994   beat Hertfordshire by seven wickets
beat Berkshire by 86 runs
lost to Lincolnshire by seven wickets
1995   beat Bedfordshire by six wickets
beat Cheshire by 13 runs
beat Dorset by 179 runs
lost to Cambridgeshire by 36 runs
1986   beat Devon by 20 runs
beat Cambridgeshire by 43 runs
lost to Cheshire by 23 runs
1997   lost to Northumberland by four wickets

ECB 38 County Cup with round robin
1998   beat Berkshire by 79 runs
beat Hampshire Board by one wicket
lost to Kent Board by four wickets
beat Sussex Board by four wickets
1999   lost to Berkshire by 36 runs
beat Hampshire Board by 72 runs
lost to Kent Board by six wickets
lost to Sussex Board by 29 runs
2000   lost to Kent Board by 30 runs
beat Oxfordshire by six wickets
lost to Surrey Board by six wickets

2001	lost to Kent Board by 173 runs
	beat Kent Board by 89 runs
	beat Surrey Board on faster scoring rate
	beat Oxfordshire by seven wickets
2002	lost to Northamptonshire Board by five wickets
	lost to Berkshire by two wickets

MCCA Knockout Cup

2003	beat Wiltshire by 76 runs
	lost to Shropshire by five wickets
2004	lost to Suffolk by nine wickets
2005	lost to Wiltshire by 33 runs

Bucks in Gillette Cup, NatWest Trophy and C&G Trophy

1965	(1st round, Lord's)
	Middlesex 269 (59 overs, R Gale 86, C Smith 3-32)
	Bucks 111 (38.2 overs, R Hooker 3-29, J Price 3-39)
1969	(1st round, Lord's)
	Middlesex 232-6 (60 overs, C Pickett 3-26)
	Bucks 104 (44.5 overs, F Titmus 4-17)
1970	(1st round, High Wycombe)
	Bedfordshire 102 (43.1 overs, C Pickett 4-20, C Lever 3-19)
	Bucks 105-1 (41 overs, J Turner 56)
	MOM: C Pickett (Bucks)
1970	(2nd round, Chesham)
	Hampshire 278-3 (60 overs, B Reed 143*, B Richards 69)
	Bucks 136 (58.1 overs, R Hooker 65)
1972	(1st round, Fenner's)
	Bucks 224-7 (60 overs, D Janes 95)
	Cambridgeshire 41 (20 overs, R Bond 5-17, F Harris 4-21)
	MOM: R Bond (Bucks)
1972	(2nd round, Amersham)
	Glamorgan 174 (58 overs, F Harris 4-33)
	Bucks 170-9 (60 overs, J Turner 65)
	MOM: J Turner (Bucks)
1974	(1st round, Canterbury)
	Bucks 223-5 (60 overs, J Turner 88)
	Kent 224-3 (57 overs, G Johnson 126*)
	MOM: J Turner (Bucks)
1975	(1st round, Lord's)
	Middlesex 267-4 (60 overs, M Brearley 124*)
	Bucks 168-7 (60 overs, S York 73*, P Edmonds 3-47)
1979	(1st round, High Wycombe)
	Bucks 133 (58.5 overs, P Done 3-9, C Rutterford 3-14)
	Suffolk 137-8 (38 overs, P Gooch 3-51)
1984	(1st round, Old Trafford)
	Lancashire 272-7 (60 overs, G Fowler 101, A Lyon 3-71)
	Bucks 199-8 (60 overs, D Smith 54, P Allott 4-34)
1985	(1st round, Taunton)
	Bucks 138 (47.4 overs, J Garner 5-18)
	Somerset 139-3 (41.3 overs, N Felton 72*)
1987	(1st round, High Wycombe)
	Bucks 154 (59.5 overs)
	Somerset 147 (59.3 overs, S Burrow 3-32)
	MOM: S Edwards (Bucks)
1987	(2nd round, Edgbaston)
	Warwicks 329-5 (60 overs, A Moles 127, A Lloyd 61)
	Bucks 128 (41.4 overs, A Harwood 57, N Gifford 4-9, A Donald 3-27)
1988	(1st round, Canterbury)
	Bucks 113 (56 overs, R Pienaar 3-19, R Davis 3-19)
	Kent 115-2 (40.2 overs, S Hinks 64*)
1990	(1st round (Marlow)
	Notts 312-9 (60 overs, C Broad 115, T Barry 3-49)
	Bucks 120 (40.3 overs, K Cooper 3-16, A Pick 3-22, E Hemmings 3-42)
1991	(1st round, Bath)
	Bucks 159-8 (60 overs, N Mallender 3-23)
	Somerset 161-4 (48.4 overs, P Roebuck 63*)

1992	(1st round, Beaconsfield)
	Sussex 327-6 (60 overs, A Wells 119, D Smith 62, G Black 3-83)
	Bucks 126 (51 overs, F Stephenson 3-8, I Salisbury 3-28)
1993	(1st round, Marlow)
	Leics 289-9 (60 overs, T Boon 117)
	Bucks 214-8 (60 overs, M Roberts 54)
1997	(1st round, Beaconsfield)
	Essex 327-7 (60 overs, N Hussain 78, R Rollins 67*, P Prichard 58,
	K Arthurton 4-53)
	Bucks 238-7 (60 overs, N Burns 51, P Grayson 3-40)
1998	(1st round, The Oval)
	Surrey 315-9 (60 overs, A Stewart 97, J Radcliffe 71, T Scriven 3-61,
	J Bovill 3-64)
	Bucks 183 (43.3 overs, A Tudor 4-39, N Shahid 3-30)
1999	(2nd round, Sheffield)
	Yorkshire Board 91 (40.5 overs)
	Bucks 92-3 (20.4 overs)
	MOM: J Bovill (Bucks)
1999	(3rd round, Marlow)
	Warwicks 249-7 (50 overs, D Hemp 110*)
	Bucks 136 (E Giddins 3-31)
2000	(1st round, Pontarddulais)
	Wales MC 212-6 (50 overs, P Simmons 82, K Arthurton 3-46)
	Bucks 201-9 (50 overs)
2001	(2nd round, Maidstone)
	Bucks 221-7 (50 overs, M Richardson 62, R Lane 55)
	Kent Board 222-5 (49 overs, J Tredwell 71, J Bowden 60)
2002	(1st round, Dinton)
	Bucks 224-7 (50 overs)
	Worcestershire Board 185 (47 overs, J Batty 3-51)
	MOM: J Batty (Bucks)
2002	(2nd round, Beaconsfield)
	Bucks 187 (47.3 overs, P Atkins 50, M North 4-26)
	Durham Board 166 (46.1 overs, Z Sher 3-23, A Thomas 3-47)
	MOM: P Atkins (Bucks)
2002	(3rd round, Beaconsfield)
	Sussex 268-6 (50 overs, T Ambrose 95, B Zuiderent 50, Z Sher 3-56)
	Bucks 143-7 (50 overs, Z Sher 55*, W Taylor 3-23)
2003	(1st round, Dinton)
	Bucks 424-5 (60 overs, D Taylor 140, P Atkins 110, P Sawyer 50)
	Suffolk 194 (40 overs, R Catley 65, A Mawson 65, A Clarke 5-36,
	Z Sher 3-50)
	MOM: D Taylor (Bucks)
2003	(2nd round, Beaconsfield)
	Bucks 160 (40.5 overs)
	Shropshire 149 (48.5 overs, A Clarke 4-28, A Saleem 3-24)
	MOM: J Batty (Bucks)
2003	(3rd round, Ascott Park, Wing)
	Gloucs 401-7 (50 overs, T Hancock 135, J Rhodes 87, C Spearman 76)
	Bucks 77 (25.1 overs, J Averis 6-23)
2004	(1st round, Bournemouth)
	Bucks 272-6 (48 overs, R Lane 95, H Marshall 66*, D Barr 51)
	Dorset
	Match abandoned - Dorset won bowl-out 4-1
2005	(1st round, Wormsley)
	Lancashire 370-4 (50 overs, A Crook 162*, M Loye 66, G Chapple 55*)
	Bucks 39-2 (10.3 overs)
	Lancashire won by 51 runs (Duckworth/Lewis)

One-Day Records

Note that these records include performances in the Minor Counties Knockout tournaments as well as the Gillette Cup, NatWest Trophy and C&G Trophy.

Centuries
140	DK Taylor	v Suffolk at Dinton	2002
129	ND Burns	v Cambridgeshire at Saffron Walden	1986
126	MJ Roberts	v Northumberland at Jesmond	1997
119*	JC Harrison	v Northumberland at Jesmond	1997
111*	AR Harwood	v Staffordshire at Stoke-on-Trent	1985
111	S Burrow	v Staffordshire at Stoke-on-Trent	1985
110	PD Atkins	v Suffolk at Dinton	2002
109	ND Burns	v Kent Cricket Board at Ashford	1998
103	PD Atkins	v Wiltshire at Chippenham	2003

Most career runs
1421	PD Atkins
882	AR Harwood
831	S Burrow
763	RP Lane
756	MJ Roberts

Most wickets in an innings
6-2	AP Cole	v Sussex Cricket Board at Milton Keynes	1998
6-24	JC Harrison	v Hampshire Cricket Board at Burridge	1998
5-17	RE Bond	v Cambridgeshire at Fenner's	1972
5-31	JNB Bovill	v Berkshire at Wing	1998
5-36	AR Clarke	v Suffolk at Dinton	2002

Most career wickets
46	TJA Scriven
41	S Burrow
40	AR Clarke
32	GR Black
31	SF Stanway

BUCKS CCC CHAMPIONSHIP CAREER RECORDS (1895-2005)

	Career	M	I	NO	Runs	HS	Avge	100	50	O	M	R	W	Avge	5i	10m	BB	Ct	St
Adams F	1920	1	1	0	9	9	9.00											3	
Adams W	1912-14	6	9	1	130	61*	16.25		1									2	
Ainge L	1980	6	9	1	123	36	15.38											1	
Alam T	1996	3	4	1	26	10*	8.67											0	
Alison CH	1911-12	5	9	0	69	21	7.67			3.0	0	21	0					0	
Allcock CH	1895-98	24	37	7	418	39	13.93			398.3	136	815	57	14.30	4		6/42	11	
Alleyne HL	1984-85	8	9	3	60	27*	10.00			230.5	51	593	29	20.45	1		7/67	3	
Amin N	2002	1	2	0	1	1	0.50											1	
Ashton FW	1907	1	2	0	0	0	0.00											0	
Ashton PDM	1977-86	21	39	1	617	76	16.24		3									7	
Astor JJ	1904-06	9	17	1	343	61	21.44		2									12	
Atkins G	1957-72	107	194	26	4689	127	27.91	4	24	83	8	339	9	37.67			1/4	45	
Atkins JD	1985	2	3	0	18	9	6.00			8.1	0	86	0					1	
Atkins PD	1985-	73	119	27	3750	160*	40.76	3	26									55	
Aubrey-Fletcher HL	1921-28	49	70	14	1083	97	19.34		3	594.3	158	1394	81	17.21	2		5/26	28	
Aubrey-Fletcher JHL	1931-48	62	93	9	1698	112	20.21	2	5	499.1	103	1573	80	19.66	1		6/23	48	
Austin H	1898-1902	3	4	1	14	5	4.67			11	1	42	1	42.00			1/42	2	
Avery RD	1950-63	27	28	7	129	14	6.14			589.3	156	1586	70	22.66	3		6/26	18	
Avery RJ	1971-72	6	1	1	0	0*				94	34	246	18	13.67			4/36	0	
Ayres AR	1909	2	3	1	9	6	4.50											2	
Ayres S	2003	1	2	0	50	43	25.00											2	
Badham PHC	1933-34	16	22	2	259	56	12.33		1	249.5	61	706	27	26.15	1		5/28	3	
Baggaley JW	1901-09	2	3	0	6	1	2.00											0	2
Baig MN	1999-2001	3	4	1	25	23	8.33			15	6	36	1	36.00			1/14	0	
Baigent RR	1989-95	22	41	3	1061	100	27.92	1	7	0.2	0	2	0					8	
Bailey RR	1975-80	46	52	14	575	40	15.13			1142	327	2875	143	20.10	5	1	6/26	12	
Baines Rev AGP	1907	1	2	0	16	16	8.00			74	19	277	13	21.31	1		5/98	0	
Baker H	1905-11	9	16	2	117	32	8.36			28.3	7	83	1	83.00			1/38	7	
Baker KB	1970	4	5	2	38	31	12.67			0.3	0	3	1	3.00			1/3	5	
Baker LG	1924-47	114	172	14	3744	131*	23.70	4	17	287.4	78	658	36	18.28	3		6/34	71	
Baker RF	1947-49	14	22	2	417	71	20.85		2									11	

	Career	M	I	NO	Runs	HS	Avge	100	50	O	M	R	W	Avge	5i	10m	BB	Ct	St
Baker RIH	1948	1	2	0	23	21	11.50											0	
Ball D	1954	3	2	0	1	1	0.50											3	
Bandy H	1901	1	2	0	0	0	0.00											0	57
Barnett BA	1951-64	80	125	15	3222	146	29.29	5	17	46	10	141	8	17.63			4/52	103	
Barnett EE	1913	1	2	0	10	6	5.00			2	0	14	0					0	
Barr DJ	2003-	11	19	2	795	103*	46.76	1	7									1	
Barry TJ	1985-94	40	54	16	700	63*	18.42		1	691.3	109	2610	67	38.96			4/26	10	
Bartlett ENN	1896-1901	14	18	3	157	50	10.47		1									8	
Barton HGM	1907	3	5	0	39	17	7.80											0	
Batt CJ	2005-	4	4	1	23	19*	7.67											0	
Battcock OG	1925-51	114	143	23	1887	79*	15.73		4	107	21	339	17	19.94	1		5/45	52	
Batty JD	2000-02	12	17	2	263	43	17.53			2829.2	1034	5701	379	15.04	26	7	9/63	7	
Beard JS	1923-26	2	3	1	45	21	15.00			311.2	69	984	25	39.36	1		5/69	0	
Beck SM	1998	1	1	0	0	0	0.00											0	
Beeson E	1931-37	4	5	0	33	17	6.60											1	
Bellew SD	1995	2								16	0	82	1	82.00			1/26	0	
Benning DHE	1976	8	16	0	453	72	28.31		2	3	0	10	1	10.00			1/10	2	
Benning JGE	2000	5	7	2	158	53	31.60		1									0	
Biedermann H	1913	1	1	0	0	0	0.00											0	
Bielby SR	1965	6	8	1	143	50	20.43		1	69	17	210	4	52.50			2/19	5	
Bilbey BE	1970-71	4	3	2	11	6*	11.00			70	15	251	5	50.20			3/62	0	
Bird FN	1896-1907	49	80	5	2043	133	27.24	2	11	4	0	19	0					35	
Bird HJ	1896-1901	11	16	3	164	50*	12.62		1	10	1	60	1	60.00			1/60	4	
Bird S	1895	2	4	0	70	24	17.50											2	
Bird SF	2003	1	2	0	2	2	1.00											0	
Bird SJ	2001	1	2	0	18	18	9.00											1	
Birrell JJ	1949	9	14	1	123	18	9.46			111	18	401	15	26.73			4/57	15	
Birtwell AJ	1934-36	23	30	8	311	67	14.14		2	371.2	71	1169	56	20.88	4	1	7/98	11	
Bishton SW	1956-58	5	6	0	23	7	3.83			42.4	9	112	7	16.00			3/37	0	
Black GR	1984-93	66	104	17	1651	91	18.98		8	824.2	174	2654	114	23.28	6	2	8/47	49	
Blair MW	1980-81	4	4	2	7	5	3.50			85	20	233	5	46.60			1/19	0	
Blake PR	1922	5	7	1	31	15	5.17			20	3	57	0					1	
Blanchett B	1900-01	1	8	1	69	15	9.86											2	
Blanchett WH	1898	1	1	0	0	0	0.00											0	
Blumire MA	1963	7	12	2	190	42	19.00			17	2	55	0					1	
Boddington JR	2004	1	2	0	39	29	19.50											3	
Boddy CH	1937-39	3	4	0	61	45	15.25			35.2	14	67	13	5.15	2	1	7/22	1	

	Career	M	I	NO	Runs	HS	Avge	100	50	O	M	R	W	Avge	5i	10m	BB	Ct	St
Boddy ES	1898-1910	33	61	2	960	113	16.27	1	2	146	39	369	16	23.06			4/76	17	
Boddy GH	1900-1910	10	15	1	277	52	19.79		1	95.3	8	399	16	24.94	1		6/35	4	
Bond RE	1965-79	72	60	22	329	37*	8.66			1863.3	494	4836	266	18.18	12	2	8/34	30	
Booden CD	1983-94	66	39	22	158	25*	9.29			1357.1	296	4027	124	32.48	4		7/17	35	
Bousfield DG	1947-49	18	30	4	970	129	37.31	1	8	23.5	2	109	2	54.50			1/9	9	
Bovill JNB	1990-2000	19	24	10	194	31	13.86			386.2	76	1209	57	21.21	3		6/38	7	
Bowen JF	1906-07	2	3	0	27	14	9.00											4	
Bowyer GEW	1905	3	6	2	35	11	8.75											1	
Bowyer IJ	1999-2000	5	6	2	143	64*	35.75		1									4	
Bowyer MJ	1996-2003	12	24	1	568	96	24.70		4	5	1	12	0					7	
Bradby GVH	1969-70	11	21	0	361	83	17.19		2	44	16	97	6	16.17			3/1	8	
Bradshaw WH	1948	4	5	1	50	20	12.50			77.3	18	177	8	22.13	1		5/25	1	
Bramwell M	1931-33	2	2	0	49	31	24.50											0	
Brand HG	1922	1	1	0	0	0	0.00												
Brandom SJ	2001-03	11	16	4	178	35	14.83			133.2	23	514	10	51.40			2/43	4	
Bray RWA	1965-75	22	39	4	794	75	22.69		5	17	3	75	4	18.75			2/26	26	
Briggs Rev CE	1909	1	2	1	5	3	2.50			12	2	38	1	38.00			1/38	1	
Brill HP	1904-05	2	3	0	5	3	1.67											1	
Brindley WT	1925-35	26	39	2	811	60	21.92		5	394.2	113	932	53	17.58	3	1	7/20	22	
Britnell ET	1928	1	1	0	9	9	9.00											1	
Brocklehurst ET	1906-21	6	11	0	98	26	8.91											1	
Brocklehurst TM	1913	2	4	0	24	8	6.00			13	4	46	4	11.50			3/14	6	
Brooke RHJ	1929-35	51	80	6	2471	164*	33.39	3	14	63	9	214	7	30.57			3/31	28	
Brooks LR	2003	2	3	0	8	7	2.67			1	0	6	0					1	
Brooks TA	2001-	7	9	2	216	48*	30.86			13.5	0	74	0					2	
Broughton-Adderley PP	1911	1	1	0	0	0	0.00											0	
Brown WJ	1904-11	2	4	1	11	5*	3.67											1	
Buchanan AG	1936	2	4	1	21	14	7.00			2.4	1	13	1	13.00			1/8	2	
Buchanan JN	1925-27	8	9	1	185	58	23.13		1	8	3	17	1	17.00			1/17	13	
Bull HE	1901-11	13	19	3	204	48	12.75			13	0	93	1	93.00			1/93	9	2
Bulteel W	1898-1903	2	3	0	21	10	7.00											1	
Burns ND	1995-99	39	68	12	2684	178	47.93	5	12									81	
Burroughs RJ	1994	1																0	
Burrow S	1984-96	80	136	25	3446	100*	31.05	1	21	1636.2	382	4895	195	25.10	7		7/55	44	28

	Career	M	I	NO	Runs	HS	Avge	100	50	O	M	R	W	Avge	5i	10m	BB	Ct	St
Busby AH	1934-39	29	50	6	994	67	22.59	2	8	65	10	268	5	53.60			2/41	4	
Busby TE	1936-51	40	61	8	1677	145	31.64		9	33.4	5	15	0					11	1
Butcher R	1958	3	3		3	3	1.50					151	4	37.75			2/34	1	
Butler GD	1939	1	2	1	13	9	6.50			3	1	19	1	19.00			1/19	0	
Butler KWA	1950-61	53	66	5	825	96	13.52		3	1202.1	425	2596	121	21.45	4		5/28	30	
Butler NV	1950-68	109	184	11	4735	157	27.37	6	21	469.4	130	1296	51	25.41	1		6/61	64	
Butler T	1986-90	20	39	10	738	87	25.45		3	0.4	0	4	0					4	
Byass BO	1930-32	18	26	2	355	76	14.79		1									4	
Byass CWR	1947	2	2	0	115	69	57.50		1	1	0	6	0					0	
Byass E	1931	1	1	1	1	1*												1	
Calvert EB	1934-35	4	7	0	97	36	13.86											2	
Calvert-Smith D	1964-65	7	9	3	86	19*	14.33											5	
Campbell A	1950	9	15	1	350	130	25.00	1										1	
Campbell AN	1970-72	14	23	3	386	37	19.30											1	
Campbell RT	1935-36	14	23	1	467	117	21.23	1										10	
Cannings VHD	1960-62	12	16	4	135	39	11.25			410.5	133	901	52	17.33	4	1	8/25	10	
Carlton E	1923-24	11	16	0	170	25	10.63			29	4	154	5	30.80			2/45	5	
Cassavetti AJS	1937	3	4	0	52	23	13.00											1	
Cavendish Hon CW	1898	3	5	0	134	87	26.80		1									1	
Champniss LJ	1971-77	43	53	29	299	31*	12.46			846.1	280	2176	106	20.53	2		5/14	30	
Charsley GH	1899	1	2	1	23	13	23.00											1	
Clarke AR	1994-2003	62	72	16	590	39	10.54			2254.1	505	7190	284	25.32	15	5	8/60	17	
Clements RE	1952-53	10	14	4	261	100*	26.10	1	1	3	0	11	0					6	
Clifford E	1958-62	20	32	5	331	85*	12.26		2	328.5	106	758	35	21.66	2		7/49	17	
Clover-Brown C	1926-33	10	14	1	209	83*	16.08			6	2	10	0					2	
Cobb CE	1895-1903	44	65	7	1419	111	24.47	1	7	22.4	3	78	4	19.50			3/39	78	
Cockett JA	1949-62	81	121	13	2715	109	25.14	1	15	155	27	569	20	28.45			6/77	33	49
Coghlan HG	1902	3	6	1	81	37*	16.20			174	26	674	14	48.14			4/39	1	
Cole AP	1998-99	14	15	2	194	52	14.92		1									12	
Coles JM	1982-84	11	10	5	12	9*	2.40											3	
Connor CA	1979-83	32	23	6	137	45	8.06			711.2	138	2205	77	28.64			4/40	12	
Cook SJ	1948	3	4	4	12	11*				93.4	15	257	17	15.12	1	1	7/63	1	
Cooper D	1947	1	2	2	22	14*												0	
Cooper PA	1984-86	6	11	2	176	28	19.56			1	0	7	0					1	1

	Career	M	I	NO	Runs	HS	Avge	100	50	O	M	R	W	Avge	5i	10m	BB	Ct	St
Cooper W	1904	1	1	0	0	0	0.00			2	0	15	0					1	
Cordaroy TM	1977-79	22	42	4	1156	86	30.42		7	4	0	32	0					18	
Cox MJJ	1982-83	5	10	2	211	48	26.38			3	1	8	0					4	
Coxon AJ	1978	1	1	1	11*	11*				17	3	66	1	66.00			1/38	0	
Cranfield-Thompson DRJ	2005																		
Crawley AM	1948	1	2	0	89	55	44.50		1	1	0	13	0					1	
Cudd RL	1963	4	7	0	100	50	14.29		1	6	3	14	0					0	
Curzon-Tompson RJ	2003-04	2	1	1	4	4				20	3	53	2	26.50			2/13	0	
Dalmeny, Lord	1899-1901	7	10	1	107	40	11.89			349	106	781	33	23.67			4/22	13	
Dare R	1958-63	20	26	5	466	70*	22.19		2									21	
Davies AG	1989	1	1	0	12	12	12.00											2	
de Montmorency RH	1907-09	3	6	0	258	90	43.00		1	15	1	80	0					0	
de Paravicini PC	1902-03	12	20	4	167	29	10.44											15	4
de Paravicini PG	1911	1	2	1	3	3	3.00											0	
de Paravicini PJ	1895-1911	69	106	7	2560	120	25.86	3	8	39.5	9	130	5	26.00			1/1	52	
de Rothschild A	1905-14	10	12	2	240	59*	24.00		2	16	2	91	4	22.75			3/63	3	
Deacon CF	1948	4	7	0	83	37	11.86											2	
Dell RJ	1979-82	11	20	2	224	49	12.44											4	
Demery TL	1926	1	2	0	47	31	23.50											1	
Deynes CJ	1902	3	2	0	3	3	1.50											0	
Dickens E	1922	4	4	0	23	10	5.75			41	16	78	7	11.14			4/29	2	
Dickens RC	1959	4	4	1	19	14*	6.33			90	14	311	9	34.56			3/46	2	
Dobson F	1897	1	2	2	5	4*												1	
Dodgson HC	1928	1	1	0	0	0	0.00											0	3
Dolphin P	1980-1990	30	60	6	1505	100	27.87	1	6									23	
Doshi ND	2001	3	5	0	65	57	13.00		1									3	3
Drepaul DR	2001-02	10	18	3	417	135	27.80	1	1	76.4	11	285	10	28.50	1		5/86	25	
Drummond AV	1921	1	2	0	16	13	8.00											1	
Duncan AA	2004-	5	9	1	234	55	29.25		1	85.3	15	321	8	40.13			3/28	1	
Durlacher PN	1920	5	8	1	232	80	33.14		1									5	

	Career	M	I	NO	Runs	HS	Avge	100	50	O	M	R	W	Avge	5i	10m	BB	Ct	St
Dyde JA	1956	6	9	3	61	42	10.17			61	13	151	5	30.20			2/17	1	
Edmunds CC	1899-1905	24	38	5	336	56	10.18		1									9	
Edwards F	1914-46	166	201	67	1099	40	8.20			5404.4	1739	11708	1059	11.06	111	35	9/29	90	
Edwards J	1908-11	6	12	1	120	33	10.91											3	
Edwards JKS	1971-86	109	191	27	4041	95	24.64		23	58	18	165	9	18.33			4/56	49	
Edwards SJ	1985-92	32	38	10	573	68*	20.46		3	749.4	209	1997	81	24.65	1	1	8/60	17	
Ellis JCW	1899	1	1	0	0	0	0.00											1	
Emery RF	1937	2	2	2	2	1*				25	1	132	2	66.00			2/61	0	
Etheridge	1908	1	2	2	0	0*				8	0	54	0					0	
Eyles EG	1910	6	12	3	61	22	6.78											7	
Eyles MJ	1999-	21	37	1	855	126*	23.75	2	3	10	0	92	2	46.00			2/16	10	
Fairbairn SG	1913-14	7	13	3	130	22*	13.00			157.3	28	532	28	19.00	1		5/30	6	
Farnon MA	1992-94	4	4	1	48	23	16.00			23	4	98	2	49.00			1/6	0	
Farr ERR	1958-60	6	7	1	97	41	16.17											7	
Farr RP	1957-67	5	8	1	98	28*	14.00											5	2
Farrow KI	1956	3	3	2	48	24*	48.00			23	9	54	2	27.00			2/2	2	
Farrow NW	1982-93	13	20	3	324	43*	19.06			309	32	1192	38	31.37	1		6/86	4	
Faulkner GM	1903-11	24	43	5	387	54*	10.18		1									7	
Faulkner L	1923	1	2	1	4	4	4.00											2	
Fawcus EA	1925-28	20	30	5	545	78	21.80		4	57.5	15	173	11	15.73			3/6	11	
Feasey IB	1966-79	36	59	7	1146	76*	22.04		3	17.2	4	45	2	16.50			2/28	25	
Field AJ	1972-82	16	21	8	131	28*	10.08			194	54	592	16	37.00			3/43	9	
Field DH	1912-13	7	11	1	232	103	23.20	1		94	23	243	11	22.09			4/21	5	
Finlay D	1905	1	2	0	1	1	0.50											0	
Floyd F	1948	2	3	0	53	26	17.67											1	
Flynn VAP	1980-82	9	10	5	74	34	14.80			34.2	10	108	2	54.00			2/40	8	
Ford Rev LGBJ	1898-99	7	12	0	229	59	19.08											2	3
Ford WE	1906-07	11	18	5	48	14*	3.69		1	37.0	6	135	3	45.00			3/27	8	
Franklin WB	1911-46	200	301	22	5191	138	18.61	4	18	181.4	26	725	25	29.00	1		5/62	220	222
Frith PL	1909-14	35	63	8	1126	102	20.47	1	5	0.1	0	0	0					21	1
Fryer GR	1990-91	2	3	2	13	6	13.00											2	1
Fuller RWB	1924-25	11	12	3	69	13	7.67			295.2	31	1377	46	29.93	1		5/88	1	
Furley NC	1962-64	6	11	2	132	34*	14.67											3	
Furley NCW	1964-68	8	11	2	60	19	6.67											3	
Gardiner TAM	1926-27	2	4	0	47	29	11.75											2	
Garforth WGW	1913	1	2	0	34	24	17.00											0	

Player	Career	M	I	NO	Runs	HS	Avge	100	50	O	M	R	W	Avge	5i	10m	BB	Ct	St
Gear ME	1983-84	8	16	2	517	57	36.93		5	5	3	14	0					7	
Gibbs T	1905-07	12	19	4	262	65	17.47		1	35.5	4	136	6	22.67			3/103	6	
Giddings A	1970-71	5	10	1	207	53	23.00		1									2	
Gilliatt Rev WE																			
Gillott EK	1904	1	2	0	28	26	14.00			329	108	865	41	21.10			4/34	0	
Gilson T	1976	12	13	6	91	22*	13.00			2	0	13	0					10	
Golding S	1900	1	2	0	9	5	4.50			304	44	982	35	28.06	1		5/39	1	
Goldsmith DJ	1899-1908	15	19	1	112	26	6.22			0.2	0	0	0					7	
Goldsmith M	1986-91	34	26	11	94	15	6.27			5	0	32	1	32.00			1/32	42	25
Gooch PA	2001	1	1	1	17	17*												2	
Graham KJ	1976-79	36	34	9	131	20	5.24			1060.4	250	3113	153	20.35	13	1	6/38	14	
Graham RM	1985-86	6	9	2	79	32	11.29											3	
Greaves GR	1981	5	9	1	59	17	7.38			18	1	83	1	83.00			1/35	0	
Gregory D	1899-1907	4	7	1	138	41	23.00			35.1	13	63	4	15.75			3/19	0	
Grenfell AM	1903-06	5	9	2	194	63	27.71		1									2	
Gresson CRH	1895-96	3	5	0	26	11	5.20			3	0	19	0					2	
Grout JR	1896-1907	69	116	8	2978	122*	27.57	4	16	25	6	47	1	47.00			1/8	42	2
Gurney H	1952-59	12	19	2	241	50	14.18		1									5	
Gwyn LW	1902	1	2	0	12	6	6.00											0	
Hames BA	1920	5	7	1	83	34	13.83			4	1	20	0					3	
Hames GE	1993-96	11	20	2	316	42	17.56			16	8	70	3	23.33			2/9	1	
Hames NG	1998-2000	6	9	0	178	66	19.78		1	10	2	29	1	29.00			1/23	2	
Hamilton RN	1977-93	109	197	27	3800	88	22.35		20									82	
Hankey LHA	1914-30	4	6	1	116	55	23.20		1									2	
Harben HD	1929-30	4	6	2	38	9	9.50											0	
Hardy MJ	1912	1	2	0	8	8	4.00											0	
Harris CR	1959-64	30	55	3	1040	102*	20.00	1	4	131.4	24	434	17	25.53	1		5/31	27	
Harris FW	1964-75	26	22	7	99	19	6.60			494.5	111	1476	44	33.55			3/44	8	
Harrison JC	1957-76	90	132	27	1489	61*	14.18		4	2556.5	784	6002	323	18.58	15	2	7/79	60	
Hartley CW	1991-	30	51	9	1960	147	46.67	3	12	292.1	52	951	39	24.38	3		6/63	26	
Harvey A	1954	2	3	0	26	22	8.67											1	
Harvey PGC	1957-61	4	8	2	107	33	17.83			19.5	4	70	3	23.33			2/31	2	
Harwood AR	1981-82	7	12	2	208	102	20.80	1		26.4	7	111	6	18.50			4/32	5	
Hastie JH	1983-95	65	119	6	3458	142*	30.60	2	19	202	71	387	16	24.19			3/17	20	
Hawes A	1938-54	27	35	4	865	102*	27.90	1	4									10	
Hawes NR	1955-56	2	4	0	92	47	23.00											1	
—	1933-36	2	2	1	5	3	5.00			9	4	20	0						

149

Player	Career	M	I	NO	Runs	HS	Avge	100	50	O	M	R	W	Avge	5i	10m	BB	Ct	St
Hawes RW	1975	1	2	1	7	5	7.00			4	1	21	0					0	
Hawkins CG	1955-65	10	15	3	250	62*	20.83		1									13	3
Hawkins FEJ	1958-61	8	7	3	52	16*	13.00											13	
Hawkins PM	1996	1	2	0	0	0	0.00											0	
Hayhurst A	1948-53	23	32	4	658	68	23.50		4	431.2	133	1018	50	20.36	5		5/18	16	2
Haynes NS	1995	1	2	1	4	4	4.00											2	
Hayward RE	1978-89	50	92	17	3320	144*	44.27	6	20	106	19	390	11	35.45			3/20	38	
Hazelton WE	1912-31	68	96	14	1541	124*	18.79	2	5	1925	504	4916	333	14.76	27	5	8/32	30	
Healey SG	1955	7	11	2	81	24	9.00											10	1
Hearne H	1911-12	8	12	3	86	40	9.56			112.1	18	444	14	31.71			4/?	2	
Henderson AA	1964-65	3	3	2	9	6	9.00			48	7	154	4	38.50			2/67	2	
Herrington AJ	1982-84	6	10	4	119	29*	19.83											5	
Hiatt E	1911	1	2	0	54	27	27.00											0	
Hickling TL	1969-70	12	23	4	451	61*	23.74		3	20	0	109	3	36.33			3/51	9	
Higgins-Bernard FT																			
Hill BJW	1895-99	23	33	4	315	53	10.86		1	7	0	17	0					5	
Hill PA	1946	1	1	0	0	0	0.00			14	1	78	0					0	
Hirst CH	2003	1	2	1	52	41	52.00			54	18	144	7	20.57			3/28	0	
Hitchings LE	1967-68	14	24	2	350	58	15.91		2	1	0	4	0					3	
Hobbs Dr AR	1956-68	43	77	6	1646	108*	23.18	2	11									39	2
Hobbs EC	1906-07	5	9	1	131	70	16.38		1									0	
Hodgson KI	1902-07	28	50	0	1071	84	21.42	1	7									31	3
Hogarth HG	1980-87	38	62	21	1128	109	27.51		3	601.4	117	1997	57	35.04			4/55	15	
Holbrooke Rev SWR	1908-09	5	8	0	47	17	5.88											1	
Holliman CA	1898-1905	8	13	1	80	17	6.67			46.4	7	172	4	43.00			2/41	6	
Hooker RW	1934-38	30	40	3	572	78*	15.46			226.1	14	1066	41	26.00			4/11	19	
Hopkins DC	1970-76	48	88	10	2349	125	30.12	3	11	573.3	158	1521	59	25.78			4/41	50	
Horlick OP	1982	2	2	0	10	10	5.00			49	14	142	5	28.40			4/41	0	
Houchin	1914-20	4	5	2	50	37*	16.67			13	0	65	1	65.00			1/13	4	
House P	1901-02	5	7	1	40	20	6.67			154	52	314	20	15.70	2	1	6/30	6	
Hubbick WE	1958	4	4	1	41	37*	13.67			80	23	195	7	27.86			3/62	1	
Hudson GD	1986	2	4	1	86	27	28.67		1										
Hughes AJ	1964-75	14	21	6	218	52*	14.53											24	2
Hughes RJA	1948-58	89	91	38	446	27	8.42			2749.5	756	5966	391	15.26	31	8	8/49	51	
Hume	1966	4	5	2	37	15	12.33											3	
Humphrey RG	1980-85	35	56	5	1301	129	25.51	2	6									47	13

	Career	M	I	NO	Runs	HS	Avge	100	50	O	M	R	W	Avge	5i	10m	BB	Ct	St
Hunt CW	1895-1904	5	9	0	73	21	8.11											4	
Huntley RH	1961-69	38	65	2	1159	65	18.40			425.5	97	1301	58	22.43	2	1	8/50	17	
Hurd RB	1992-98	16	29	3	797	105*	30.65			9	0	108	0					7	
Hurst AV	1950-52	9	8	0	62	12	7.75			4	1	7	0					7	
Hutchison RW	1973-75	31	54	10	1366	102*	31.05	1	10	718.1	254	1712	118	14.51	9	2	7/44	23	
Irving GR	1957-59	6	5	0	8	4	1.60			131.4	35	361	9	40.11	1		5/32	5	
Isherwood P	1939-60	61	89	12	2033	116	26.40	4	8	217.5	59	564	25	22.56	1		5/25	12	
Jackson C	1988	1								19	2	65	1	65.00			1/46	2	
Jackson JW	1950-54	5	8	2	137	46	22.83											2	
Jackson PF	1952-60	17	28	4	352	61	14.67			23	1	157	3	52.33			2/94	6	
Jackson WL	1911-24	26	45	1	1083	86	24.61											3	
Jacques GH	1904	1	2	2	3	3	1.50											0	
Jaggard CM	1995-97	17	32	4	888	68	31.71		4	2	0	9	0					6	
James AE	1947	4	4	1	45	17	15.00			15	5	30	0					0	
James AJS	1926-37	42	57	4	871	64	16.43		6	19	0	81	2	40.50			1/6	21	
Janaway RGL	1957	8	15	2	207	73*	15.92		1	5	2	15	2	7.50			2/15	6	
Janes BC	1957-66	35	56	13	723	53	16.81		2	310.2	81	882	47	18.77	2		6/15	17	
Janes DA	1960-76	94	161	19	3805	133*	26.80	3	14									58	
Janes HR	1933	1	2	1	7	7	7.00											0	
Janes RA	1904-21	8	13	2	98	22	8.91											5	
Jean-Jacques M	1983-88	9	10	5	84	39*	16.80		1	198.4	42	616	18	34.22	1		6/40	5	
Jennison H	1911-21	11	20	1	327	87	17.21		1									4	
Johns DFV	1950-66	83	126	10	4270	191	36.81	8	19	1444.2	365	3328	168	19.81	4		7/48	52	
Johnson AW	1901-08	8	13	0	56	20	4.31			139.5	20	580	22	26.36	3		6/76	2	
Johnson TL	1952	4	4	1	26	17	8.67			45	9	152	6	25.33			3/23	1	
Jones GA	1972-79	57	113	9	2915	114	28.03	2	20	349.1	89	959	41	23.39	1		5/20	37	
Jones H	1900-06	12	17	2	140	48	9.33			32.1	4	121	6	20.17			3/34	3	3
Jones HR	1964	3	3	1	31	24	31.00											4	
Jones RA	2000-03	8	15	1	153	48	10.93											1	
Joy PL	1967	3	2	0	49	31	24.50			59	16	129	8	16.13			4/43	4	
Judge G	1928	1	1	0	2	2*												1	
Katinakis N	1901	1	1	1	6	6	6.00											1	
Kearsey AHC	1913	2	3	0	14	11	4.67											3	
Keen AW	1901-13	12	20	3	206	79	12.12		1	175	45	549	19	28.89	1		5/73	3	
Keen GF	1953-60	6	5	4	71	32	71.00			24.2	4	90	2	45.00			2/33	3	
Kemp AH	1956	2	2	1	21	19*	21.00											1	
Kemp WP	1956	5	6	1	96	46	19.20											4	

	Career	M	I	NO	Runs	HS	Avge	100	50	O	M	R	W	Avge	5i	10m	BB	Ct	St
Kempster BJ	1995	1	2	0	25	21	12.50			9	1	40	0					1	
Kent TR	1908-33	38	68	4	1158	123	18.09	1	4	6.3	0	46	1	46.00			1/19	18	
Kentish	1901-03	8	13	1	125	32	10.42			131	35	341	18	18.94	1		6/85	5	
King D	1951	1																	
Lane RP	1995-	42	74	8	1785	112	27.05	2	12	492.1	90	1622	61	26.59			4/31	38	
Langley C	1908	2	3	0	53	33	17.67											4	
Langley F	1895-1905	13	22	2	322	77*	16.10		1	3	0	19	0					6	2
Lawford TM	1951	1	1	0	1	1	1.00											2	
Lawman SF	1907	1	2	1	14	12	14.00											0	
Lawner TM	1958	4	5	0	79	41	15.80											3	
Lawson RL	1980	1	2	0	14	11	7.00											1	
Le Gros PW	1911-30	80	132	11	3050	155	25.21	2	17	4	0	11	0					64	
Leach CW	1966-71	16	28	2	635	80	24.42		3	246.5	43	980	36	27.22	1		5/96	17	
Leat EJ	1908-11	17	31	4	588	57	21.78		3	38.4	8	105	6	17.50			4/21	8	
Lees FA	1952	1								31.3	1	145	0					0	
Leigh EB	1934	3	5	0	80	25	16.00			7	0	35	0					0	
Leigh-Bennett TJ	1934	3	5	0	63	50	12.60		1									0	
Lennox IS	1963	2	3	1	14	10	7.00			18	7	62	1	62.00			1/18	1	
Lever C	1962-78	92	155	19	4074	158*	29.96	6	21	2046.1	653	4660	234	19.91	10	1	7/30	54	
Lines BJ	1969	3	1	0	0	0	0.00			28	7	53	0					0	
Lishman JWD	1991-93	3	3	0	6	6	2.00			4	1	19	0					2	
Lister CW	1913	2	4	0	11	7	2.75			34	5	131	4	32.75			2/20	1	
Locke KJ	1998-2003	29	42	5	867	56*	23.43		3									12	
Lomax IR	1949	1	2	0	8	8	4.00			4	2	3	0					0	
Lowndes WF	1908-13	30	50	6	802	139*	18.23	1	1	22	4	79	1	79.00			1/9	25	
Lucas BJ	1951-64	40	57	8	1030	100*	21.02	1	3	19	3	77	4	19.25			2/27	17	
Lund VE	1929-47	42	52	19	238	32*	7.21			924.3	297	2148	159	13.51	13	3	7/9	37	
Lunnon WH	1895	1	2	0	16	12	8.00											0	
Lynch PS	2000-03	4	5	1	42	23	10.50											8	
Lynch SG	1984-2001	46	71	28	1076	91	25.02		7	445	65	1637	56	29.23	1		6/28	25	
Lyon AW	1977-88	109	83	31	567	39	10.90			3021.4	832	7846	367	21.38	13	3	6/12	38	
McAdam KPWJ	1966-68	7	10	0	121	32	12.10			1.3	0	9	0					4	
McCoy-Hill L	1923	3	5	1	46	37*	11.50			11	0	37	1	37.00			1/19	2	
Macindoe DH	1937-47	18	24	3	402	63	19.14		3	350.1	77	995	25	39.80	1		5/57	11	
McKelvie RD	1947	1	1	0	15	15	15.00											0	1

Name	Career	M	I	NO	Runs	HS	Avge	100	50	O	M	R	W	Avge	5i	10m	BB	Ct	St
Mackey DLL	1908-20	7	14	1	115	69	8.85		1									4	
Mackinnon D	1956-57	12	18	1	324	66*	19.06		2									2	
Mackintosh DS																			3
Macleay KH	1971-76	44	78	9	1754	69	25.42		5	5	0	22	0					45	
Mallender NA	1980	9	16	2	332	69	23.71		2	134	32	422	13	32.46			3/41	2	
Mann FN	1997	4	3	2	25	11*	25.00			82.1	25	186	14	13.29	1		5/14	1	
Marvin BL	1913	1	2	1	3	3*	3.00											0	
Mason LS	1976	1	2	0	21	21	10.50			24	6	91	0					0	
Maul SD	2000	1	1	0	0	0	0.00			14	3	55	1	55.00			1/34	0	
Mayhew JFN	1897-1902	23	37	4	856	83*	25.94		5	28	1	119	8	14.88			4/26	11	
Mayne SN	1947-48	11	16	3	57	23	4.38											12	3
Medlycott KT	1998	1	1	1	0	0	0.00			4	0	28	0					1	
Mehar SA	2004	12	21	1	854	136	42.70	2	6	757.1	184	2094	85	24.64	4		7/17	7	
Melville JH	1979-83	31	45	13	727	54	22.72		1	30	6	109	4	27.25			2/37	22	
Millar Logan W	1937	3	4	0	27	10	6.75											0	
Mills JWC	1934-39	3	5	4	48	16*	48.00			26	3	68	1	68.00			1/36	3	
Milton ME	1959-72	23	19	5	57	15*	4.07			593	145	1636	86	19.02	6	1	8/22	10	
Mitchell FH	1979-89	45	88	7	2845	128*	35.12	6	14	719.2	196	2047	80	25.59	1		5/53	37	
Mitchell HR	1897-1907	7	12	2	287	98*	28.70		2	45	7	153	6	25.50			3/27	0	
Mobbs ER	1895	1	2	0	20	14	10.00											0	
Molloy M	1912	3	1	0	14	14	14.00			38	4	153	7	21.86			3/62	0	
Montague JG	1904-05	3	4	0	25	25	6.25											2	
Morgan RN	1907-09	3	12	3	50	12*	5.56			64.1	20	158	8	19.75			3/26	5	
Morrison JW	1976-79	3	5	1	35	16	8.75			1	1	0	0					1	
Murfin MA	1895	1	2	0	14	12	7.00			80	23	254	5	50.80			2/39	0	
Nash G	1983	5	5	1	61	24	15.25											7	
Naylor SP	1895-1903	42	55	23	228	30	7.13			1519.2	471	3427	259	13.23	27	12	8/28	17	
Newberry WJ	2000-01	15	23	5	541	74*	30.06		3	164.5	21	658	29	22.69	1		7/22	8	
Newell JJ	1921-26	6	8	1	62	27	8.86			233.2	64	608	25	24.32	2		7/99	2	
Newell TW	2005-	5	9	3	44	12	7.33			193	54	518	23	22.52	2	1	5/57	1	
Newitt R	1899-1900	7	7	5	27	13*	13.50											3	
Newport PJ	1921	1	2	1	9	9	9.00											0	
Nickless R	1981-82	8	9	4	73	21	14.60											2	
Noyes SJ	1949-57	11	12	3	42	10	4.67			170	35	503	15	33.53				10	
	1992	3	6	0	68	28	11.33											3	5

	Career	M	I	NO	Runs	HS	Avge	100	50	O	M	R	W	Avge	5i	10m	BB	Ct	St
O'Callaghan RFB	1939-49	13	21	0	277	61	13.19		1									7	
O'Connor J	1946-47	17	24	1	742	165	32.26	2	3	123.1	28	407	20	20.35	2	1	6/25	8	
O'Dowds	1909	1	2	0	7	6	3.50											1	
O'Reilly MJ	2002	2	4	0	36	20	9.00											2	
Orton RW	1905-1910	36	67	2	1302	75	20.03		6									20	2
Osborne DR	1913	4	7	1	106	31	17.67			59	12	233	9	25.89			3/55	4	
Outram JI	1920-22	8	12	2	205	48*	20.50											8	
Owen DM	1993-99	27	28	6	120	16	5.45			564	97	1853	62	29.89	1		5/28	16	
Packard EAJ	2003	2	4	0	23	22	5.75											0	
Packer	1901	1	1	0	0	0	0.00											1	1
Page H	1896-1913	54	83	25	515	39	8.88			1156.5	335	2848	143	19.92	7	1	7/46	48	
Palmer JE	1966	5	9	1	66	32	8.25			22	4	68	2	34.00			1/12	5	
Palmer RWM	1986	3	3	0	0	0*	0.00			38	6	154	3	51.33			2/24	2	
Parez AH	1910	1	2	0	16	12	8.00			2	0	16	0					0	
Parkinson SDH																			5
Parry CJ	1981	10	9	2	55	25	7.86			211.3	39	641	23	27.87			3/47	4	
Parry JT	1968-77	71	71	32	667	40	17.10			1803	622	4329	233	18.58	9	1	7/57	60	
Parsons GJ	1905-06	4	8	3	79	34*	15.80											0	
Parton J	1977	4	1	0	0	0	0.00			3	0	18	0					0	
Paskins GDT	1954	3	4	0	120	113	30.00	1										3	
Paxton GN	1993-	39	69	6	1825	123	28.97	2	8									45	
Payne AU	1933	37	52	5	594	32	12.64			509.1	161	1074	79	13.59	4		7/41	31	
Peachell GE	1923-29	1	2	0	9	9	4.50											0	1
Peppiatt DR	1903	34	47	11	520	58	14.44		2									23	
Percy BS	1948-65	50	79	17	2229	123	35.95	3	15	215.1	73	539	21	25.67			4/15	27	
Perkins TE	1986-2000	28	38	7	436	51	14.06		1	123.1	20	466	10	46.60			2/24	42	
Perry S	1969-80	19	32	6	327	37*	12.58											21	12
Peters SS	1903-06	62	93	2	2398	131	26.35	3	11	12	3	55	2	27.50			2/32	23	
Peto HE	1932-46	11	16	5	166	37	15.09			7	0	49	0					8	
Philps WRN	1922-27	15	25	2	250	34	10.87			2	0	12	0					8	
Phipps DD	1952-53	10	12	3	77	29	8.56			136	30	330	7	47.14			4/42	6	
Phipps RP	1967-70	8	8	5	5	4	1.67			138	13	539	16	33.69			4/35	0	
Pickett CA	1949-70	69	84	18	911	80	13.80		2	1780.2	557	4023	219	18.37	10		6/24	61	
Pierce WM	1927	1	2	0	3	3	1.50											3	
Pitchford H	1913-29	50	80	9	1220	78	17.18		3	504.4	157	1109	82	13.52	4		7/45	16	

	Career	M	I	NO	Runs	HS	Avge	100	50	O	M	R	W	Avge	5i	10m	BB	Ct	St
Pitchford J	1926-27	3	5	1	42	19	10.50											1	1
Plested RJ	1954-61	25	28	15	300	57	23.08		1	661.3	168	1656	84	19.71	5		6/23	6	
Plummer PJ	1973-77	15	25	3	365	59	16.59		1	139.4	32	535	15	35.67			4/41	18	
Poll BW	1966-80	132	170	45	1801	56*	14.41		4									288	33
Pont IL	1983-84	4	4	2	27	16*	13.50			49	4	187	4	46.75			2/29	0	
Popplewell NFM																			
Porter D	1975-78	2	3	2	29	28	29.00			17	1	55	0					0	
Potter JN	1991-92	3	4	2	8	4*	4.00			62	20	209	8	26.13			3/44	0	
Poulter SJ	1982	2	4	0	58	29	14.50											1	
Powell AP	1984	1	1	0	14	14	14.00											0	
Powell CF	1932-38	25	41	5	997	100	27.69	1	2									16	
Powell CJ	1920-33	65	102	13	1382	60	15.53		5	146	7	690	35	19.71	1		6/33	42	
Powell GA	1999	5	8	0	132	40	16.50											4	
	1898		2	0	4	4	2.00											0	
Pratt DA	1964-67	12	10	5	47	17*	9.40			406	139	950	40	23.75	3		5/29	5	
Price K	2005-	2	4	0	97	64	24.25		1	27	2	128	4	32.00			3/34	2	
Priestley HW	1907	1	2	0	38	27	19.00			4	3	2	4	0.50			4/2	2	
Prince CA	1946-49	36	54	3	1165	105*	22.84	1	4	2	0	8	0					11	
Prior CL	1897-1900	3	5	1	24	11	6.00											1	
Pusey AE	2001-	7	11	0	168	64	15.27		1	1	0		0					3	
Raffety CV	1924-32	17	21	4	329	53	19.35		2	134	33	426	6	71.00			2/31	10	
Ralph IE	1949-53	14	20	1	275	49*	14.47			20	2	85	2	42.50			1/23	14	
Ramage PF	1970-72	8	10	4	74	16*	12.33		1	1	0	10	0					5	
Rance GD	1994-95	10	17	1	313	74	19.56		1									4	
Ratcliffe A	1937-39	12	16	2	318	68	22.71		2	24.5	3	89	3	29.67			2/24	3	
Rawlings W	1963-66	3	1	0	5	5	5.00											0	
Read CW	2003	1	2	0	13	8	6.50											0	
Read SD	2003-04	5	6	0	30	18	5.00			93.5	11	399	4	99.75			3/98	0	
Renshaw SJ	1982-83	8	12	2	147	38	14.70			54	6	249	3	83.00			2/42	0	
Reynolds D	1948-50	5	10	1	143	43*	15.89											0	
Reynolds G	1947-61	62	101	11	2016	119	22.40	3	9	559.1	132	1637	68	24.07	2		6/52	27	
Rickard D	1951-56	24	25	5	175	32	8.75			354	78	995	45	22.11	2		5/57	15	
Ridge SP	1980-82	5	5	2	3	3	3.00			85.1	21	304	11	27.64			3/26	6	
Risden DC	2000	4	4	0	9	7	2.25											1	1
Ritchie GM	1981	4	8	0	433	85	54.13		6	10	1	42	1	42.00			1/24	0	
Ritchings R	1921-22	4	6	0	30	10	5.00			7.2	2	21	2	10.50			2/21	0	
Roberts AW	1902	2	4	0	16	11	4.00											1	

	Career	M	I	NO	Runs	HS	Avge	100	50	O	M	R	W	Avge	5i	10m	BB	Ct	St
Roberts D	1937	5	7	1	20	8	3.33			40	6	155	6	25.83			3/59	6	
Roberts KC	1986	1	2		14	13	7.00											1	
Roberts MJ	1987-1997	75	145	13	5989	193*	45.37	15	35	12	6	30	3	10.00			2/21	57	7
Robertson AD	1933-36	7	10	0	59	20	5.90			131.4	19	477	13	36.69			4/30	1	
Robertson GK	1980	6	7	2	106	49	21.20											2	
Robey CJ	1937	1	1	0	0	0	0.00			60	10	212	8	26.50			3/21	2	
Robins RVC	1950-51	5	8	0	63	31	7.88											3	
Robinson	1900	1	2	0	4	4	2.00											0	
Robinson CD	1895-1907	5	8	0	130	36	16.25											7	
Robinson N	2004																	0	
Robson EF	1925-28	15	20	5	119	17*	7.93	1		4	1	8	0					5	
Roe WN	1923-24	4	6	0	269	115	44.83	1	1									0	
Rogers C	1905	3	5	0	60	38	12.00											2	
Rogers ND	1973-74	17	13	5	81	26	10.13			345	86	976	41	23.80	2		9/50	12	
Romaine AN	1999-2000	4	5	1	99	33	24.75											3	
Roshier PG	1991-93	12	16	5	175	29	15.91			307.4	71	985	27	36.48			3/42	2	
Ross NDC	1910-12	12	21	1	523	144	26.15	1		13.1	1	79	0					7	
Rudd CRD	1946	1	1	0	1	1	1.00											1	
Russell TP	1981-2000	61	85	22	1125	77	17.86		3	2104.2	594	5347	366	14.61	26	6	7/22	69	21
Rutter RH	1928-47	82	103	19	846	106	10.07	1		1	0	4	0					40	
Ryan D	1958	1								157.4	35	497	17	29.24			4/48	1	
Saleem A	2002-	9	13	1	266	72	22.17		1	27	6	73	6	12.17	1		5/17	1	
Sales HE	1937-38	3	4	0	27	19	6.75			112.2	9	522	17	30.71			3/31	4	
Salmon ECH	1923-24	9	12	1	158	31	14.36			350.2	77	1133	48	23.60	4	1	6/75	4	
Samms WJ	1912	1	1	0	0	0	0.00			5	0	28	2	14.00			2/28	1	
Sampson PJ	1999	7	9	4	66	30*	13.20			26.2	4	88	4	22.00			1/12	2	
Sant MR	1973-76	16	23	8	224	30*	14.93											9	
Saunders FG	1962-65	9	14	1	198	30	15.23											47	1
Saunders J	1895-1900	44	70	3	1487	114	22.19	1	6									5	1
Sawyer MR	1949	2	2	0	0	0	0.00											7	
Sawyer PR	1997-	26	40	4	1198	181	33.28	1	8	100	13	446	7	63.71			2/22	26	
Sawyer SA	1988	6	7	1	88	34	14.67			14	3	49	3	16.33			3/25	2	
Saxby RB	1932	1	1	0	3	3	3.00											0	
Scoggins R	1933	2	4	1	6	4	2.00											2	
Scott GLT	1959-61	10	20	3	337	70	19.82		1	27	6	68	2	34.00			2/23	9	
Scott-Murray A	1900-01	6	8	0	33	11	4.13		1									7	

	Career	M	I	NO	Runs	HS	Avge	100	50	O	M	R	W	Avge	5i	10m	BB	Ct	St
Scriven JR	1961-62	5	7	2	87	36*	17.40			13	2	51	1	51.00			1/15	3	
Scriven TJA	1986-99	98	149	29	3574	94	29.78		25	2076.2	482	6886	265	25.98	14	3	7/68	31	
Sear MD	1973-81	21	34	4	526	82*	17.53		1	19	7	64	6	10.67			3/27	10	
Sears D	1946	1	1	0	8	8	8.00											0	
Sewell DAD	1912-22	30	39	12	313	46	11.59	2	2	200	25	831	33	25.18	1		6/44	19	2
Sewell EHD	1912-14	16	28	3	794	109	31.76		2	463	70	1610	83	19.40	9	2	7/80	25	6
Shaw BHG	1911-13	11	17	0	235	65	13.82											2	
Shaw EA	1908-14	17	30	1	574	117	19.79	1	3									21	
Shaw Rev ED	1897-1909	9	17	0	273	44	16.06			2	1	4	0					0	
Shaw RJ	1928	1	2	0	30	23	15.00			12	1	36	1	36.00			1/23	6	
Shearer RDJ	1997	1	2	1	15	15*	15.00											0	
Shearman SM	1988-95	40	73	15	1681	94	28.98		8	9	2	58	0					34	
Shepherd M	2003	7	2	0	33	30	16.50											5	
Sher ZA	2001-	26	11	1	552	200	55.20	2		218	43	707	24	29.46	2		6/83	12	
Sidaway BG	1964-71	66	32	8	130	15	5.42			523	156	1298	58	22.38	1		5/51	44	
Skinner AG	1927-52	40	100	12	2515	104*	28.58	2	17	258.1	48	781	33	23.67			4/19	17	
Slack JKE	1964-69	12	60	12	1030	74*	21.46		3	6	0	18	0					10	
Slack WN	1976	2	24	0	748	70	31.17		6	1	0	8	0					0	
Slocock HL	1908-09	1	3	1	26	25	13.00											0	
Smith AJ	2003		2	0	20	10	10.00												
Smith CW	1954-67	58	72	27	481	41*	10.69			1768.3	551	4381	202	21.69	11		7/18	35	
Smith DE	1967-88	141	246	44	4922	109*	24.37	2	25	253.3	59	756	29	26.07	1		5/45	99	
Smith DJ	1979-80	9	10	1	67	19	7.44			160.1	43	443	14	31.64			4/35	3	
Smith EF	1926	3	4	2	18	7*	9.00			81.3	19	207	5	41.40			2/15	2	
Smith KW	1964	2	1	1	11	11*												3	
Southall E	1907-09	7	12	2	431	90	43.10		5	9	0	31	2	15.50			2/20	3	5
Southall WHC	1926-31	8	9	1	98	37	12.25											2	
Spiro RMF	1950	8	11	1	55	11*	5.50											6	
Stacey T	1901-12	26	44	6	713	58	18.76		3	278	41	997	37	26.95	1		5/130	9	
Stanway SF	1989-	79	65	26	267	32*	6.85		1	1883.4	495	5300	164	32.32	6		6/39	22	
Steel DMA	1957	6	9	0	150	62	16.67											2	
Stephenson FMR	1927-31	6	8	1	140	68	20.00		1									2	
Stephenson JWA	1927-32	18	25	1	566	79	23.58		4	125.4	31	321	24	13.38			3/17	11	
Steptoe GR	2000-02	4	6	1	131	52	26.20		1									1	

Career	M	I	NO	Runs	HS	Avge	100	50	O	M	R	W	Avge	5i	10m	BB	Ct	St
Stevens-Davis BH 1928-37	35	46	6	687	56*	17.18		2	9	0	47	1	47.00			1/29	14	
Stillman LT 1910	2	4	0	25	7	6.25			3	1	18	0					0	
Stoddart PLB 1955-67	77	124	14	3097	104	28.15	2	14	49	6	186	10	18.60			2/8	50	4
Storie AC 2000	1	2	1	44	37	44.00											0	
Stott DS 1927	1	1	0	1	1	1.00											0	
Stratton JW 1895-1901	27	39	8	387	30	12.48			328.3	80	861	45	19.13	2		7/54	12	
Streatfeild-Moore AM 1897	1	2	0	2	1	1.00											0	
Strong PFJ 1993	1	2	0	82	54	41.00		1									0	
Sullivan ME 1995-96	5	4	1	32	20	10.67			40	11	155	1	155.00			1/15	1	
Sutherly H 1895	4	8	0	127	44	15.88											3	
Sylvester SA 1991-96	6	6	2	40	18	10.00			110.2	12	478	13	36.77			4/40	2	
Symes-Thompson Rev F 1905-07	9	13	0	207	62	15.92		1	124.5	30	345	12	28.75			4/60	8	
Taylor BL 1958-63	6	5	4	25	8	25.00			61	11	204	5	40.80			4/94	5	
Taylor CH 1946-47	16	21	4	869	131	51.12	3	4									7	
Taylor DJS 1961-63	23	32	18	409	50*	29.21		1									31	
Taylor H 1954-55	17	28	4	694	150*	28.92	2	3									13	
Taylor MNS 1961-62	5	9	0	116	62	12.89		1									4	
Taylor SJ 1981	2	2	1	10	10	10.00			41	10	150	4	37.50			2/35	0	
Taylor Z 2004	2	2	1	12	12	12.00			4.3	0	28	0					2	
Theed NH 1926	2	3	2	12	9*	12.00			18	7	42	1	42.00			1/20	2	
Theed ST 1928-30	2	3	0	16	15	5.33											4	
Thomas AW 1996-	24	28	7	216	44	10.29			588	88	2099	76	27.62	3		8/83	9	
Thompson LT 1922	2	3	0	4	2	1.33			16	6	42	2	21.00			1/1	2	
Thompson R 1959	1	1	1	2	2*				11	1	62	2	31.00			1/15	0	
Thorpe H 1921	6	8	1	131	61	18.71		1									2	
Tibbles EJ 1920-37	8	13	1	255	81	21.25		1									7	
Tilbury JMH 1954-57	25	33	4	472	113	16.28	1										15	
Tilley NW 2001	3	5	1	78	40*	19.50			0.1	0	1	0					2	
Tomlin SJ 1960-62	14	25	4	296	36*	14.10			10	2	33	1	33.00			1/6	13	
Tompkins RS 1934-53	36	48	6	557	94	13.26		1	262.3	53	771	30	25.70	1		5/46	11	
Tomson AH 1899	1	1	0	13	13	13.00			80	18	207	8	25.88			3/50	0	
Topliss SM 1981	1	3	1	5	5	2.50											3	
Tovey JR 1939	3	2	0	22	17	11.00											1	
Tredwell RWM 1986-89	11	5	1	14	5	3.50			164.4	28	592	11	53.82			2/33	4	

	Career	M	I	NO	Runs	HS	Avge	100	50	O	M	R	W	Avge	5i	10m	BB	Ct	St
Trevor SL	1914-26	27	39	4	471	60	13.46		1	77	16	269	13	20.69	1		6/54	12	
Trumper J	1963	1								2	0	12	0					0	
Tungate CJ	1987-90	13	17	4	142	26	10.92			126	33	409	13	31.46			4/35	25	
Turner JB	1968-83	151	286	16	7524	117	27.87	4	34	12	4	32	2	16.00			2/26	197	2
Tustian BJ	1966-71	30	52	5	874	67*	18.60		4	51	8	184	7	26.29			6/52	21	
Umpleby AS	2002	2	4	0	71	27	17.75			20.2	6	67	3	22.33			3/27	0	
Ussher B	1899	1	1	0	15	15	15.00			10	1	49	1	49.00			1/24	1	
Ussher S	1902	2	3	0	34	29	11.33			29	2	154	4	38.50			2/41	0	
Vaughan RH	1903	4	7	1	44	11*	7.33											2	
Vickerstaff SJA	1905-10	48	77	24	317	25	5.98			989.1	153	3717	154	24.14	8		8/54	41	
Vine DR	1928	1	1	0	1	1	1.00											0	
Waite AC	1965-74	61	60	26	217	25	6.38			1338.1	326	3572	166	21.52	7	1	6/30	23	
Walker GS	1936-39	21	29	1	590	70	21.07		4									16	
Walker LM	1929	3	4	1	56	44	18.67			3	0	15	0					1	
Ward AB	2005-	2	4	1	22	7	7.33											0	
Ward AJ	2002-	17	27	4	381	63*	16.57		1	98	20	297	16	18.56	1		5/52	28	
Ward AS	1900-05	9	12	2	150	40*	15.00			35	7	104	2	52.00			2/104	4	
Watson A	1904	1	2	0	6	4	3.00											1	
Waugh E	2003	1	2	0	0	0	0.00											0	
Weatherby F	1902	1								3	0	12	0					1	
Weatherby JH	1896-98	4	4	0	53	40	13.25											5	
Weatherby JT	1896-02	6	10	0	135	49	13.50											3	
Weaver-Adams Dr E	1903-12	35	62	6	1472	162	26.29	2	6	73	6	271	15	18.07	1		5/35	34	
Weaver-Adams ER		9	13	1	119	26	9.92			5	1	18	2	9.00			2/13	4	
Wells AV	1923-26	13	15	1	148	32	10.57			132.5	19	513	17	30.18	2		6/80	3	
West E	1924-28	7	12	2	120	32	12.00			11	1	55	0					9	
Wharton SJ	1997	1	2	1	0	0	0.00											0	
Wheeler W	1906-11	14	22	2	198	51	9.90			62	7	283	5	56.60			1/9	2	
White OC	1906	3	5	0	17	11	3.40											1	
Whiting F	1920-22	13	21	2	342	62	18.00		1	5	0	23	0					8	
Whiting F jnr	1948-49	3	6	0	42	25	7.00			5	1	22	1	22.00			1/10	1	
Whiting JGB	1920-22	13	17	7	99	19*	9.90			282	53	750	60	12.50	5		8/23	3	
Wilkins CWA	1923	2	4	0	1	1	0.25			30	8	68	1	68.00			1/26	1	
Willes H	1903	1	2	0	22	22	11.00			13	1	45	1	45.00			1/45	1	

	Career	M	I	NO	Runs	HS	Avge	100	50	O	M	R	W	Avge	5i	10m	BB	Ct	St
Williams JM	1972	8	14	3	101	32*	9.18			103.4	23	327	8	40.88	1		5/35	4	
Williams JR	1977	2	3	2	3	3	3.00			28	7	70	5	14.00			3/44	0	1
Williams RA	1895	1	2	0	10	7	5.00											1	
Wilmot HG	1933	2	4	0	81	30	20.25											0	
Wilmot TP	1904	1	1	0	17	17	17.00											2	
Wilson GA	1907-08	10	18	1	241	42	14.18			383.3	73	1355	81	16.73	10	4	8/109	12	
Wilson JG	1989	4	2	0	0	0	0.00			41	5	184	3	61.33			2/37	1	
Woodbridge CM																			
Woodroffe PJ	1895-97	8	12	1	124	49	11.27			15	5	35	2	17.50			1/17	3	
Woolliams PJ	1994-2003	28	28	5	232	60	10.09		1	465	122	1280	37	34.59			4/26	8	
Worsley END	1899-1906	3	4	0	14	5	3.50			54	10	175	2	87.50			1/40	2	
Wright EE	1926	2	3	0	15	8	5.00											0	
Wright HJW	1900	1	1	0	0	0	0.00			29	6	82	2	41.00			2/82	1	
Wright MJW	1975-78	13	20	3	195	41	11.47			169.1	26	576	21	27.43			4/47	6	
Wright MW	2005-	1	2	0	25	15	12.50			10.1	0	34	1	34.00			1/34	1	
Wye CW	1895-1913	143	241	27	4762	148	22.25	4	20	6184	2480	11584	811	14.28	68	18	8/27	75	
Wyld HJ	1923	1	3	2	25	12	25.00			2	0	15	0					0	
Wynd AJ	1899	1	2	1	20	13*	20.00			8	2	30	1	30.00			1/30	5	
	2005-	2	4	0	61	24	15.25												
Yates W	1946-52	23	32	2	607	117*	20.23	1	1	88.4	15	299	16	18.69	2		5/34	15	
York SE	1971-79	35	67	3	1185	118*	18.52	1	3	87	14	333	6	55.50			2/86	31	6
Young KE	1969	4	5	1	133	83*	33.25		1	6	1	17	0					2	

Note: All statistics are based on scorecards except where details of bowling analyses are deficient, in which case the averages published at the time have been used to assist computations. In seasons where complete bowling analyses have not been found there have been some incompatibilities between the known figures and the published averages. The most notorious instance is for 1921, where some 'constructive accounting' has been necessary to compile the most likely figures for CF Powell and DAD Sewell. An arbitrary 13 overs have also been assigned to Le Gros for one match with no record of his overs bowled. In the match against Kent at Chesham in 1957 it has been possible to identify only four of the Bucks players taking part. In the match against Suffolk at Chesham in 1962 only ten Bucks players are known.

Index of People Mentioned in the Text